PENGUIN BOOKS

Garry Linnell is one of Australia's most experienced journalists. A Walkley Award winner for feature writing, he has been editor-in-chief of *The Bulletin*, editor of the *Daily Telegraph*, director of news and current affairs for the Nine Network and editorial director of Fairfax. He spent four years as co-host of the Breakfast Show on 2UE and is also the author of three previous books – *Football Ltd: The Inside Story of the AFL*; *Raelene: Sometimes Beaten, Never Conquered*, and *Playing God: The Rise and Fall of Gary Ablett*.

BUCKLEY'S CHANCE

GARRY LINNELL

PENGUIN BOOKS

PENGUIN BOOKS

UK | USA | Canada | Ireland | Australia
India | New Zealand | South Africa | China

Penguin Books is part of the Penguin Random House group of companies
whose addresses can be found at global.penguinrandomhouse.com

Penguin
Random House
Australia

First published by Michael Joseph, 2019
This edition published by Penguin Books, 2020

Author photo © Fairfax
Cover photography/illustrations courtesy of Getty Images and Shutterstock
Cover design by Alex Ross © Penguin Random House Australia Pty Ltd
Map by Ice Cold Publishing
Typeset in Adobe Garamond Pro by Midland Typesetters, Australia
Printed and bound in Australia by Griffin Press, part of Ovato, an accredited
ISO AS/NZS 14001 Environmental Management Systems printer

 A catalogue record for this
book is available from the
National Library of Australia

ISBN 978 0 14379 576 6

penguin.com.au

MIX
Paper from
responsible sources
FSC® C009448

CONTENTS

PART II

PART III

PART IV

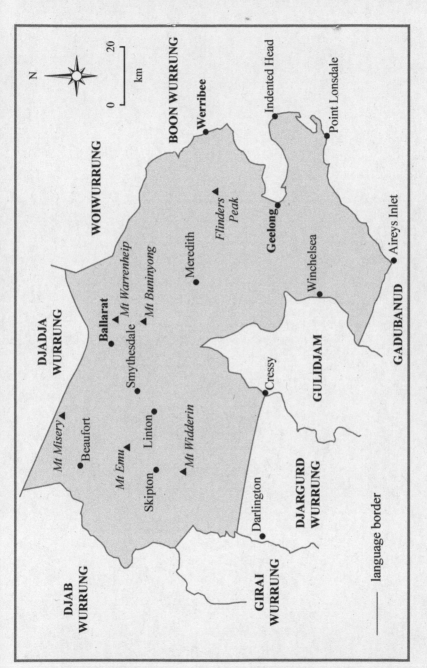

Land of the Wadawurrung people

'What is history after all? History is facts that become lies in the end; legends are lies which become history in the end.'

Jean Cocteau

———————————————————————

FOREWORD

Tracing the footsteps of William Buckley is not easy and not just because his strides were so long. Few historical figures in this country are shrouded in as much myth and speculation. His illiteracy undoubtedly contributed to this. But it is the nature of his life that has left him stranded in a shadow world. To some, his 32 years living with Australia's Aboriginals and ultimately becoming one of them is a bizarre footnote in the early colonisation of Australia. Others have embraced him as the early embodiment of reconciliation.

Part of the problem is that so many people insist on peering into history through a modern lens, applying the standards of the present to the past. Because of this, Buckley's legacy leaves many feeling uncomfortable, in the same way the man's imposing physical presence made those around him feel uneasy. He made some awkward observations about the black and white worlds in which he lived. Both societies could be cruel and inhumane. He lived in a time when Indigenous people were labelled savages and their presence seen as an impediment to so-called progress. He also lived in a period when orphaned white children were treated as slaves and where unspeakable atrocities were carried out on the poor and defenceless. Buckley was consigned to a no-man's-land between these two vastly different cultures. Was he a traitor to the Aboriginal people? Or did he betray white people?

So much about the man is in dispute. Even etymologists, that diligent band who study the history of words, do not unanimously agree on the true origin of the phrases 'Buckley's chance' and 'You've got two chances – Buckley's and none'. Some have suggested it may be a play on 'Buckley & Nunn' – a Melbourne department store first established in the early 1850s. But the weight of opinion now leans heavily toward the man as its source. By the early 1870s there was a racehorse called Buckley's Chance and the phrase itself was being used in print by the 1880s to indicate long odds.

What is not in dispute is that this man led one of the most extraordinary lives imaginable. Which is what this book is about. Even by the standards of the 18th and 19th centuries, when epic feats of endurance and courage were commonplace, his tale still borders on the unbelievable. He fought against Napoleon's army. He endured the hell of England's festering prison hulks. He was shackled for six months while being transported to Australia. He escaped and was adopted by the Wadawurrung people. And then, more than three decades later, he returned to live among white people as they set about seizing Aboriginal lands and doing their best to erase from existence the world's oldest continuing culture.

I grew up in Geelong and heard tales about the so-called Wild White Man. But they were just stories. No-one I knew had any real idea who he was or that he had ever really existed. I have no memory of learning about him in school, which is no surprise given the unimaginative and embarrassed manner in which Australian history is often imparted in our classrooms.

All I knew was that a huge and immensely strong man with a long beard and a spear in his hand had apparently spent decades roaming the nearby countryside.

Family outings sometimes found us at Point Lonsdale, staring up at the gnarled, wind-whipped sandstone cliffs where Buckley's Cave sits beneath the lighthouse, its tantalising entrance barricaded to discourage vandals and amorous couples. The site has long been dismissed as nothing more than an imaginative attempt at attracting tourism. But recently my uncle, Ken Bell, came across a letter written by the Irish botanist William Henry Harvey when he was in Australia in the early 1850s. Harvey writes about finding a small cave at Point Lonsdale and 'it is said that Convict *Buckley*, who first explored these parts, lived there when he first landed as a runaway'. There were no tourism spruikers in 1853, so it seems probable that the cave actually was used by Buckley. Let's hope they take down the iron bars protecting the cave and look at opening it to the public.

William Buckley seems to be riding a new wave of respectability he could never have imagined. In 2018 several original documents relating to his discovery by John Batman's party sold at auction for more than $40,000 – far more than papers written by Batman and other more prominent explorers. He has had a beer dedicated to him and numerous trails and locations in and around Geelong now carry his name. Why, all the man needs now is an Instagram account . . .

In life no-one ever quite knew where William Buckley stood. In death we have no idea where he truly lies. In Hobart, a small grove of maple trees and newly laid lawn form Buckley's Rest, a quiet corner in a busy section of Battery Point. He was buried around there in 1856. But a large primary school now sits on the site of the old bone yard and the small park commemorating his life is about as physically close as anyone will ever get to him.

Which brings us to this book. *Buckley's Chance* is not a conventional historical biography. William Buckley's life rubbed up against events and characters that changed human history. I was staggered by just how many there were. Along the way I fell in love with the 19th century. Despite its cruelties and racism it was the last true epoch of human exploration on this planet. It produced an unprecedented array of the brave, the stupid, the reckless and the appalling. It also inspired mountains of excessive verbiage, which is why some have dubbed it the 'Era of Windbags'. Read many of the memoirs and journals of the day and you will discover writers who relentlessly hurled commas at their pages like darts, who capitalised every noun with compulsive obsessiveness and were skilled in the unfortunate art of telling any short story long. Because of this I have made some grammatical changes to quotations in order to make them easier to read by 21st century standards. Any conversations quoted directly have either been sourced in the text or in the Endnotes.

There are more than one hundred variations on the spelling of 'Wadawurrung'. I have chosen to use the most commonly accepted form, along with other Indigenous words and phrases.

A book like this leans on the work of many. But my biggest thanks must go to my wife, Maria. Patient as ever, she was always there, even when I wasn't. And when I *was* there, my mind was often adrift in the first half of the 19th century. William Buckley certainly took his chances. But Maria took the greatest chance of all and I love her for it.

Garry Linnell, October 2019

PROLOGUE

December 1803

There is a full moon in hell. It hangs low in the western sky on this warm night, casting shadows with its dull light. The seeing is good. There is a trail of snapped twigs and bent undergrowth that leads down to the beach where his enormous feet have gouged large holes in the sand.

Can't be too long now before they corner the ungrateful bastard.

What to do then? Put a lead ball through his back or head? Or drag him back to camp and have him flogged so hard next morning the hot sand will turn red and he'll never be able to straighten that huge frame of his again?

Perhaps they can manage something crueller. Trying times always motivate men when it comes to devising new methods of inflicting pain on others. He is not a man known for his words. Brooding silent type, he is. A man his size doesn't really need to say much, after all. But by God, once they finish with him the bush will echo with his pain. They will have him crying out for the mother he barely knew. And maybe the father he never knew.

No punishment can be fitting enough for a man who decides to escape in the days over Christmas, forcing the King's men to put down their rum and pick up their muskets and pursue him through this wretched scrub. They have only been here for two months but already they have come to know this as the devil's land, parched and crawling with snakes and bugs and hostile tribes. The only drinkable water has come from wooden casks sunk in the sand – and even that has been making them sick. The heat scalds, the dry winds from the north leave even convicts, grateful to have escaped the horrors of England's prison ships, pining for home. It is an ancient land, this one, its bones so old you can hear them crunch with each step. They will leave this world very soon and search for sanctuary elsewhere, a better place where a free settler won't wake in the morning looking like a sufferer of the pox from all the mosquito bites, a land where a true colony can be founded and have a decent chance of surviving and even flourishing.

But first they must capture the big bricklayer and the others who have escaped into the bush.

Heavy boots thud on dry soil. Shouts drown out the gentle lapping of waves on the nearby beach. Nearby, the sound of a musket being fired. Not long after, a whiff of acrid burnt powder. And then silence, broken only by the odd curse. The trail has turned cold and lifeless. William Buckley is long gone.

He will always be a hard man to find. No wonder the Aboriginals will call him a ghost.

—

Decades later he will be easier to find. There he is, walking down the street with his Irish wife, Julia. You don't need to listen to the whispers of passers-by or follow their furtive glances. How could you miss them? He looms so large, she so tiny, the tips of their fingers barely meet.

He has come up with a solution for this, of course. A lifetime of being forced to adapt does that to a man. He might not be able to make up the age gap separating them. But this? He has looped a handkerchief around both their wrists so they can remain connected. She has already lost one husband and in these lean times, when money and food are scarce, she cannot afford to lose another.

Particularly an extraordinary man like this one.

And William is extraordinary, even if he is finally beginning to feel and show his age. He is now in his 70s – more than 30 years separate him from his bride. She has nursed him through a battle with typhus, cooling his fevers and tending to the painful rashes. It was the first time he could remember falling ill and for a time there it was touch and go. But once again his remarkable strength and constitution pulled him through. It may have weakened him but when he strolls down the streets of Hobart Town, with Julia by his side, he insists on carrying himself straight and erect. Like the soldier he used to be. Like the free man he has become.

He has no wealth, the pair of them barely getting by on his paltry pension. But he has been a good husband. A patient man, devoted to her and her daughter. Look at how he steps slowly, shortening his stride so Julia doesn't have to run to keep up.

She knows what they say behind their backs. She has seen the fingers pointing, heard the snide laughter, registered the wry smiles. There are men who regard her husband as stupid, a simple buffoon no smarter than the Aboriginals he lived with for so many years. Others are not so sure. They suspect William Buckley knows far more than he lets on.

He is, after all, the great survivor, perhaps the greatest of them all. His name is known from Sydney to London. Even now, so many years after his escape and his disappearance, the newspapers still refer to him as the Wild White Man. See the modern Hercules who survived for 32 years among the savages! Be amazed at how long he went without ever seeing a civilised white face! Ponder the depravities he endured, the loneliness he suffered!

Who could have imagined that a boy from a village whose people never journeyed more than a few miles in their lives would one day travel the globe? Who would have thought a child from rural Cheshire, cast out by his mother and stepfather, destined only for the chapped, coarse hands of a bricklayer, would go on to fight Napoleon's army? Who could even begin to imagine the horrors he experienced while shackled on a stinking, filthy prison hulk? Or the long and rough sea journey to the other side of the world and, soon after that, all those years living with Aboriginal tribes, becoming one of them until he forgot his own language?

It's true. No other man has seen or experienced anything close to that. No man has been tried and tested like William Buckley.

Yet his silence and reticence baffles and exasperates. What man does not want a hand in his own epitaph? What man who makes history would prefer to vanish from its pages? There was an offer once to put him on stage and take the plaudits of the crowd. A stupid man might have walked straight into that trap, dazzled by the lights and applause and all those eyes gazing upon his big frame in admiration and awe. There was no way William Buckley was becoming an exhibit in a freak show. What many don't understand is that all those years without seeing a white face or sleeping on a soft bed were easy compared to what happened when he came back. He has been used enough, torn in so many directions and pummelled by the motives of others so often that he wants no part of it.

Besides, he has already had his say. Didn't he sit down with a newspaper editor, John Morgan, and allow him to write his story? Not the full story, of course. But enough to at least feed those inquiring minds a few morsels and tidbits about his life. God knew both of them needed the money.

But even in these, his last remaining years, a time when so many men feel the urge to remind the world they lived and did things that deserve to be remembered, he will shy away from marking his place. And all those frustrated souls who never get to really know him, let alone understand him, will be left with the memory of this big lumbering man, joined to his tiny wife by a small handkerchief, his heavy face staring ahead, 'aimlessly walking the streets . . . with eyes fixed on some distant object'.

Centuries later, after all the extraordinary facts and lies and myths have merged into one, when historians sift through the torpid memoirs of men who did far less than Buckley, searching for a hint of his character, a small trace of his personality, he will remain that distant object.

A ghost.

Come, William. It is time to give up your secrets.

PART I

WILLIAM ENTERS
THE WORLD

1

SENTENCED TO DEATH; REPRIEVED; IMPRISONED ON A HULK

It is dark and damp, the air sour with sweat and shit and rot. No point trying to stand; the ceiling is so low you can only stoop. No point trying to move; a 12-pound iron connected to a heavy chain has been bolted around one of your powerful ankles. All you can do is sit amid the filth and listen to the constant cries and whimpering.

And hope. A man can always hope.

Damn hard thing to do in a place like this, though. A man would have to be a saint to find a glimmer of optimism in this fetid hole. Or find himself in the grip of madness – and there is no shortage of that around here. And just where, exactly, would you even begin to find a little positive *something* that might give cause for hope? Try looking in the eyes of the young children, manacled and hungry, calling out for parents who will never come, all because they stole a loaf of bread. Or how about the women with bruised faces and swollen lips and missing teeth who flinch whenever the heavy boots on deck grow louder with each step? Surely not among the old men with their sunken jaws and backs whipped so often the cobwebbed scars are all that hold the sinews together.

No. Not much here to inspire confidence in the future. But that's the whole point, isn't it? Punishment can be counted in sentences of months and years but *real* punishment – the sort judges are quick to hand out in these times – strips away the optimism as quickly as a leering guard can flay your skin with his knotted whip.

You want hope? Best go searching for it on those nearby banks of Langstone Harbour, where skinny dogs nose around among the scraps with their ribs pressed tight against a thin layer of fur, wearily lifting their heads whenever they catch a faint scent of food on the breeze. That's hope for you.

Besides, consider yourself lucky, William Buckley. They were going to put a rope around your thick neck and hang you in front of the usual gawking crowd, until those judges handed down a last-minute reprieve before climbing into their carriage and heading back to London. Some rope it would have been, too. You're a huge man. When they let you out each morning and allow you to shuffle on to the deck, blinking in the sunlight, sucking in air that no longer reeks, you stand, what? Six feet, six inches? Measurements of your height will vary over the years, depending on who is telling the story. Some will even suggest you nudge seven feet but they will be the newspapermen trying their best to extract a shilling or two from some-one's deep pocket. So let's settle on six foot six and untold pounds of pure, hard muscle. It has been a cold winter and you have lost weight because you are never warm and the daily rations are never enough. But you still tower over everyone else, convicts and captors alike.

It has always been this way. Maybe that is why you have so little to say. Everyone gets it wrong about big men, portraying them as loud and swaggering, soaked in self-belief and conviction, every pore of their skin oozing confidence and testosterone. Truth is, most big men are all too aware of their size. In crowds many of them try to shrink their presence, perhaps by bending over a little, by saying less than others. That's what you do, isn't it?

Problem is, there's just no place to hide when you're on a prison hulk like this one in Langstone Harbour, no way to shrink into some quiet corner, no chance of slipping into anonymity. And it's not just your height, either. There's that snub nose and low bushy eyebrows hanging above hazel eyes. The mass of dark hair. The mole high on your left cheek. The skin pocked in places. The 'W.B' tattooed on one of your arms. In years to come someone will write that you are 'just such a man as one would suppose fit to commit burglary or murder'. Well, they will get it half right. Two pieces of stolen cloth, that's all it took to land you here. Broke into Mr Cave's shop thinking you and your mate William Marmon would get away with it. Well, that's what the law said. You will say you were framed. Twenty years old and hardened by a few years in the army and a battlefield wound that quickly healed. Must have left you feeling invincible.

But not anymore, not after what you have seen in the past few months.

For six months the routine for you and Marmon and the others has been the same. Hauled out of the dank hold at daylight along with the rest of the prisoners. A biscuit for breakfast, hard enough to crack your teeth, or a tasteless slop of boiled barley. Then you are rowed ashore to work on fortifications or clean up the putrid banks. Passers-by gaze at convicts like you and there may have been a time, back in those first few weeks, when you burned with embarrassment when you felt their stares. Now just being alive is something in which to take pride. But this is what those passers-by see when they stare, all of you working with 'fetters on each leg, with a chain between that ties variously, some round their middle, others upright to the throat. Some are chained two and two; and others whose crimes have been enormous, with heavy fetters. Six or seven [guards] are continually walking about them with drawn cutlasses, to prevent their escape and likewise to prevent idleness . . . so far from being permitted to speak to anyone [convicts] hardly dare speak to each other.'

Well, talking is hardly your strength. You're illiterate and will always struggle for the right words. Better to let others find them for you. George Lee can do that. He's a 22-year-old clerk who was found guilty of trying to pass forged bank notes in Worcester, just a few months before you were hauled into court. Lee is well educated and full of himself – and his life will soon become bound to yours in ways you cannot yet imagine. But he's a handy man with words and in recent months there has been no shortage of them spilling from his quill. Imprisoned on the *Portland*, waiting to be transported for 14 years, Lee has begun corresponding with a member of parliament, Sir Henry St John-Mildmay. There's a subtle shift taking place in England over the way the criminal classes are being treated, particularly in the hundreds of squalid prison hulks that are anchored in Portsmouth Harbour and line that fetid sludge of a river they call the Thames. Most of the hulks are decommissioned merchant or Navy ships, their masts removed, their sides battened down to prevent escape, floating wrecks housing nothing but despair and disease, a catchment for the spill from the country's overcrowded prisons. Now there are murmurings that a more humane approach is needed.

The *Portland* is home to 440 prisoners. About half of them, Lee writes to Sir Henry, are 'Johnny Rays' – 'country bumpkins in whose composition there is more of the fool than the rogue'.

Country bumpkins. That pompous airbag is not talking about you, is he?

Lee trusts few on board the *Portland* and detests the officers in charge more than he does his fellow uneducated convicts. He writes to Sir Henry that those officers are regularly turning a blind eye to the criminality flourishing below decks, including 'the unnatural crime' which has become an initiation rite for new prisoners.

'The horrible crime of sodomy rages so shamefully throughout that the surgeon and myself have been more than once threatened with assassination for straining to put a stop to it . . . it is in no way discountenanced by those in command.'

But rape and the constant brutal violence of the guards is just the start. It will be decades before the hulk system is abandoned. Here right now at the turn of the 19th century, the mortality rate on these ships is nudging 30 per cent. Bacterial diseases, including cholera and typhus, move through the holds quickly and fatally, killing thousands.

Lee has seen days when nine or 10 bodies have been hauled out of the hulk and taken to the shore – 'pictures of raggedness, filth and starvation'. You must have seen them too.

In the years to come you will say that during your stint on the hulks you were once put to work on the fortifications at Woolwich, the biggest arsenal in the kingdom. Workers digging in the area a few decades later will feel the crunch of human bone at the end of their shovels as they uncover one mass grave after another.

George Lee cannot contain his outrage at the atrocities being committed deep below the decks of the hulks. And his resentment over the way the guards condone what is going on will burn inside him over the next 12 months until it turns into an uncontrolled rage against all authority.

So best leave the most colourful description of life on the hulks to another prisoner, James Hardy Vaux. He's a true rake of his times: thief, swindler, gambler and all round ne'er do well. Hard not to like the man, though. He's incorrigible. He's on his way to setting some kind of record – the only man to be transported to New Holland on three separate occasions. God only knows what his father, Hardy, a respectable butler to a politician, must think of him. James fell into gambling and a bad crowd in his mid teens and has been paying off his debts by stealing and duping the gullible ever since. But his bad luck – he will marry three times – will finally turn later in life when he publishes a successful memoir and a companion volume called *A New and Comprehensive Vocabulary of the Flash Language*.

You probably know most of the words, William, all the street lingo. But Vaux's book will become an eye-opening tome for all those upper-class swells wondering what on earth those nasty people on the streets of London are saying. Vaux will pull open the curtain on the 19th century criminal world and its unique language: spectacles are 'barnacles', to 'Betty a door' is to pick a lock, to 'spank a glaze' is to break the window pane of a store. Perhaps, like Vaux, you like to gamble, maybe even roll the 'tatts' (dice). And always, as within any ecosystem, there is a bottom feeder. And that happens to be the 'tinny hunter', a profession reserved for the special few lacking any empathy. They can always be found attending the many house fires around London and, under the pretence of helping the victims remove their property, plundering whatever remains of value.

Vaux's guide to the criminal classes is a riot of colour and detail that historians will lap up over the coming centuries. But Vaux is at his best when describing the hulks. He knows them more intimately than just about anyone else.

On one of his stays on the Thames before another journey to New Holland, Vaux is imprisoned on the *Retribution*: 'There were confined in this floating dungeon nearly 600 men,' he writes, 'most of them double-ironed . . . the reader may conceive the horrible effects arising from the continual rattling of chains, the filth and vermin naturally produced by such a crowd of miserable inhabitants, the oaths and execrations constantly heard amongst them.'

Vaux will always remember arriving on board, being stripped and washed in large tubs of water before putting on a suit of coarse cloth, shackled to leg irons and sent below. And there, well, who should he meet but many old acquaintances 'who were all eager to offer me their friendship and services, that is, with a view to rob me of what little I had, for in this place there is no other motive or subject for ingenuity'.

But it is the guards and the putrid conditions that Vaux will never forget.

'These guards are the most commonly of the lowest class of human beings; wretches devoid of all feeling; ignorant in the extreme, brutal by nature, and rendered tyrannical and cruel by the consciousness of the power they possess . . . they invariably carry a large and ponderous stick, with which, without the smallest provocation, they will fell an unfortunate convict to the ground and frequently repeat their blows long after the poor sufferer is insensible.

'If I were to attempt a full description of the miseries endured in these ships, I could fill a volume . . . besides robbery from each other, which is as common as cursing and swearing, I witnessed among the prisoners . . . one deliberate murder . . . and one suicide; and that unnatural crimes are openly committed.'

They say you can smell the hulks long before you see them; at night you can hear the screams and cries and not even the rain beating down and the wind gusting across the water can muffle the despair and sadness.

And if you listen closely enough right now you might also hear the sound of oars breaking water and the grunts of sweating men. There's a boat being rowed across Langstone Harbour. It is coming for you, William Buckley – you and many of your fellow convicts. William Marmon and George Lee and the rest are to be taken from the hulks and placed on board HMS *Calcutta*, a 56-gun former Navy cruiser under orders to take more than 300 convicts, 30 wives and children of prisoners, and marines and a crew of almost 170 to the other side of the world.

It is April in the Year of Our Lord, 1803.

See? Perhaps a little hope lives here, after all.

2

BEHEADED; AND THE KING LOSES HIS HEAD

Escaping and surviving. If there are two things you're good at, two things you're going to be better at doing than just about anyone else, it's the art of disappearing. Not bad for a big man who finds it impossible to blend into a crowd, whose face and features are forever imprinted on anyone whose path you cross. Thing is, becoming a great escape artist is not about how anonymous you look, or how clever you might be at picking a lock. It's all in the timing, isn't it? When that opening comes, when that chance finally presents itself – often out of nowhere – you just have to take it.

You've done it in the past. If you hadn't taken chances you could still be laying bricks back in that rural village in Cheshire and siring bastards like yourself all over the countryside. Or your bones could be rotting beneath the soil of a foreign country courtesy of a French bayonet or musket ball. But there was always a moment – maybe you will call it luck – that steered you in another direction.

Being accused of breaking into Mr Cave's drapery . . . well, that didn't turn out so well. But you can call getting out of that prison hulk a great escape by any measure and, now that you have made it out before a drunken guard belted you senseless just to make a name for himself, or a fellow convict slid a knife into your guts for the very same reason, or one of the rampant diseases claimed even your strong body, how do you fancy your chances here on the deck of HMS *Calcutta*?

Not good, are they? There is an attachment of guards from the marines watching all of you shuffle aboard in your leg irons. Just before they take you below to the two big prison rooms you get a quick look around, enough to know things are going to be awfully cramped for the next six months. More than 500 of you – 300 convicts – all living and eating and shitting in a world made of oak and tar 230 feet long and 41 feet wide. That's not much more than six square feet for each of you – a world less than half a soccer field, held together by nail and rope and more than a little of, yes, hope.

She's an old ship, this one, a 15-year sea veteran the Navy purchased from the East India Company a few years earlier. She has undergone a major refit for this journey to New Holland and you can smell the pine tar and turpentine and linseed oil and wonder just how long it will last before the stench of all those lives on board takes over. But her bones are solid. She was built in John Perry's yard on the Thames and it took more than 2000 wagonloads of oak dragged all the way from the forests of Sussex to put her together. Still, it is going to be an awfully small world as it heaves its way through some of the most treacherous oceans on the planet. Not everyone is going to make it; the death toll on convict ships heading to New Holland has been appalling since the First Fleet sailed away in 1787. But look at the world you are leaving. It makes about as much sense as the one you are entering.

—

Two men are losing their heads in early 1803 and they perfectly sum up the manic world of extremes England has become at the turn of the 19th century.

London is still awash with debate about the first head; just a few weeks earlier, as rain fell on a miserably cold morning, this head had been hanging by its hair from the hand of an executioner.

He had then thrust it forward, blood mingling with the icy rain, and yelled out to the 20,000-strong crowd: 'This is the head of a traitor, Edward Marcus Despard!'

Well, they hadn't liked that. They began hissing and jeering and the jail warden began nervously eyeing off the six skyrockets he had been ordered to fire if public disquiet turned to insurrection. The rockets and their trail would activate hundreds of soldiers on standby.

Yet the squalls of rain and the sheer awfulness of Despard's beheading had sucked all the energy and most of the anger out of the crowd. Still, 20,000 braving the conditions to witness an execution was an extraordinary number. It told you the people were restless and a suspicious man might very well smell revolt in the air. Well, there could be none of that. Even murmurings of dissent hinted at weakness and vulnerability, something Napoleon Bonaparte, plotting away in Paris and about to become the first Emperor of the despised French, could exploit and use to his advantage.

A rare and uneasy peace exists between England and France. No-one believes this paper-thin Treaty of Amiens can last and, sure enough, within a few months, the old enemies will be at each other again. But for now, in the vacuum peace often creates, distrust and suspicion are everywhere.

Despard's trial exposed this. Irish born, he had fought for England in the American Revolution and then led his forces to a famous victory in the Battle of Black River, which had handed Britain control of Honduras. But Despard, spurred on by his Irish nationalism and rankled by the British parliament's refusal to repay him money he had used to fund the Honduran campaign, had started wondering – loudly at times – about the righteousness of the French Revolution.

People were tired of kings. Liberty – now there was an idea. In late 1802 the authorities identified Despard as a key conspirator in a plot to trigger a revolution on London's streets by seizing the Tower of London and assassinating King George III. During his trial Despard maintained his innocence. Little strong evidence was tendered against him and he had also received extraordinary support with a character reference by Horatio Nelson.

But despite all this he had been found guilty of high treason. What came next stunned everyone. The Lord Chief Justice handed down his verdict, announcing that Despard and six of his co-conspirators were 'to be drawn on a hurdle to the place of execution, there to be hanged by the neck, but not until you are quite dead, then to be cut down and your bowels taken out and cast into the fire before your faces; your heads to be taken off and your bodies quartered'.

The verdict astonished just about everyone except those within the King's circle. The last man in living memory hung, drawn and quartered had been a Scotsman, David Tyrie, a clerk in the Portsmouth Navy Office convicted in 1782 of selling secrets to the French. But hours after the carpenters began erecting the gallows just south of the Thames on the roof of the gatehouse at Horsemonger Lane jail, Despard's sentence was softened. No quartering or burning of the bowels would take place. Just a simple hanging and beheading, fit for a traitor.

The crowd was the largest public gathering in London in decades and the handling of the execution would be talked about for years to come. After making a speech once again declaring his innocence, Despard stepped back and a noose was placed around his neck, the hangman ensuring the notch was tightened behind his left ear to ensure a quick death. One of Despard's colleagues looked out at the vast execution audience and said: 'What an amazing crowd.'

Despard looked up at the skies and uttered his last words: ''Tis very cold. I think we shall have some rain.'

It ended brutally. Despard's body was taken down after hanging in the freezing air for more than 40 minutes. The surgeon responsible for the beheading tried to cut through a joint in the neck vertebrae but botched it and was quickly reduced to hacking. He was joined by the executioner who twisted Despard's head back and forth until the surgeon's blade finally severed it from the body. No wonder the crowd hissed. No-one really took offence when a traitor lost his head.

The more humiliation the better. But this? There were many in the crowd who saw Despard as a patriot rather than a Judas, a loyalist trying to protect the nation from the real enemy.

Which brings us to the second head that helps make some sort of sense of England at the turn of the 19th century. It belongs to King George III, the man Despard had been allegedly plotting to kill.

But George doesn't need any help when it comes to losing his head. He can do that all by himself.

—

No wonder you're happy to leave this country. You're not one of the ruling class. Unlike them, you still had to trudge through streets strewn with horse dung while you were a free man. No carriage or footman for you. Unlike many of them you have not been a beneficiary of the enormous profits being made by the British East India Company as it plunders the world with its private army of 26,000 soldiers and fleet of powerful ships. The Age of Enlightenment, that era when philosophers and artists and scientists shone their lights on the human condition and celebrated a new age of scientific reason and discovery, never quite reached those parts of rural England where you grew up. The elites in their parlours and reading rooms can do as much thinking and measuring and studying as they like, but in Cheshire people know there are still ghosts and fairies and witches lurking in the countryside. Cunning folk – healers and magicians – still ply their trade through the small towns and villages. The sight of a white horse means you have to spit on the ground to avoid bad luck. Even a squinting neighbour can hint at misfortune to come. Seventy years earlier, just as the Enlightenment began, the parliament had made it a crime to accuse someone of witchcraft. But in most villages and hamlets there is an old crone everyone knows is hatching some sort of mischief.

And now the Enlightenment is coming to an end. A new era of cold reason is replacing the age of curiosity. The first Industrial Revolution, with its steam-powered machines and grinding iron cogs, is underway. Massive swathes of the rural population are moving into the cities. London is already seething with more than a million people. Tens of thousands of prostitutes work its squalid streets, vying for trade in the thousands of gin houses and gambling dens.

England might be the greatest power in the world – within a few decades the Empire will rule over one in four inhabitants of the planet – but much of the nation's gold-embossed livery is falling apart. War has long been its greatest industry – more than 60 per cent of the government budget is allocated to the Navy and Army to support the never-ending hostility with France and others amid Europe's constantly shifting alliances. But the treasury's coffers could do with a lift. Only a year or two ago crop failures after a freezing winter and a rainless summer led to bread riots and mutterings that perhaps the French are not so wrong when they play at revolutions. In Essex, a recipe for turnip bread circulates among the poor. The effects of this new Industrial Age can be seen in Regent's Park. There, with its 400 acres of rolling paddocks leased to farmers, smart men can tell how long the sheep have been grazing by the amount of soot blackening their wool.

And ruling over this divided kingdom is Mad George. Nervous courtiers wonder when his next bout of insanity will strike. Days and weeks of mania have been happening more frequently in recent years and will only worsen. The King will be known to write sentences of more than 400 words – a considerable achievement even by the florid writing standards of the day. He will speak and roar for hours until, foaming at the mouth, his voice finally grows faint and he collapses. A rumour will spread from the elites to the streets that the King has shaken hands with a tree, mistaking it for the King of Prussia. Doctors will place him in straightjackets and apply poultices to draw out the 'evil humours'. One manic bout will see him speak continuously for 56 hours.

It will take another 200 years before the inheritors of the Enlightenment and the Industrial Revolution – scientists in white coats in sterile laboratories – test a strand of the King's hair and discover abnormal levels of arsenic, built up through 40 years of powdered wigs and make-up.

To think it had all begun so promisingly. There's a portrait of George not long after his coronation, painted just after 1760 when he was 22. It shows a soft-looking young man with pale and slender fingers, cherubic lips and slim body swathed in an enormous fur cloak and gold finery. No hint of the madness to come, no sign of the flushed red face and narrow eyes and foam forming in a corner of his mouth. Say what you like about kings being disposed to madness and how all that damn inbreeding makes it inevitable, but don't say George is not for England. He has ruled since 1760 and in his many saner moments has been keen to make his mark. Eager to shrug off concerns that his German predecessors of the last 200 years were more loyal to Hanover than London, he told the nation after his coronation that 'born and educated in this country, I glory in the name of Britain'.

George has seen England through a period of unprecedented change. There have been many conflicts; success over the French in the Seven Years War and bloody battles throughout Asia and throughout Europe. But he also carries the blame for the loss of the 13 colonies during the American War of Independence and that scar still runs deep.

It's one of the reasons why you, William, now find yourself chained on HMS *Calcutta* and bound for New Holland. Those American colonies had proved to be a rich dumping ground for England's criminals; from the early 1700s almost 50,000 convicts had been shipped to the New World and the Caribbean. Many were sold to private contractors who used them as nothing more than slave labour. But victory had given the American revolutionary leaders a deter-mination to end their role as receivers of unwanted English goods. Cheaper fodder to pick their cotton had come with an endless supply of imported black slaves.

George had been stubborn to the end. When negotiations began over a settlement to the revolution, he had written to his advisers saying he would not allow the Americans any favours but 'permitting them to obtain men unworthy to remain in this island I shall certainly consent to'.

So many had proven to be unworthy of remaining on English soil. And now, with a new century underway, the prisons are overflowing. It is estimated up to one in eight Londoners survive on the proceeds of crime. There are more than 160 offences listed as worthy of capital punishment and if those soft magistrates showed a little less mercy then perhaps all those ships of the damned, clogging up the Thames with their 100,000 chained and tortured souls, would not be needed.

But this is the problem with rapid progress. You know it from your days as a soldier. A fast march leaves the unfit and the unlucky behind, vulnerable to attack.

In the reign of George III, the real madness takes place in the cities and towns where those left behind struggle to survive. We know a great deal about the bleak lives they lead from the work of Henry Mayhew, a rare journalist of his time who gets his hands dirty by delving into the reality of London street life in the 19th century.

It must have taken Mayhew some work to win the confidence of London's underclass. Pudgy and balding with hair hanging loosely over his ears, Mayhew hardly resembles an investigative reporter keen to expose society's underbelly. He will become a co-founder of the satirical magazine *Punch* and go on to experience the life of many an editor in the 19th century – fleeing debtors, sometimes overseas. But his book *London Labour and the London Poor* is the work of a patient and observant anthropologist.

And one who treads carefully. Mayhew discovers the 'pure-finders' – treasure hunters who haunt any area with a stray dog population in order to collect their faeces. Those who make a living from collecting it in buckets know dog turds as brown gold. It is a vital ingredient when it comes to softening leather used in the bookbinding process. Why, this is the sort of thing that gets economists excited. Here, surely, is a great by-product of the Age of

Enlightenment – the ruling class and its voracious reading habits creating income for the illiterate poor!

A few blocks away you might find crossing sweepers, paid to remove the horse dung and mud from the streets so that the very same ruling class can cross the street without dirtying their shoes. There are mudlarks – usually old women and young children – sifting through the refuse and sewage on the banks of the Thames for anything that might be of value. Who knows, a bloated corpse could be sold on to a medical school for dissection. London is a tumult of noise and bodies pressing against one another, eking out a living in the biggest and filthiest city in the world.

There is already talk of new laws to protect workers, but for the moment it is just that – talk. For now, children work 12-hour days in factories and six-year-olds are sent up chimneys to ensure dinner parties are not ruined by smoke and soot. The best of the sweeps, Mayhew learns, know how to navigate their way up the inside of the wider flues – elbows and knees out, edging carefully upward. But for the inexperienced, injuries and death come with the job. 'I niver got to stay stuck myself, but a many of them did,' one sweep tells Mayhew. The boy began his apprenticeship at the age of seven. The dead 'were smothered for want of air, and the fright, and a stayin' so long in the flue'.

And always, the putrid smell of rotting food and the open sewer that is the Thames, its murky waters a depository for bodies, industrial waste and sewage. 'Through the heart of the town a deadly sewer ebbed and flowed, in the place of a fine fresh river,' Dickens will write sombrely. But others just shrug. 'He who drinks a tumbler of London water has literally in his stomach more animated beings than there are men, women and children on the face of the globe,' writes the humourist Sydney Smith. Is it any wonder that regular cholera epidemics sweep through the poorer parts of London? The smell will reach its climax with The Great Stink of 1849 when parliament is shut down; its MPs huddled behind curtains soaked with chloride of lime to avoid the nauseous stench. Nosegays – posies of flowers and scented herbs like rosemary and thyme – will become not just a fashion accessory but a necessity, particularly for judges not only battling the stink of the city but the lower classes who fill their courtrooms.

No, you don't need this world, William Buckley. It certainly doesn't want you. And this new home of yours for the next few months, the *Calcutta*. It might be small and stifling. And lives will certainly be lost before this journey across the world is completed. But it feels solid. Reliable. Years of salt water and rain have flowed down through the decks, seeping through cracks and knots, all the way into the bilges where the wood has swelled and sealed itself into a thick, impenetrable skin.

That's oak for you, doing what oak does best. You're not a shipbuilder, even though you're good with your hands. But oak is something you know about. It feels and smells of home.

3

YOUR MOTHER, 16 AND UNWED

In late 700 AD, in the cold autumn soil in the kingdom of Mercia, the shell of a small acorn begins to crack. Above ground, King Offa is in the midst of his long and bloodthirsty reign as one of the most successful rulers of the Dark Ages. Viking raiders are about to begin plundering the coastline of Britain. They will look upon many of the English as easy pickings; soft worshippers of a Christian god with no concept of Valhalla, no idea about the glory of death with an axe in your grip and the blood of an opponent on your hands.

But Offa is a man the Vikings can easily admire. He is ruthlessly stitching together an empire that will make him the greatest English monarch history has yet known. Offa has set about uniting many of the seven kingdoms that now make up Britain. Rival kings not interested in bending the knee are quickly disposed of. Even a son-in-law who grows too powerful is assassinated.

Maybe that's why this small acorn is already growing, its emerging root feasting on the nutrients and moisture below. The land around here is fertile, thick with the blood and bone of Anglo-Saxons and Celts and Romans and all the tribes that came before them. It will take Offa decades to build his kingdom. For this acorn, it will only take six months before its first small green shoot breaks the surface to be greeted by a spring sun. But it will still be there more than a thousand years later, still dropping acorns, still feeding off the rich soil as, not very far away, a young, unwed woman, scared and lathered in sweat, exhausted from the endless contractions, finally pushes a very large baby boy out of her womb.

A few years later two well-educated brothers from London, the antiquarians Daniel and Samuel Lysons, will begin an ambitious and epic series on the topography and history of Britain they will call *Magna Britannia*. Hitching a wagon loaded with supplies, they travel throughout rural England, arriving one day in the small village of Marton in Cheshire, once a part of the kingdom of Mercia. 'Not far from the chapel is a very fine oak,' they will note, '. . . which although but little known is believed to be the largest in England.'

Little known elsewhere, perhaps. But, William, you know that oak. Every child – every person – in Marton is aware of the Oak and its secrets. In the early 1780s, long after Offa has turned to dust, it has become one of the oldest sessile oak trees in the world, still grimly holding on to life, still sucking out the last of the marrow from those medieval bones. Its girth is more than 50 feet and decay has long set in, eating away at its heartwood and splitting the trunk, leaving it resembling three separate trees that have come together, arms embracing but with a respectable amount of space between them, like reluctant relatives at a family reunion.

The Lysons brothers, true sons of the Enlightenment, have measured and examined this oak. But like all city types with their heads buried in books, they've missed the obvious and no-one in the village is likely to let them in on the secret. The Oak is an old sage from a past era, a dispenser of wisdom and medicine. Who needs word getting out that the bark from the Oak – just a small piece – can cure warts and other skin diseases if you rub it on your skin? Farmers hang the bark in their homes for good luck, warding off evil spirits. The grand old tree is a relic from those Dark Ages when magic and mysticism were as feared as Offa's sword.

Even two centuries after your birth, the village of Marton will not have changed that much. The ruts from the wooden wheels of carriages might be covered in bitumen but the small lanes will still be there, hugged by native hedges blended with hawthorn and blackthorn and holly, a little elder and dog rose here and there, the lush rolling country filled with shallow valleys and lazy dairy cows until the open plains meet the Pennines to the north, a range of hills and small mountains known as the backbone of England.

Even the half-wood house you are supposed to have been born in, down in Marton Lane not far from that gnarled old tree, is still there. No longer recognisable, perhaps. But it will make a visitor wonder why on earth you would want to escape from this place. That feeling of being trapped, that need to get free, must run deep. How often did you wander past the Davenport Arms Inn as a young man and look up at the crest – a serf's head with a rope around his neck? From the 1300s the land around here was ruled by the Davenports, the game wardens appointed to protect the King's forests and hunting grounds. Thieves caught poaching deer or hares and captured highwaymen who had been plundering passing carriages would be hauled down to the inn and put on trial in one of the upstairs rooms. Once that guilty verdict was announced – and the Davenports, zealous guardians of their fiefdom, didn't waste time with due process – a small crowd would gather outside. Once the rope had done its work, the body would be placed in a gibbet and suspended outside for all to see, rotting until the crows had pecked it clean and the bones had bleached in the sun.

So much beauty around here. And just as much horror never far from the surface.

A faded document shows William Buckley is baptised on 31 March 1782, just down the road from Marton in Siddington at the All Saints church, an old timber-framed building going back to the 1300s. The good Lord must be looking carefully after the place. When the bishop welcomes you into the house of God and dabs your head with holy water, the walls of the church are bulging; someone years earlier decided to replace the centuries-old thatched roof with heavy Kerridge stone slabs, and now the church's sides are swollen and buckling under their enormous weight.

The woman holding you is Elizabeth. She is 16 and unwed. Your father has already vanished from history's pages and not even his surname will linger. Instead, you will take on the name of your mother and her parents, farmers Jonathan and Martha. In five years' time Elizabeth will marry James Stanway, a 22-year-old shoemaker from nearby Middlewich. She will be pregnant when she weds and will leave you in the care of your grandparents.

Now that, surely, is something you will wonder about over the years. Elizabeth and James will go on to have four children of their own. You will call them your brothers and sisters . . . but Elizabeth never came back to raise you herself. Why was that? Were you too much of a handful? Or did her new husband not want the seed of another man in his presence? It could hardly have been the shame of having brought a bastard into the world – in the late 18th century illegitimate offspring are everywhere.

It's a subject that must be touchy because, years later, when you are asked about your childhood, all you will say is that 'from some circumstance or other, I was adopted by my mother's father'. Well, whatever the reason, Jonathan and Martha take you into their home and raise you on their small farm of one acre, three roods and 30 perches, which is almost two acres of that lush Marton ground. They are not the strictest of parents, old Jonathan and Martha, even you will admit that. They send you to evening school where you are taught to read. But William Buckley isn't much of a student. You will have forgotten what you were taught and for the rest of your life your signature, your mark, will be an uncertain cross, pressed against paper with a nervous hand, as if you are trying carefully not to make a mess of something as simple as two intersecting lines.

As for all those years here in Marton . . . you won't remember much. 'The wandering, extraordinary life I have led has naturally obliterated from my memory many of the earlier scenes of my childhood,' you will say many years later. But you will never forget old Robert Wyatt, will you? In a way, he's the man who stokes those early desires to escape, to get away.

—

You will never be a scholar. But as you enter your teens Jonathan has obviously seen your huge hands and those massive feet and the way you cannot enter any doorway without stooping. It's as if the grand old Marton Oak has taken on human form. A man would need two acres just to keep you fed. So Jonathan has started thinking that if your brain is not going to provide for your future, then certainly that body can – and will. And suddenly you find yourself indentured to Robert Wyatt, a bricklayer in the nearby village of Butley.

If Jonathan and Martha have been a tad soft with you, your new master will make up for it. 'Master Wyatt'. Or just 'Master'. Isn't that what you must call him? Apprenticeships in the late 18th century usually involve a contract between the parents and the craftsman for seven years. The master takes on his 'prentice not just at the work site but in his home as well, providing food and lodging and constant instruction. Old Wyatt must have thought he'd hit the jackpot when he first laid eyes on you. He probably has a workhorse the same size tethered to the ring pit, walking in circles shackled to a trough, mixing the clay mortar before it is moulded.

It's a real craft, this one. A bricklayer has to know how to fire the kiln and bake the bricks, increasing the heat until they are cooked and hardened and won't crumble when you apply the slurry and fix them in place. He must have a feel for straight lines. Hard work, too. It can leave a man hunched and broken as he grows older. It soon becomes apparent to you that this is not the life for you. Wyatt is a disciplinarian. He has rules and expectations and you start to simmer with resentment. Not as bad as the shackles and leg irons on those prison hulks, or life deep in the hold of the *Calcutta*.

But it's enough to get you thinking. It might be time to escape.

4

THE SCUM
OF THE EARTH

The scum of the earth. Is that really you, William? One of England's greatest heroes will say that about men like you. This hero, this legendary figure, is Arthur Wellesley, the first Duke of Wellington, the man who will finally end Napoleon's dreams of conquering Europe. There, at the battle of Waterloo, as the squat Frenchman squirms in his saddle unable to keep his mind on the battlefield because of the pain shooting up his backside from his ever present haemorrhoids, Wellesley will take charge and lead his alliance with Prussia to victory, a triumph that will end the First French Empire, the Napoleonic Wars and the rule of Napoleon himself.

Wellesley might come from Irish aristocratic stock but he's not that different to you. He's a late bloomer. He might have gone to Eton but he was no scholar. His newly widowed mother would often complain about his inability to concentrate or focus, saying once: 'I don't know what I shall do with my awkward son Arthur'. Well, she needn't have worried. Arthur becomes a hero of the Empire and will go on to serve twice as Prime Minister.

The Duke will offer up more than his share of sanguine quotes to history. When the Battle of Waterloo begins he will turn to his troops and say, 'Hard pounding this, gentlemen. Let's see who pounds the longest.' Of course, the Duke is also a bit of a pounder himself, a notorious womaniser who will confront a publisher threatening to reveal one of his affairs with the words: 'Publish and be damned!'

But 'scum of the earth'? Wellesley is talking in 1813, not long after his forces have routed the French during a crucial battle and, instead of pursuing the retreating rabble, stop to loot the enemy's convoy of wagons.

'The scum of the earth – the mere scum of the earth,' snorts the Duke about England's finest. It's easy to picture him, the corners of his mouth drawn tightly in disgust, peering down over his large Roman nose, that very same beak kind artists will always try to disguise in portraits by painting him head-on. Won't fool the common folk, though. They will celebrate Old Nosey in ballads for years to come.

But as for the scum, 'It is only wonderful that we should be able to make so much of them afterwards. The English soldiers are fellows who have all enlisted for drink – that is the plain fact – they have all enlisted for drink.

'People talk of their enlisting from their fine military feeling – all stuff – no such thing. Some of our men enlist from having got bastard children – some for minor offences – many more for drink.'

It's not drink that has lured you to enlist, although by your own account it may contribute to many of your problems in a few years' time. But signing up with the Cheshire militia – an 18th century version of the army reserve – means an escape from the monotony of bricklaying and all of Master Wyatt's rules and discipline. And that bounty of 10 guineas – have you ever seen a fortune like it? You've never had money like this and you must think it will last forever. But it's all gone within a year and so you take another bounty by signing with the 4th or King's Own Regiment of Foot. Easy decision. Guaranteed salary and a promise of a great adventure, travelling the world and fighting for your country.

Problem is, the public mood has soured by the 1790s when it comes to all of Mad George's warmongering. Decades of it have taken their toll. When deserters from the army flee into the countryside mobs often assault and even stab the officers trying to apprehend the runaways. There's a growing suspicion that the desire of the King and his parliament to boost army numbers has less to do with enemies from other shores and more to do with maintaining domestic peace and keeping an eye on possible traitors like Marcus Despard.

And let's face it. The Duke isn't wrong when he laments the lack of quality men at his service. The Secretary of War will stand up in the House of Commons in 1795 and admit that the process of recruiting has lured 'men of very low description'. But you would hardly call it a process. More like a circus. That same year in St George's Field more than a dozen men are found shackled in a cellar awaiting sale to the army recruiters, victims of a local agent who has plied them with rum and perhaps a little coin too, and then obtained their drunken signatures in order to earn his commission. Those men wake the next morning with a headache and the knowledge they have signed on for life – for the King's shilling.

The small towns and rural areas are prime hunting ground for the army's recruiters. Perhaps that is how they found you there in Marton, not far from the old oak, the arrival of the regiment heralded by drums and trumpets. Some of them seem to have studied the promotional techniques of Philip Astley, the father of the modern circus who becomes the first to use clowns and acrobats in his amphitheatre between acts. One regiment employs the 42-inch 'Yorkshire Dwarf' John Heyes, who carries out a sword drill in town squares to lure the crowds. Or how about the battalion whose recruiting campaign centres on Sergeant Samuel Macdonald? Big Sam – now here's a man who makes William Buckley look . . . almost normal. He's six foot 10 inches and his legend is well known. He was the soldier ordered one night to act as sentry over a large cannon. Tired of standing guard in the bitter cold he slung the huge weapon over his shoulder and carried it into the warmth of a nearby guardhouse.

There is little they won't try in the quest to provide fodder for the slaughterhouses of Europe. In 1794 the Marquess of Huntly begins assembling what will become known as the 100th Foot. He uses his mother, the Duchess, a woman known as 'Bonnie Jean' for her ravishing looks, to ride the countryside, visiting farms and hamlets with a shilling on her lips, transferring it with a kiss to any man who signs up.

Well, many of them can't actually *sign* their names but then, the men recruiting them are hardly better educated. One soldier who joins the ranks, Tubal Cain, will find himself forever designated in the books as 'Two Ball Cain'.

But you have your shilling. And they have issued you the famous red waistcoat, a pair of breeches and two pairs of shoes, although God knows how they managed to find the right size. You will have to take that long hair of yours and form it into a 'club'. That takes some doing, doesn't it? You'll have to plaster it with grease, thicken it with flour and then use a small bag of sand to roll it into place at the back of your head. That can take more than an hour and if it falls out of place you have to go through the same routine again.

Little wonder John Gaspard Le Merchant, a cavalry commander during the Napoleonic Wars, will never forget that evening when he arrives in a Flemish barn where his troops are spending the night. 'They were . . . lying on the hay. But to preserve the form of their clubs for the next day, they were all prone on their faces, trying to sleep in that pleasant posture.' One man always had to act as sentry, though. That heavy dusting of flour on each club often drew rats.

But you will have plenty of time to get your club in place each day. Life in the barracks in England is monotonous. Best to avoid indoors during the day. Squalid and cramped, beds are often shared and that bucket of stale piss in the corner of your room should be cleared more often than it is. First morning parade in summer is just after four in the morning. Then breakfast. Then the sergeant's daily sobriety check. The Duke isn't wrong. Alcohol has become a peculiar British disease, cheap gin distilled from the remnants of corn crops is everywhere and the nation's thousands of illegal gin houses barely cope with demand. An average soldier will receive up to a pint of rum or wine with their regular issue of bread or biscuit and beef.

The wounded are regularly plied with booze before surgery. Why, its restorative qualities are endless – a surgeon with the 71st Foot will insist it helps even more in defeat: 'The exhilarating and beneficial effect of liqueur in distressing circumstances is also well known, and often exemplified on the retreat.'

Problem is, they encourage you to drink, to down as much grog as you like. Then they call you the scum of the earth, don't they?

5

FIGHTING THE FRENCH
IN THE DUTCH RAIN

Listen closely. Hard to do that when someone near you is screaming because half their leg is missing and they can't find it no matter
how hard they drag their ruined body through the bedlam and
chaos.

The battlefield is shrouded in smoke from the opening barrage
of cannons and muskets. Your mouth is dry and tastes of powder,
your face blackened, your hearing dulled by the roar of war and the
constant explosions. Your heart, it's thumping so hard it rattles your
ribs and forces your hands to shake.

But listen you must.

There. It's faint at first and only the most experienced hands can
hear it. Then the noise grows, from a low hum to a buzzing sound.
A swarm of bees, here on the battlefield? The veterans know what it
is: incoming musket fire. Old soldiers know to listen because you
can tell by the pitch whether the musket balls still have enough force
to penetrate your body or have lost just enough momentum to leave
a bruise. You flinch and want to drop to the ground but know that
would be breaking formation and if you manage to survive this,
you might not survive the lashes that will come later. So you stand
here, no longer sure where north and south are, lost in the fog and

wondering if a musket ball or a bayonet will be the first to pierce your red coat.

Is this what you wanted, what you thought it might be like when you signed up with the 4th? Your height means you have been made a point man, out here on the flank helping to keep the line straight. But it doesn't matter that much anymore. Another battle on another rain-drenched field somewhere in the Netherlands. More bloodshed before another embarrassing retreat as you nurse a wounded hand and a head filled with unforgettable scenes of carnage. This is not one of those times in the Napoleonic Wars that veterans and historians will recall with relish. No glory here, no opportunity to add even more pain to the little Frenchman's sore arse. He's not even here; Bonaparte is enjoying the warmth of Egypt, basking in a campaign that will ultimately serve as a springboard into statesmanship and the Emperor's throne. But his forces are here and they have combined with the Dutch to give the English and their Russian allies an almighty flogging.

It is October 1799. William Buckley stands at the crossroads of history. Four years earlier the Netherlands had seen one of those popular uprisings against its monarchy, just the sort of grass-roots rebellion against established royalty the rest of Europe had feared after the French Revolution.

French fingerprints were all over this revolution, too, as the Dutch rebels ousted Prince William V and established the Batavian republic. Mad George and his advisers were apoplectic. The French now had access to the Dutch fleet, which meant they were within striking distance of invading Britain.

Restoring Prince William to power seemed the only solution. So in late August 1799, a ragged 40,000-strong coalition of British and Russian troops head to the Netherlands, led by King George's inexperienced son, the Duke of York, Prince Frederick.

The sea crossing provides a taste of things to come. Storms and heaving seas separate the English fleet. Troops are 'packed like a parcel of pigs in an Irish boat' and after landing one naval officer will observe that 'nothing looks more picturesque than to see a parcel of men with powdered heads and cocked hats puking'. It's easy to find you here on the Dutch peninsula as the rain begins to fall. They say only two per cent of most regiments stand six foot or more and around you are hundreds of soldiers more than a foot shorter. Some of them had placed leather pads in their shoes to make themselves look taller when they signed on; others were more ingenious, hiding blocks of wood beneath clumps of hair.

Not that anyone cares that much. You're all battlefield fodder. There will be some early success; the Dutch fleet will be seized in the Battle of Callantsoog and the French-Batavian forces pushed back. Perhaps this is when the Duke of York should stop. Glory might come to all of you. But no, onward you push and as the rain gets heavier, the already patchy roads are washed away, cutting off supplies. The retreating Dutch flood the surrounding farmland, turning it into malarial swampland. The death toll from marsh fever and hunger begins to rise.

These nights must be the worst. It will be another decade before the English army issues tents in the field. So in the darkness you must squat on your knapsack, a greatcoat and a single thin blanket the only thing separating you from the ever-present damp.

Just what the hell was the Duke of Wellington thinking when he sneered at the scum of the earth? It's a miracle any of you can even stand in those sodden uniforms, empty stomachs churning, holes in the line already forming because so many have succumbed to the conditions. This is the sort of fortitude that will inspire Samuel Johnson – yes, *Dr Johnson* himself, the great essayist and moralist – to talk about an epidemic of bravery within the nation's ranks. 'We can shew a peasantry of heroes, and fill our armies with clowns, whose courage may vie with that of their general,' he will write.

This courage, this glue that holds motley regiments together under so much pressure, can be found at night as you huddle against the rain just as often as it is on display on the battlefield. Hard to think of something that can actually prepare a man for that, though.

'Every minute seems an hour and every hour a day,' says a wistful George Gleig, a Scottish soldier and military writer, about those awful moments before battle begins. 'The faces of the bravest often change colour and the limbs of the most resolute tremble, not with fear but anxiety. It is a situation of higher excitement, and darker and deeper feeling, than any other in human life . . .'

And then the trumpets sound. Look at the French once the signal to start fighting is given. They will have had an officer whipping them into a frenzy with a passionate speech about liberty and freedom and all those ridiculous notions the French think should be the way of things. And then they will charge into the fray, hollering and screaming, eyes bulging, looking and sounding like Bonaparte as those haemorrhoids torment him during another arduous stint sitting on the pot.

The English, that stiff upper lip always on show, prefer silence and stillness, believing it might unnerve the opposition.

It doesn't quite have that effect by early October. A few weeks earlier British fears that their Russian allies were riddled with incompetent officers were realised during an attempt to take the village of Bergen. A mix-up saw the Russians attack far too early before the English – stranded by rain and washed-out roads – could support their attack. More than 4000 men had been killed and that is when the finger-pointing had begun in earnest, the acting Russian commander accusing the Duke of York of poor communication.

Small victories followed that debacle as bloody battles raged in vast networks of sand dunes, some of them 200 feet high and held together by dense scrub. No-one there will forget the ferocity of the fighting, much of it descending into hand-to-hand combat with bayonets and fists. It all comes down to this day, the 6th of October, when the allies find themselves under attack from the full forces of the French and Dutch forces outside the town of Castricum. In the afternoon rain falls so hard soldiers can barely see one another let alone the enemy. In the nearby town of Alkmaar one of the Duke's officers climbs the spire of a church tower with a telescope to see what is taking place.

Nothing, neither the rain nor the oncoming darkness, can disguise the carnage. More than 3000 allies dead. One chaotic retreat has left two field hospitals behind with hundreds of wounded. William, count yourself lucky. Your hand may be hurt – you will never say if it was from a bullet or a bayonet – but once again you have found a way out. Two battalions of the 4th have not been so fortunate. They have been lost after stumbling behind enemy lines without any clue where their commanding officers were taking them.

More than 12,000 men in this campaign have been lost. The full retreat after midnight offers little respite. Heavy artillery must be hauled through mud. The Dutch cavalry keep up a constant harassment of the rear. Some English units, unable to tell the difference between sodden tracks and nearby dykes, lose dozens from drowning.

—

The Duke of York – George's son – will learn from this. He will go on to reform the military and turn it into the machine that will dominate the 19th century. But it will take a long time for memories to fade and soldiers like you will be singing the same song in taverns for years to come:

The grand old Duke of York,
He had ten thousand men.
He marched them up to the top of the hill
And he marched them down again.
And when they were up, they were up
And when they were down, they were down.
And when they were only halfway up,
They were neither up nor down.

The Duke has no option but to negotiate for terms. By 18 October these will be signed – Britain agreeing to release 8000 French prisoners of war and the allies allowed to evacuate.

It's a sombre and far smaller fleet that sails home toward a new century. For you, the next two years are going to be hard. Your right hand will heal but what about your mind? You're a paid-up member of the Scum of the Earth and it will be impossible to put aside what you have seen and endured in the past couple of months.

You say your commanding officers have respect for you, although that may have a little something to do with your size. But it won't take long before the restlessness returns. And then things will rapidly go downhill, won't they? What is it you will say, long after you have become an old man and that magnificent mane of hair has begun to recede? 'Feelings of discontent' will descend upon you. That's what you will call them. And that will lead you to become 'associated with several men of bad character in the Regiment, who gradually acquired an influence over my conduct, which very soon led me into scenes of irregularity, and riotous dissipation'.

Now that, given the times, sounds like a polite way of saying the next two years – much of it spent in the barracks as Europe settles into an uneasy peace – descend into a wild stint of drinking and whoring. Don't take it the wrong way. It's hard to pass judgement on a young man who has just lived through the horrors you have seen.

But it cannot possibly end well, can it?

6

A DOUR LEADER;
A SNEAKY BOY

David Collins stands on the deck of the *Calcutta*. Perhaps you catch a glimpse of him as you and the rest of the convicts are taken below, down two levels into the dark hold for prisoners where the ceilings are low and the air is thin. Good-looking man this Collins, tall and broad shouldered. He's just turned 47 but there's not a fleck of grey to be seen in that head of curly sandy hair. Handsome, no doubt about it, not like the weather-beaten faces of the sailors hauling ropes and getting this ship ready to leave England. Important man, too. You only need to see that scarlet coat, with all its brass buttons and gold lapels, to know he wields power. No wonder so many women find him attractive. Within a few days, once the *Calcutta* has made it into the open sea and is well and truly on its way to New Holland, the wife of a convict, fair to the eye herself, will be seen visiting his cabin, where she will keep him entertained through the long nights ahead.

Surely the man is blessed. So why is David Collins feeling as trapped and as miserable as the prisoners parading in front of him?

He's not a bad man. God, no. Fact is, Collins is a man with more empathy than most in this era. Hannah Power, that 26-year-old convict's wife he will soon be sleeping with . . . because he is David Collins he will grant her cuckolded husband, Matthew Power, special privileges; the ability to roam the ship almost at will, along with a place to sleep a long way from the rest of the rabble. Surely that will give the man a good night's rest, a chance to put to one side the thought of his wife keeping the Lieutenant-Governor up all night.

In just six months' time Collins will stride ashore to set up a new colony in an alien world. At the King's behest, too. He should be excited. But all he can feel is that familiar devil of disappointment gnawing at his insides. Once more he must do his best to disguise it. Yet with each passing year it gets harder. It was not meant to be this way, not for a man blessed with intelligence and the luck of being born into a respected military family. Collins is growing weary of it all: the years of unfairly being passed over for promotion, the empty promises of patrons and superiors, as well as what seems like half a lifetime apart from his constantly ailing wife, Maria. Not to mention the unspoken disappointment of his family and having to watch his younger brother George marry into a prosperous family and become a successful farmer.

And Collins? He has taken on this role to return to New Holland – to set up a new colony at Port Phillip, more than 500 miles south of Port Jackson where he and the rest of the First Fleet had landed 15 years earlier – because he has no choice. After years on half-pay, financial ruin is certain if he remains in London.

Resentment eats away at him. It has almost swallowed him whole. He once penned letters home that were filled with the soft language of a man who viewed the world through a far gentler lens than men like his father, good old Arthur Tooker Collins. Now there was a man of his times, a stern and unemotional former marine who had never felt more alive than dodging storms of cannonballs. It is only 10 years since Collins wrote to Tooker to confide that: 'I have always thought that nature designed me for the tranquil rather than the bustling walk of life . . . I know I was meant by that unerring guide to wear the gown rather than the habiliments of a soldier. Nature intended and fashioned me to ascend the pulpit and there I think I should have shown ability.'

You can only begin to imagine how that went down with Tooker. Probably the same way it did back in 1775. Collins, who had been drafted into his father's marine regiment at the age of 14, had gone on to fight in the famous battle of Bunker Hill. The American Revolution was at its height and Collins had been involved in a bayonet charge – one of war's most frightening experiences. When it was over he had looked across a battlefield littered with a thousand broken bodies. But nothing managed to extinguish his enthusiasm for military life more than a couple of barbs from his father.

'I have just had two letters from my father,' Collins wrote to his beloved mother, Henrietta, 'which gave me a great deal of uneasiness as it first informed of your illness and next of my having displeased him; I know not which gave me the most pain. Believe me, dear Madam, it has destroyed the little happiness I was beginning to enjoy here. I flattered myself that I was very well liked among the officers . . .'

Always, this sense of failing to live up to expectations. Always, this growing bitterness that he has served King and country and deserves far better. Thirty years earlier he had been on the frigate HMS *Southampton* during its secret mission to rescue King George's sister, Queen Caroline Matilda. Now that had been the sort of swash-buckling assignment any young ensign could only dream about. The Queen had been married off to her first cousin, King Christian VII of Denmark, another monarch tormented by voices in his head. He could sometimes be found banging that head against a wall until it bled. There were hallucinations and vast mood swings and unprompted bursts of laughter. He'd turned his back on the young Queen almost from their wedding night, taking on a courtesan as his mistress and spending his evenings in Copenhagen's brothels. Caroline, isolated and unloved, began an affair with her husband's surgeon and confidant, Johann Struensee. He, of course, ended up losing his head. After lengthy negotiations it was agreed the English could send a ship to collect Caroline and escort her to a castle in Hanover where the woman who had brought such embarrassment to both royal families could live out her life in exile. When the *Southampton* docked in the port city of Elsinore, it had been a 16-year-old David Collins who stepped forward, bowed, took her hand and kissed it gently as she came on board.

But all that was so long ago. It is now late April 1803. The journals and letters of David Collins are no longer filled with delicate sentences and soft reminiscences. He has seen the convicts loaded on to the *Calcutta* and will write despairingly that they 'are a collection of old, worn out, useless men, or children equally as useless'.

Who else can he turn to, who else understands the depth of his frustration more than his beloved mother, Henrietta? He has just sent a letter to let her know he must submit 'to another separation, which I trust will be more blessed with good fortune than was the past . . . I think and hope that my evil genius is weary of persecuting me and resigns his place to a better.'

Evil genius? If you heard that, you would probably throw back your head and unleash your loudest laugh in years. Collins has his looks and standing and a fine scarlet coat and a cabin with a comfortable bed of his own that will be kept warm at night by one of the best-looking women on this ship.

Yes, hard to compare that with your leg irons and your thin and frayed trousers and the slop that will serve as food over the coming months. But let's get things in perspective. You could also have a rope around your neck.

—

Have you seen that small boy who has been brought on board the *Calcutta*? Yes, there are quite a few, many of them in irons. But there is one in particular you should keep a close eye on because in 30 years' time he is going to make your life difficult. If only you knew how difficult. You could try showing him a little kindness; perhaps throw a portion of your ration his way from time to time. Might make things much easier down the track. Take a good look at him scampering about the deck, sticking his nose into other folks' business, getting in the way of the sailors as they load the last of the supplies before you leave Portsmouth. Little Johnny Fawkner. He's only 10 years old and looks half his age with his pasty face and short legs but already there's a touch of arrogance about him. You can see it in the way he lurks and listens in on conversations. Raised by his grandparents for a few years – wealthy folk who no doubt spoiled him. But they have just died. His old man is being transported for 14 years for receiving stolen goods – a diamond necklace and a gold snuffbox full of more diamonds worth more than 400 quid – and little Johnny now has to accompany his parents to the other side of the earth. Just be careful with him if he ever crosses your path. He has a ferocious memory and an even greater appetite for exaggeration and duplicity.

The Fawkners – John senior, his wife Hannah and their nosey kid – have been desperate to stay out of the prison rooms below and thanks to those wealthy grandparents they have negotiated with one of the ship's carpenters; for 20 pounds they will take his room in the fore cockpit with a convicted counterfeiter, James Grove, and his wife and son.

That's how it works, isn't it? If you had a little coin then maybe you and your mate from the regiment, Will Marmon, could also be living it up in more salubrious quarters. But two years of that 'riotous dissipation' after coming back from the Netherlands must have left you a little short. Is that why you and Marmon broke into John Cave's drapery? You will be a little vague about the events so many years later and a lot of that will be understandable given what happens to you. Perhaps, along with those memories of the battlefield, you preferred to tuck it away in the deepest recesses of your mind. Or maybe – just maybe – you have been telling the truth all along and the entire thing was a set-up.

A well-meaning reverend, George Langhorne, will try to get to the bottom of it with you more than 35 years later and all you will offer is that one day while you were crossing the barrack yards in Horsham 'a woman whom I did not know requested me to carry a piece of cloth to a woman of the garrison to be made up. I was stopped with it in my possession. The property had been stolen. I was considered the thief and though innocent sentenced to transportation for life.'

But that's not quite the story that makes its way into *The Sussex Weekly Advertiser* on 2 August 1802. A keen reader will have scanned the reports of local vegetable prices and magical elixirs for coughs and bad skin. And they will have no doubt been horrified by the remarkable detail on the front page of artillery Captain Mazot, who, having eaten a 'hearty dinner with his mistress, shot himself a few days ago under the chin with a pistol loaded with three balls. His head was shattered in a frightful manner; one of the bullets took out one of his eyes but the other two, which no doubt reached the brain, could not be found. The unfortunate man had full knowledge enough to perceive that he had not fully perpetrated his crime and with a dagger again wounded himself in several parts of his body . . .'

Compared to Captain Mazot's troubles, your situation rates a simple paragraph on page three. The *Advertiser* reports that the shop of Mr Cave in nearby Warnham 'was broken open and robbed of several pieces of printed linens and cottons, stockings &c. and on Tuesday last a woman, wife of a soldier of the 4th regiment of foot, was taken into custody . . . on suspicion of being concerned in the robbery. The woman, it seems, had offered several of the stolen articles for sale . . . she was immediately suspected and secured. She has since impeached two men of the above regiment as principals and they were all on Wednesday committed to Horsham Gaol, for trial at our next assizes.'

You might be innocent after all. This woman – her name is Margaret Harris – knows she is in deep trouble. Stealing cloth is one of those 160 crimes punishable by death. Almost a third of all offences across England involve cloth and other material. The wars have hurt trade with the traditional fashion houses of France and Italy and, while Britain's textile industry is churning out material as fast as it can thanks to those oiled cogs and steam machines of the Industrial Revolution, a well-cut outfit can be worth a year's average wage.

And now Margaret Harris has fingered you and Marmon. It doesn't take long for the next Sussex assizes – courts held periodically all around England usually dealing with serious offences – to be called to order in front of the visiting judges, headed by Baron Hotham. The hearing is surely not a long one and it's unlikely anyone represents you and Marmon.

The following week the *Sussex Advertiser* is back on the streets reporting the outcome: 'At our assizes, which ended on Tuesday last, ten prisoners were tried, four of whom were capitally convicted and received sentences of death, viz . . . William Buckley and William Marmon, the former aged 20 and the latter 25, for burglariously entering the shop of Mr Cave, of Warnham, and stealing therein two pieces of Irish linen.'

Death. How does it feel? You have faced the prospect before on the battlefield. But not like this. Hanging is not the swift form of execution it will become later this century when science will dictate the position of the knot and the length of the drop based on a man's weight, all designed to instantly snap the neck. No, to be hanged is often a drawn-out affair, a slow and agonising strangulation that is sometimes only brought to a merciful close by the hangman pulling down on your legs. So this is how it finishes, at the end of a rope, because of a simple piece of cloth? You are left shackled for hours with nothing else to think about.

And then, as the judges head back to London, they will issue a reprieve and reduce both your and Marmon's sentences to transportation for life. They often do that these days. A nice touch of humanity, even if it has turned those prison hulks into reeking, overflowing cesspits. And as the pair of you are hauled away and sent to the hulks in Langstone, what do you discover? Margaret Harris is 'discharged by proclamation'.

That's how it works. No-one really believes in the concept of fairness, do they? Certainly not here in these early years of the 19th century as the *Calcutta* finally sails from England with its cargo of more than 500 souls and a morose man called David Collins expected to lead them into a new world.

7

'THE TREATMENT ON THE PASSAGE WAS VERY GOOD'

Say what you like about David Collins – and they will be lining up with all sorts of uncomplimentary complaints in the years to come, led by a nasty piece of work called William Bligh – but don't mistake his distaste for military life for softness. Collins knows how difficult it is to establish a new colony on the other side of the world and he has been as diligent as usual in his preparations. As the *Calcutta* embarks on the first leg of its journey to New Holland, down the west coast of Africa before crossing the Atlantic toward Rio de Janeiro, secured in the hold is a second-hand printing press Collins insisted the Navy buy for the voyage. It wasn't long ago that he took up his quill and penned another letter in his flawless handwriting asking for additional, often-used letters such as 'A' and 'E' and 'R' and 'T' to be supplied for the press. Just in case.

It's the small details that matter. He'd shaken his head when preparations for the *Calcutta*'s voyage were underway and all those bureaucrats in the naval office – the same men occupying the sort of comfortable, well-rewarded positions he so fully deserved – kept sending him a constant stream of orders and suggestions. Didn't they understand he, of all people, knew the importance of looking after all those sacks of seeds destined for the new land? Of course those sacks of turnip and peas and lettuce seeds had to be regularly brought on deck and aired so damp did not set in.

This is a man, after all, who, while stationed in Halifax in Nova Scotia as the war against the American colonies drew to an end, busily wooing Maria Proctor and keeping a close eye on the progress of his career, still had time to write to his mother regarding a recent letter he had received from his younger sister.

'Nancy must mind her spelling, and not stick her letters too close together, nor too upright, but give them an easy inclination to the left,' he'd said, before signing off with 'Oh, how I long once more to clasp them all to my bosom.'

The details are important because when Collins sailed with the First Fleet back in 1787 so many of them were overlooked. He'd gone to New Holland as an aide to its first Governor, Arthur Phillip. They had known, even then, that a new colony would need builders and engineers – and what had they been given by the admiralty? A horde of diseased and malnourished prisoners whose hatred of authority was ingrained after months and years of being flogged on the hulks. What incentive was there for them to help lay the foundations for the metropolis Phillip imagined might one day become a major trading and export hub for the Empire?

Collins and Phillip were kindred souls. Phillip had made it his business to know the background of every one of the almost 1500 people who had undertaken one of the greatest mass sea journeys in history. He'd argued with the public servants over the number of razors they had requisitioned. And he had been just as angry and bitter as the convicts when they discovered Duncan Campbell had been up to his usual tricks and shortchanged the fleet when it came to food supplies for the prisoners.

Duncan Campbell. Now there's a name you might like to roll around your mouth before spitting it out, William. He was the Scottish merchant who had overseen the prison hulk system, appointing all those brutal overseers and presiding over all that misery. Campbell changed the meal allowance for the First Fleet's 736 convicts without consulting anyone, substituting half a pound of rice each week for the previously agreed pound of flour per convict.

Well here's some good news. Campbell has just died at home in Kent. A little hard to hear the cheering on all those hulks back in Portsmouth and on the Thames when you are in the middle of the Atlantic . . . but good riddance to a man who had profited from so much misery.

Collins had remained at that first settlement in Port Jackson for eight long years, many of them closely by Phillip's side. He'd been there that day in Manly Cove when an Aboriginal had sent a 12-foot spear through the Governor's shoulder. He'd been there that legendary evening in Sydney Cove when the female prisoners from the fleet were finally allowed onshore and a riotous orgy fuelled by rum and heat and relief at finally being on land went on all night.

The next day it had been David Collins who had broken the seal of King George III and opened two leather cases to read aloud Phillip's royal instructions. They had herded the convicts together and forced them to squat under the harsh sun as Collins, relaying the King's wishes, told Phillip he could build as many 'castles, cities, boroughs [and] towns' as he deemed necessary. After that, and after Phillip had scolded the convicts and marines for the previous evening's excesses, Collins had joined the rest of the senior officers under a shady tent for a lunch of cold mutton. The sheep had only been slaughtered the night before but already it was flyblown and crawling with maggots, a taste of what lay in store for the fledgling colony.

See what happens when a man does not pay attention to details? The *Calcutta*'s journey will be different. Collins and the ship's skipper, Daniel Woodriff, will allow the convicts on deck whenever conditions allow. Hammocks and bedding will be washed, the holds inspected daily and cleansed as often as possible. There will be no repeat of the nightmare that became the remnants of the Second Fleet that Collins watched limp ashore in Sydney Cove back in 1790. More than a quarter of the convicts perished during the journey and more than half were diseased when they arrived.

Several of the ships had been so ancient and in need of repair that during the journey sea water regularly seeped into the convict hold as the prisoners lay shackled, shivering from the cold, their bodies festering with sores from scurvy and the abominable food the private contractors dished out in miserly portions. One convict who managed to survive wrote home to tell his family of the ordeal: 'When any of our comrades that were chained to us died, we kept it a secret as long as we could for the smell of the dead body, in order to get their allowance . . . and many a time have I been glad to eat the poultice that was put to my leg for perfect hunger. I was chained to Humphrey Davies who died when we were about halfway, and I lay beside his corpse about a week and got his allowance.'

'The misery I saw amongst them is indescribable,' recalled a witness who watched the survivors – boat loads of living dead with hollowed cheeks and clumps of missing hair – rowed ashore after they finally arrived. 'Their heads, bodies, clothes, blankets, were all full of lice. They were wretched, naked, filthy, dirty, lousy and many of them utterly unable to stand, to creep, or even to stir hand or foot.'

All those years of hardship hardened David Collins. Eight years away from the asthmatic Maria, who had lost their only child shortly after birth. At least there was some consolation – he could momentarily put aside all those wretched images and bury his head in the bosom of Ann Yates, a convicted burglar with whom he fathered two children.

But all those years away from home, money always a problem, watching his career ambitions slowly vanish as he became just another figure in a forgotten backwater of the Empire . . . no wonder a man became despondent. 'I find that I am spending the prime of my life at the farthest part of the world,' he'd written to Tooker Collins, '. . . without credit, without . . . profit, secluded from my family . . . my connections . . . under constant apprehensions of being starved.'

All those years in that land of thin soil and poisonous snakes and hostile Aboriginals and recalcitrant convicts saw a callus develop over that tender heart. As Judge Advocate of the colony, Collins ruled over civil and military trials and liked to consider himself a fair man. But he rarely thought twice about using the rope.

James Bennett, an 18-year-old transported for highway robbery, was one of those who had to appear before Magistrate Collins after being charged with stealing biscuits and sugar from the transport ship *Friendship*.

On a cold autumn morning at Sydney Cove, Collins informed Bennett he was to be hanged immediately. The young man, who had pleaded guilty to some but not all of the charges, was led to a tall eucalyptus tree nearby, blindfolded with a handkerchief and helped up a ladder where a noose was then placed around his neck.

Once tightened, the ladder was kicked away. Bennett jerked and died quickly. Collins had made sure a large group of convicts was gathered to watch. These were the lean famine years in the colony and it was time a lesson for stealing supplies was handed out for all to see. But there was more to come. As it began to rain heavily another group of thieves Collins had found guilty of lesser offences were tied to the old gum tree and flogged. Bennett's body dangled slowly above them, a puddle of rainwater forming below his feet.

—

Good thing your grandfather sent you off all those years ago to learn the art of bricklaying. Without that you might still be stewing on those hulks and not here on the *Calcutta*. At least you get to suck in the fresh salty air and put that big body to good use. 'The treatment I received on the passage was very good,' you will remember, 'and, as I endeavored to make myself useful on board, I was permitted to be the greater part of my time on deck, assisting the crew in working the ship.'

You and Marmon were selected by the ship's surgeon, Edward Bromley, from a list of 400 convicts to make the trip. There will be some who will become suspicious about Bromley and whether he has the best interests of this mission to Port Phillip at heart; he receives a 10 pound bounty for every convict he lands in the new country, so naturally he has gone looking for the healthiest and least damaged specimens he can find. But they have you listed as a bricklayer – one of six – and there are carpenters and cabinetmakers and butchers and ropemakers also making the journey. Huge improvement on the First Fleet and another example of how so many of the small details were overlooked, despite Phillip's best intentions. London had expected that fish would supply a significant amount of food for the new colony – but no-one had thought to give a berth to a single fisherman.

Still, it's nowhere near what Collins had wanted and as he looks out at the convicts shuffling about on deck there is little that might change his judgement about this collection of 'old, worn out, useless men, or children equally as useless'.

It's certainly no place for a nine-year-old boy. What was Bromley thinking? William Appleton is barely four feet tall, his face so pasty he looks jaundiced and in desperate need of a good feed and a warm, comforting arm. In June last year he was taken from his father's care in Westminster and shackled and hauled before Justice Conant at a hearing in Middlesex. Been pinching money from a milkman – six shillings and a bloody apron. That's all. Kid should have been kicked up the arse and told some sphincter-tightening stories about what happens to little boys in jail before they sent him home. Instead, Conant sentenced him to seven years' transportation and they had taken little Will to the infamous Newgate prison before sending him down to the hulks at Woolwich until the *Calcutta* was ready. God knows what he saw and suffered through in that hell hole but at least now he might finally catch a break. Collins and Woodriff will let him go without irons for the entire trip and one of the marines – the very decent Sergeant Thorne – will effectively adopt him once they settle in the new world.

There you go. A happy ending just when you were thinking this bleak world had run out of them. Young Will, once he's grown up, will actually make his way back to England.

There's another nine-year-old convict on board – William Steel.

Steel was sent down the same day in Middlesex as Appleton. Justice Conant was having a decent outing with badly behaved children that day. Steel was convicted for the same crime as you – stealing Irish cloth. No rosy outcome here, however. Steel is never going to make it to adulthood. In a little over a decade he will be executed for exchanging stolen goods and assisting bushrangers in Van Diemen's Land. His body will be hanged in chains to serve as a warning to others.

Three hundred and eight convicts, sharing this ship with officers and seamen – and just behind the *Calcutta* sails its supply ship, the *Ocean*, with dozens of settlers on board. So many of you, some with no birth date, no idea who their parents really were, and who will soon vanish back into the wash of history, leaving little trace they were ever here. Some are destined to rise up and leave their mark – perhaps not as famously as you – finding wealth and even, on rare occasions, greatness. Others, already bludgeoned and beaten down by life's vicissitudes, will keep surviving the only way they know – by stealing and forging, then feeling the lash once more on their backs. Some of the world's first bushrangers are on this ship; others will become pirates and at least a couple will undergo such a reformation they will be appointed police constables.

By far the smallest of the convicts is 12-year-old William Jones. Another cloth stealer. Another *William*. He has a dark complexion and a pair of legs so crooked that even if you straightened them he still wouldn't reach four foot. They have already marked him out as a servant for the officers' mess – see, David Collins hasn't run out of empathy yet – and in the years to come Jones will overcome his handicap to become a fine hunter of kangaroo and emu before embarking on a career as a sailor.

The oldest convict – and he must seem ancient to you – is 57-year-old gypsy Robert Cooper. He's come from the *Captivity* hulk in Portsmouth after being sentenced to seven years on suspicion of stealing seven donkeys. Cooper won't be seeing the wife again. Despite his years he still has a full head of black hair. But a nice cut above his left eyebrow and another on his forehead has him marked as one to watch by the guards, who have listed him as 'lusty'. Some gypsy he will turn out to be. He will survive well into his 90s in Hobart Town, running a handful of cattle on a 30-acre land grant.

You will form friendships with some of these fellow convicts. Men like Joseph Johnson, a 26-year-old labourer from Derbyshire, transported for life for horse stealing. You won't see him for almost 35 years but when you do – both of you well into your 50s with so many stories to tell – Johnson will extend a hand when you need it most. Hard to believe but the man will own thousands of acres and have servants of his own.

George Lee is on board somewhere, too – the well-educated passer of forged bank notes who wrote all those letters complaining about the buggery going on in the hulks. Probably not your type, though, constantly spouting quotations from the Classics and impersonating the officers of the *Calcutta* just to draw a few laughs.

You don't want to upset the officers. This journey is going to be long and hard enough without them all over your back.

8

A STOPOVER; THE WOMEN OF RIO; THE DEAD THROWN OVERBOARD

Another one dead. The corpse, wrapped in canvas and weighted with a cannonball, lies on the deck of the *Calcutta* as the good Reverend Robert Knopwood prepares to send it over the side and down into the black depths. It is late Saturday morning, 7 May. A northerly wind carries showers and gloom. This is the third death in four days and Knopwood is becoming a dab hand at this.

'Unto Almighty God,' he says, as the ship sways and heaves through a north-easterly swell. 'We commend the soul of our brother departed, and we commit his body to the deep, in sure and certain hope of the Resurrection unto eternal life, through our Lord Jesus Christ, at whose coming in glorious majesty to judge the world the sea shall give up her dead . . .'

The body under that shroud is Stephen Byrne, a 36-year-old silk weaver and thief. The *Calcutta*'s third lieutenant, Nicholas Pateshall, is about to scribble in his diary that Byrne has died from 'mere disability brought on by seasickness'. Yesterday it was John Thomas, a butcher sentenced to seven years for stealing seeds. The day before, Knopwood had sent Ann Stocker into the deep. That had been an upsetting afternoon for everyone. The first death of the journey, little more than a week from home, and a heavily pregnant woman at that. Ann had decided to make this trip with her husband while he served 14 years for possessing forged bank notes. But she had fallen sick immediately after leaving Portsmouth and her deterioration had been swift.

She is not the only one to fall prey to the roiling seas. It has been rough and wild and even experienced sailors have been looking a touch green. A few nights ago the officers were forced to sleep in the wardroom. You've experienced conditions like this before – that ocean crossing to the Netherlands was almost as bad as the battles that followed. But there are hundreds of convicts here who have never been to sea before and that smell rising up out of the decks below . . . it no longer carries with it the strong scent of tar and turpentine, does it?

You're going to meet more than your share of reverends and priests and other servants of God in the years to come. But none of them will come close to good old Bobby Knopwood. That nosey kid scampering around on deck – little Johnny Fawkner – will regard Knopwood as a fraud in the years to come, a man who can never look you straight in the face, who always tilts his head to the side and peers elsewhere while you're talking to him, as if he has a dark secret that someone might see by looking deep into his eyes. Might be one of the kid's more accurate character assessments. Could be that Knopwood is hiding something. He's certainly one of those old school reverends, a sermoniser who will invoke the wrath of God from the pulpit, then that night reach for a second bottle of wine as a busty woman reclines in his lap.

The man has a daughter back in England he has hardly seen. He's the third and only surviving child of a well-off family from Norfolk who blew much of his inheritance gambling and drinking with a crowd of royals and had to become a naval chaplain to make ends meet. He knows how to cosy up to power, does Bobby. In his cabin is a copy of David Collins' book. What better way to win a seat most nights at the Lieutenant-Governor's table?

When he is not carousing into the night – 'Where I dine I sleep,' he likes to say – Knopwood is a fastidious diarist with a maddening habit of misspelling names and obsessively recording weather conditions he crimps from the ship's log. When the *Calcutta* and *Ocean* arrive at Tenerife in the Canary Islands off Africa's west coast for a brief stay, he accompanies Collins and Captain Woodriff on land to meet a British shipping agent. They make their way into the centre of town when Knopwood realises they are treading on ground reeking of history. 'We landed on the very place where Lord Nelson lost his arm . . . Here it was that British seamen and Marines were repulsed when they attached [sic] Santa Cruz . . .'

Is there anyone in Britain who is not familiar with what happened six years earlier? In a battle with the Spaniards for control of Santa Cruz de Tenerife, Horatio Nelson had stepped ashore to personally take charge after several British attacks had been fought off by the Spanish. Nelson was immediately hit by a musket ball in his right arm. Bleeding heavily, the rear admiral was taken back to his ship where he refused to be helped aboard.

'Let me alone!' he yelled. 'I have got my legs left and one arm. Tell the surgeon to make haste and his instruments.'

The surgeon, seeing the ball had caused a compound fracture above the elbow and severed an artery, amputated Nelson's arm without anaesthetic. Within 30 minutes the admiral was back shouting orders, ignoring the pain. This was old school stuff and Nelson a tough old bastard, even by the standards of the day. A year later he is shot in the head during the battle of the Nile, and despite a three-inch hole exposing the inside of his skull leaves hospital after just a few weeks.

It will take more than that to stop him. In 1805 – when you have used up your fair share of luck, too – Nelson will run out of his. Up against the weight of a combined French and Spanish fleet in the battle of Trafalgar he will be shot through the spine by a marksman and fall to the deck of the *Victory*.

But even then he will remain true to form. Kneeling on the deck, one hand supporting him from totally collapsing, he looks up and says with some surprise in his voice: 'I do believe they have done it at last . . . my backbone is shot through'. He will linger below decks for a few more hours; still shouting orders until his body finally surrenders and is taken back to England in a casket filled with brandy, camphor and myrrh.

This is an age for such men. There are fools and tyrants aplenty, of course. But it's also a time for heroes, no matter how absurd and ridiculous they may act and sound. It's as if some of them have sprung to life from the dulled imagination of a hack novelist, wielding their swords and refusing to blink as they charge forward into perils unknown. Perhaps they all sense that an era is coming to an end, that the world is shrinking, that their maps with uncharted territory will no longer be marked with 'Here be Dragons' and that all too soon there will be fewer places left to discover and explore. Wars will be fought from a distance; enemies will remain out of sight. It's as if they know this and have decided to go out in style with preposterous displays of courage and bravery. Horatio Nelson is hardly in a league of his own. You, William Buckley, are about to undergo an experience they will talk about for centuries. And you're not alone on the *Calcutta* when it comes to such things, either.

Have you met the ship's first lieutenant, James Hingston Tuckey? Easy to find, although probably not the sort of fellow you would feel comfortable lounging about with on the swaying deck, helping to keep him steady as he fills his journal with the sights and sounds of this voyage. He's a tall, 27-year-old Irishman clinging to handsomeness. But years at sea in service to the Crown are taking their toll. His hair is thinning and greying and his right arm is next to useless. It was broken six years ago by a gun burst during a native uprising just off a small island in Indonesia. There was no doctor on board so he set the snapped limb himself as best he could and waited until he returned to England to have it broken and reset. His liver is a bigger problem. 'Hepatic derangement', they call it – chronic liver disease that has kept him invalided for the past two years. He is only now returning to sea and the complaint will plague him for the rest of his life.

But if his body is failing him, Tuckey, a keen diarist, remains an optimist. Even by the flowery writing standards of the day there is more than just a dollop of the Romantic poet in him; he could be an apprentice to Wordsworth or Coleridge, roaming the world's seas, wide-eyed and consumed by the rapture of the endlessly curious traveller.

Here he is observing you and the other convicts boarding the *Calcutta* as she leaves England: 'Among the convicts on board were some who, by prodigality and attendant vices, had degraded themselves from a respectable rank in society and were indebted to the lenity of their prosecutors alone for an escape from the last sentence of the law.'

'Some of these men were accompanied by their wives who had married them in the sunshine of prosperity, when the world smiled deceitfully and their path of life appeared strewed with unfolding flowers; in the season of adversity they would not be separated but reposed their heads upon the same thorny pillow . . .'

'. . . those alone who know the miserable and degraded situation of a transported felon can appreciate the degree of connubial love that could induce these women to accompany their guilty husbands in exile . . .'

While you're stuck here on the *Calcutta*, Tuckey goes ashore when the ship anchors off Santa Cruz. But don't worry. He's taking notes and his journal will not disappoint. He visits a local church and will wonder at the 'deeply imprinted superstition' of the Catholic faith: 'Children, before they can scarce speak, are taught to set a sacred value on the ridiculous grimace of devotion and a father brings his boy, not three years old, to lisp his Ave Maria and count his little rosary before the altar.' And having stood through those ceremonies on deck as Knopwood sent all those bodies into the deep, Tuckey is . . . well, he's become a downright *enthusiast* for the way the locals treat their dead. Bodies in coffins with no lids that are then 'filled up with quicklime which, decomposing the flesh, the bones are afterwards removed to a general charnel-house. This example deserves to be universally followed but the prejudices of education, which teaches us to consider disturbing the dead as a species of horrid sacrilege, still wars against our better judgment and perpetuates the noisome and acknowledged evil of crowded churchyards.'

While the officers enjoy the layover on land in Santa Cruz, there is respite, too, for the convicts, an opportunity to wash clothing with fresh water – 'an indulgence,' writes Tuckey, 'the benefits of which cannot be too highly valued . . . cleanliness is the only preventative of disease'.

That, and the decent quantity of lemons and vegetables being hauled on board.

They call scurvy the sailor's disease and there are already early signs of it among some of the convicts: a handful with bleeding gums, others who can feel their teeth beginning to loosen. Nothing too serious, however, not like the full-blown effects when the fever sets in and the mouth and eyes are constantly dry and before you know it the sufferer is experiencing delusions and massive personality swings as their skin turns yellow and the convulsions set in.

Remarkable how a disease like this – a chronic lack of vitamin C so easily cured by citrus and vegetables – has remained one of the great mysteries in the Age of Sail for so long. It is only in the past few years that the British Navy has made it mandatory for ships on long voyages to be well stocked with remedies. For hundreds of previous years the Navy assumed it would lose up to half of its sailors on any lengthy sea journey. One estimate puts the number of deaths at sea between the years 1500 and 1800 at two million.

The *Calcutta* leaves Santa Cruz and sails toward Rio, the Atlantic an endless, watery bone yard of forgotten souls.

—

The Reverend Knopwood sends another couple of bodies into the deep and then watches with great interest as a marine found guilty of sleeping at his post while supervising the convicts receives 24 lashes for neglect of duty. Knopwood may be a man of God, but he is not merciful. He will act as a magistrate in the coming years and never flinch from ordering a prisoner to be whipped.

So he must be avidly looking on as some of the crew with the help of a few convicts go fishing for sharks. Here is something just as grisly, just as absorbing, as watching a man having his back flayed.

Best leave it to Tuckey to describe the feverish scene: 'Often the day's allowance of meat is sacrificed to bait the hook intended to trap their hungry adversary; while . . . harpoons attend their operations and the deluded victim is dragged on board, no pack of hungry fox-hounds can be more restless till they receive the reward of their labours, than the sailors to tear out the bowels and examine the stomach of the shark.'

When the equator is finally crossed after days of alternating calm and squalls, the tedium of the voyage is broken by the time-honoured ceremony of 'crossing the line'. Tuckey watches on as 'the ugliest persons in the ship are chosen to represent Neptune and Amphitrite (but the latter name being rather too hard of pronunciation is always familiarized into Mrs Neptune); their faces are painted in the most ridiculous manner and their heads are furnished with swabs well-greased and powdered . . . a large tub of salt water is prepared with a stick across it, on which the visitor is seated; Neptune's barber, after lathering his face well with a mixture of tar and grease, performs the operation of shaving with a piece of rusty iron hoop and when clean scraped . . . he is pushed backwards into the tub and kept there until completely soaked.'

Within days the *Calcutta* is in Rio, stocking up with sugar, rum, coffee and livestock. But the South American city – the key port for ships sailing the Atlantic – has a more exotic attraction. Not that you will be given an opportunity to indulge in its offerings. So let Tuckey describe it to you. The geographer inside him has been nudged aside by an amateur anthropologist.

'The women wear their waists very short, their bosoms much exposed . . . the features of the females can in no instance that I saw claim the title of beautiful and even very few reserve the epithet of pretty . . . their eyebrows are fine arched, their eyelashes long and silken, their hair is long, black and coarsely luxuriant; and if we may judge from . . . frequent application of fingers, not always without inhabitants.' Tuckey has done his research while on land in Rio and thinks the 'premature ripeness' of the local women is all down to the delicate soil and the genial warmth of the sun which, after 'a momentary bloom sinks them towards decay; at fourteen they become mothers, at sixteen the blossoms of their beauty are full blown and [at] twenty they withered like the faded rose in autumn'.

Tuckey is a single man. He does not have many years left to live – a little over a decade – and it's as if he, too, understands time is short and he needs to cram as much into life as he can, to forge a reputation as one of the 19th century's true adventurers. In just two years' time the *Calcutta* will be captured by the French – hostilities resumed shortly after the ship's departure from England – and Tuckey will be imprisoned for eight years until the war with France finally ends. He will marry a fellow prisoner during his long incarceration and two of their children will die once they are released and endure a difficult journey home. But once he is back in Britain he will be named commander of one of the first expeditions to explore the mysterious Congo in the deep heart of Africa.

There will be some back in England who will question why a man so severely weakened by chronic liver disease and a useless arm is appointed to such an important role, despite his impressive credentials as a geographer. Others will suggest it will be compensation for all those years as a prisoner of war.

Whatever the reason, it is easy to picture Tuckey there in the dense, almost impenetrable jungle, pith helmet and calf leather boots to his knees, face red from the heat, intoxicated by the perils of what lies beyond, notebook in one hand to record any sudden inspirations of purple prose, the other weakened arm helplessly swatting away mosquitos, all the while urging his lads to push further into the unknown.

Deeper they will go, too, more than 150 miles inland. But there's something missing in Tuckey's journal about this African expedition.

There's none of the usual whimsy, no poetry or soft observations from the heart that fill his journal on this voyage to Port Phillip. He is worn out. The majority of his men are dying of fever and eventually Tuckey will have to be carried back to his ship where, at the age of 40, he will die of 'exhaustion'.

—

It's starting to grow cold. The *Calcutta* has gone from Rio down to the Cape of Good Hope for a final chance to replenish supplies before the long, torturous leg across the Indian Ocean to Port Phillip. It is late August and you have been at sea for almost five months. Misery – never far away – is beginning to set in. A 16-year-old forger from London, Johnny Cashman, has thrown himself overboard after stealing the watch of surgeon Bromley. Nerves are strained – a Dutch commodore threatens Woodriff and Collins that he will seize their ship because war has been declared. But Woodriff, who receives unanimous support from his crew and the convicts that they will defend the *Calcutta* to the last man – stares down the threat and the Dutchman capitulates, saying he does 'not wish to capture such a large number of thieves'.

By the time you leave the Cape pessimism is growing. The *Ocean*, with its cargo of supplies and cranky settlers, has not been seen since Rio and there are fears the slow-moving ship already lies in a frigid grave. Small irritations escalate into full-blown fights among crew, convicts and marines, some of which can only be resolved by the cat-o'-nine-tails.

The seas grow rough and are littered with chunks of ice. Cattle on board will soon die from the conditions and on the horizon the dark sky will merge into the equally dark, swirling water of the Indian Ocean. It will look as if the *Calcutta* is sailing straight toward a black wall.

The Reverend Knopwood has been reading David Collins' account of the First Fleet's journey to New South Wales – what better way to prepare for another evening of flattery and fawning at the

Lieutenant-Governor's table? A passage from that book has caught Knopwood's eye. It's the voice of a much younger, more idealistic Collins from 16 years earlier. Knopwood appropriates it for himself for his own diary entry on this Thursday, 16 August 1803.

'On our departure from the Cape it was natural for us to indulge at this moment a melancholy reflection . . . the land behind us was the abode of a civilized people. That before us was the residence of savages. When, if ever, we might again enjoy the commerce of the world was doubtful and uncertain. The refreshments and the pleasures of which we had so liberally partaken at the Cape and Simon's Bay were to be exchanged for coarse fare and hard labour at Port Phillip, and we may truly say all communication with families and friends now cut off, we were leaving the world behind us to enter on a state unknown.'

9

LAND AT LAST; PREDATORS
AND MISFORTUNE;
THE NATIVES APPEAR

Six months since you felt land under your feet. Can you feel the sand grinding beneath your hardened soles, the cold salt water embracing your waist? As you wade toward shore you can see the beach and, beneath one large tree, Lieutenant-Governor Collins' much-loved printing press. How fortunate is it that Matthew Power, whose wife has kept Collins company throughout the journey, is a printer and is already at work putting the press together? With Hannah comfortably berthed in a tent conveniently placed behind Collins' marquee, Matthew will soon have the press spitting out daily proclamations from the Lieutenant-Governor, including the first beach warning ever posted in this land they will eventually call Australia.

'This bay and the harbor in general being unfortunately full of voracious sharks and stingrays . . . it is recommended to the convicts not to go into the water without the utmost precaution, and they are positively prohibited from bathing in front of the encampment.'

See, Collins hasn't lost his empathy. He doesn't want you losing your life by ending up as fish bait. The *Calcutta* has finally arrived in Port Phillip; the *Ocean*, despite all those fears, had beaten it by two days and had already successfully navigated the turbulent rip lying in wait outside the entrance to the bay. Collins should be enthused and optimistic. The worst, surely, is over. But everywhere he looks he sees predators and misfortune. After entering the bay the *Calcutta* had turned right and sailed for several miles before anchoring a long way off a beach dubbed Sullivan Bay. The water is so shallow even the supply boats must pull up hundreds of yards before the shore. All the cargo must be carried to the beach, a tiresome and time-consuming task and, of course, a large man like you was never going to avoid being given the task. The wheels of the carriages needed to cart wood back to the settlement for huts become stuck in the sand and break.

Poisonous snakes slide unseen through the undergrowth. That strange animal called the kangaroo, which Collins hoped would boost the meagre meat supplies, is rare and finds it easy to elude gunfire. Worst of all, there is no nearby supply of fresh water, so perforated oak casks have been sunk into the sand to filter the salt water and provide something drinkable, although given the dysentery that will follow in the next few days it will be hardly worth it.

Hard to believe the mandarins back in London thought this a good place for a colony. Just goes to show what happens when you don't pay attention to the little details. The decision to come to Port Phillip was a hasty one. Port Jackson, now a settlement of 6000 always on the verge of rebellion, was overcrowded and its third governor, Philip King, had been keen to ease the pressure by forming another colony further to the south.

Collins knows the background and that Governor King's entreaties were finally being heard. In a letter to Joseph Banks, Lord Hobart had written: 'If you continually send thieves to one place it must in time become supersaturated. We must let it rest and purify it for a few years and it will be again in condition to receive.' The influential Banks had quickly agreed and urged that a road between the two settlements – which he estimated correctly to be roughly 500 miles – be built as soon as possible.

Of course, it wasn't just the inexhaustible supply of convicts that King was keen to stop. The damn French had been seen with increasing frequency in the southern waters of New Holland, their naval cartographers mapping Van Diemen's Land and Bass Strait and many of its islands. It could only be a matter of time before they established a strategic base and, from there, use it to dominate the Pacific. A year earlier King had sent an expedition south on an exploratory mission. Its leader, Lieutenant John Murray, had discovered Port Phillip Bay and, apart from an incident with some worked-up natives who resented his presence, had been immediately impressed with its spacious harbour and 'bold, high land . . . not clothed as all the land at Western Port is with thick brush but with stout trees of various kinds and in some places falls nothing short, in beauty and appearance, of Greenwich Park'.

Well, nothing pleases the English eye more than an alien landscape with a nod to well-known features back home. King, aware how hungry the British Navy was for wood for new masts and flax for its ropes and sails after years of constant war, wrote to Lord Hobart extolling Port Phillip Bay's assets. A few months later the explorer Matthew Flinders would find the same, a place that had 'a pleasing and, in many parts, a fertile appearance'.

But what Collins doesn't know – he hasn't seen many of these later reports – is that there is an abundance of fresh water to the northern end of the bay, a river that, 30 years later, will become the site of a village. Had he asked Woodriff and the *Calcutta* to keep sailing straight ahead after entering the bay they might have found it. But no, they went right. And now, as he swats flies away in the heat, Port Phillip Bay seems to Collins the last place on earth an empire would want for an outpost.

Well, thank the Lord that James Hingston Tuckey is still about. Takes a great deal to dull the shine of the man's ever-present optimism. As the *Calcutta* entered the bay and Collins saw only misery lining the shores, Tuckey was overcome by the sight: '. . . we were presented with a picture highly contrasted with the scene we had lately contemplated: an expanse of water bounded in many places only by the horizon and unruffled as the bosom of polluted innocence, presented itself to the charmed eye which roamed over it in silent admiration. The nearer shores, along which the ship glided at the distance of a mile, afforded the most exquisite scenery and recalled the idea of "nature in the world's first spring . . ."'

Best stop him right there because Collins, if he hasn't already tired of Tuckey's endless cheerfulness, has a job for him. Tuckey is to take a small party and boat and head off on an exploratory trip around the bay to see whether a better option than Sullivan Bay exists.

It starts well: Tuckey and his party have several peaceful encounters with the local Aboriginals. Presents of blankets and beads are handed over and Tuckey insists all guns are kept back in the boat out of view. 'They appeared to have a perfect knowledge of the use of fire arms and . . . they seemed terrified even at the sight of them,' he will record in his journal.

But as they travel north-west toward a plain that reaches to the horizon they see almost 200 Aboriginals gathering with 'obviously hostile intentions'. Three of them step nervously forward to receive gifts of fish and bread. The presents appear to have calmed any tensions, so Tuckey leaves a crew on shore and takes the boat further up the bay to continue his survey. But while he is gone things quickly sour; the natives return with reinforcements and an apparent chief being carried on the shoulders of two others. They surround the small group of men on the beach, steal a tomahawk, an axe and a saw and by the time Tuckey returns bedlam has broken out.

An Aboriginal seizes the master's mate, holding him fast in his arms. 'Fire, sir,' pleads the mate, 'for God's sake, fire!'

Two musket volleys are fired over Aboriginal heads. They do nothing to disperse the angry crowd. Tuckey dispenses any thought of a peaceful resolution, almost as quickly as he discards his lyrical prose: 'Four muskets with buck shot, and the fowling pieces of the gentlemen with small shot, were now fired among them and from a general howl, many were supposed to be struck.

'This discharge created a general panic and, leaving their cloaks behind, they ran in every direction among the trees.' But Tuckey, the closet anthropologist, is never far from the surface. 'A very great difference was observed in the comparative cleanliness of these savages,' he writes, 'some of them were so abominably beastly that it required the strongest stomach to look on them without nausea, while others were sufficiently cleanly to be viewed without disgust.'

The feeling appears to be mutual. Tuckey tries to calm the situation, laying down his gun and moving slowly toward the man he regards as a chief, whose head is adorned 'with a coronet of the wing feathers of the swan, very neatly arranged and which had a pleasing effect'. He offers him a cloak and a necklace but the chief remains angry at the intrusion of these white outsiders, 'his spear appeared every moment upon the point of quitting his hand'.

Within moments the army of natives begin rushing down the hill, shouting and flourishing their spears, whooping and hollering as loudly as the damn French. 'Our people were immediately drawn up and ordered to present their muskets loaded with ball . . . it was deemed absolutely necessary for our own safety to prove the power of our fire arms before they came near enough to injure us with their spears; selecting one of the foremost, who appeared to be the most violent . . . three muskets were fired at him at fifty yards distance, two of which took effect and he fell dead on the spot.'

Tuckey's party hurry to their boat and return to Sullivan Bay to brief Collins, who is already close to deciding he does not want to remain here. Tuckey's report helps him make up his mind. Collins has already begun talking about packing up and heading further south to Van Diemen's Land, where a small detachment from Port Jackson has already set up a camp. Some of the free settlers he is charged with supervising have told him they would prefer to stay and farm the land in a valley behind the bay. 'I am sorry to observe that in general they are a necessitous and worthless set of people,' Collins writes in a letter back to London.

There is nothing but darkness everywhere Collins looks. There are the useless convicts like you, even if your bricklaying skills are finally being used as you put together a store for the settlement's ammunition. Others have already escaped, or tried to, proving yet again the unrelenting stupidity of the criminal class. There is Daniel Woodriff, the skipper of the *Calcutta*, who has just told Collins he will soon be departing for Port Jackson before returning to England, leaving Collins with just the *Ocean* and its reduced capacity to haul almost 500 people south to Van Diemen's Land. Not only that, but under Collins' command is an undermanned and largely worthless group of marines who seem more intent on drinking and squabbling than keeping the peace.

And to top it all off there is that infernal Tuckey, wandering about on his carpet of perfumed rose petals, his enthusiasm never waning, his optimism shining warmly in any direction he turns.

So let's take one more look at him. It will be the last time we see him as the *Calcutta* prepares to leave. Even two centuries later it will be easy to picture him sitting on the carriage of a gun in front of the camp, prim and buttoned up, perhaps his chin resting reflectively in the palm of his only good hand, contemplating 'with succeeding emotions of pity, laughter and astonishment the scene before me'.

The convicts are at work. 'When I viewed so many of my fellow men, sunk, some of them from a rank equal or superior to my own, and by their crimes degraded to a level with the basest of mankind; when I saw them naked, wading to their shoulders in water to unlade the boats while a burning sun struck its Meridien rays upon their uncovered heads, or yoked to and sweating under a timber carriage, the wheels of which were sunk tip to the axle in sand, I considered their hapless lot, and the remembrance of their vices was for a moment absorbed in the greatness of their punishment.'

He's not finished, yet. Never is. Have you been watching him, William? He's now worked himself into such a lather that he begins to speak aloud, spouting with great enthusiasm a line from William

Cowper, one of the forerunners of the Romantic poetry movement and a writer even Coleridge rates as the best modern poet of the era.

> *Tis liberty alone that gives the flower*
> *Of fleeting life its lustre and perfume*
> *And we are weeds without it.*

Well, he's not wrong. It's all about liberty. Always has been with you. And thoughts of escape are never far from your mind.

10

DARING ESCAPE
UNDER A FULL MOON

You're going to forget a great deal as you become an older man. The English language, for one thing. But that won't really matter. Being a man of few words you've never had any great passion for it, never really felt the need to push it to its limits the way men like Tuckey do. You'll also forget much about your childhood and even your memories of your time on the prison hulks will slowly recede.

But you won't forget tonight, will you?

The moon, near full, low in the western sky. The silence of the camp. The tightness in your gut and the panic that sets in when you realise you are being chased by men with guns. How the bush suddenly comes alive with screams and shouts and the sound of musket fire as you and Will Marmon and four others are hunted down like animals. Those red-coated marines are cursing and they want to put a musket ball right through the back of your head. Some of them have had to put down their rum; others probably have a scantily dressed woman convict in their tent who is wondering where in hell everyone has gone.

Of course you will remember this night. Many years later you will concede it was a stupid idea, hatched by men so lacking in geographical knowledge they thought Sydney was just a few miles to the north and China just a brisk walk from there. 'The attempt was little short of madness,' you will say, 'for there was before me the chances of being retaken and probable death or other dreadful punishment.'

It's not as though you haven't known what happens to convicts who decide to do a runner from Sullivan Bay. In the last few weeks up to a dozen of them have fled, including that annoying, Classics-spouting George Lee. Well, Lee will never be seen again. His mate, David Gibson, wandered back into camp more than a week later, a 'mere skeleton from his privations in the bush'. Some have been recaptured more than 60 miles away and are happy to return and be tied to the flogging post rather than endure another night on the run.

But despite all this – and all the warnings the Lieutenant-Governor kept pumping out of that little second-hand printing press down near the beach – you insisted on doing it. On Christmas Eve when revelries were in full swing Daniel McAllenan (Irishman, horse stealer) broke into the commissary's tent and stole a gun. The theft alerted Collins that something might be in the air and so he doubled up on the night patrols and increased perimeter security around the camp. That wasn't so much of a problem for you – as a bricklayer you had been given special privileges, including a tent on the edge of the settlement.

Just after 9 pm you and Will Marmon and McAllenan, along with several others, launch your escape. The night is suddenly plunged into a maelstrom of noise and chaos. There's a loud shot and some shouts. One of your group, Charles Shore, has been wounded, a pellet lodging in his stomach. They will send a wagon to collect him soon, but the pursuit will continue.

And you? Those huge feet are propelling you through the bush at an almighty pace. 'After running the greater part of the first three or four hours to make our escape more certain, we halted for rest and refreshment,' you will recall. 'We were now fairly launched on our perilous voyage and it became necessary to reflect on our position and to examine our resources.'

Let's see. What do you have there? Apart from the gun there's an old iron kettle, a very small collection of tin pots – what is this, an escape party or a group of jam-preserving enthusiasts? – and barely two or three days' worth of rations. The next morning you come face to face with a tribe of spear-carrying Aboriginals, but they depart fairly quickly after you fire a warning shot from the gun.

Still, the enormity of your plight begins to set in. It doesn't take long before McAllenan, taking the gun from you, begins to have second thoughts and turns to make the long journey back to the settlement. Even your mate, Marmon, is struggling. He might be fit but scurvy is starting to slow him down and, not long after, he says farewell, the whipping post back in Sullivan Bay far preferable to this.

But there's no way you're going back. You and two others – most likely George Pye, a sheep stealer from Nottingham, and James Taylor, who stole a horse in Lancaster and joined you on the hulks at Langstone – push on. The heat gives way to a cold change sweeping in from the south bringing heavy rain and an abrupt drop in temperature. You come to a river – perhaps the one that Collins should have discovered two months ago when the *Calcutta* first made its way into the bay – and, being the strongest swimmer, help the other two to cross it.

The days are long and your rations are running out. You have almost completed a full circuit of the bay – more than a hundred miles. But surely the nights are the worst. For a small group of ignorant Englishmen constantly looking over their shoulders for pursuers, listening to the creaking of old gum trees and surrounded by the sheer melancholic emptiness of the country around you, the desolation is almost suffocating.

—

Say what you like about David Collins, but don't say the man does not have a temper when he is pushed far enough. On New Year's Eve – several days after your escape – the Lieutenant-Governor has Matthew Power hunched over the printing press publishing his latest missive to the Sullivan Bay camp. He cannot, he says, but 'pity the delusion which some of the prisoners labour under, in thinking that they can exist when deprived of the assistance of government. Their madness will be manifest to themselves when they shall feel, too late, that they have wrought their own ruin. After those who have absconded he shall make no further search, certain that they must soon return or perish by famine.'

As if constant desertions are not enough, Collins has an even greater problem on his hands. Since Christmas there has been growing drunkenness and – far worse for a man who has lived with a reverential respect for authority – insolence. He has had two marines arrested, suspected of plotting a mutiny, and sentenced them to 900 lashes.

It is by far the most brutal punishment handed out since leaving Portsmouth back in April. Collins demands everyone gather in the parade ground shortly after seven in the morning. Two floggers – one right-handed, the other left-handed – carry out the Lieutenant-Governor's orders. Skin and blood soon cover the ground. The doctor on duty will stop one of the floggings after 500 lashes, the other after 700. Days later, when the skin has healed, the pair will be hauled back for the remainder.

Collins is running out of patience. He wants to leave this place and head south before he has a complete insurrection on his hands. His hunch that some of the convicts will return is correct. McAllenan has stumbled into the settlement and handed back the stolen gun.

It prompts another notice to the camp. 'The Lieut. Governor hopes the return of . . . McAllenan will have convinced the prisoners of the misery that must ever attend those who are mad enough to abscond from the settlement. To warn them from making an attempt of a similar nature they are informed that, although this man left his companions on the fifth day after their departure hence, they all began to feel the effects of their imprudence, and more of them would have returned had they not dreaded the punishment which they were conscious they deserved . . . their provisions were nearly expended and they had no resources. They lived in constant dread of the natives, by whose hands it is more than probable they have by this time perished.'

Well, not quite. There are three battling hunger and fear. But you're still running. You have long since left the place they will one day call Melbourne and moved south-west, down through the You Yang hills, discovering a small bay connected to Port Phillip where you eat shellfish that affects 'us all very seriously'. After 10 days on the run you reach the opposite side of the bay and can see the *Ocean* – you mistake it for the *Calcutta* – at anchor.

By this time Pye and Taylor have had enough. But none of you can possibly swim the handful of miles across the bay and through such rough water. So you set about making signals – 'by lighting fires at night and hoisting our shirts on trees and poles by day'.

At one stage a small boat leaves the *Ocean* and begins making its way toward the beach. 'Although the dread of punishment was naturally great,' you will recall years later, '. . . the fear of starvation exceeded it, and they anxiously waited her arrival to deliver themselves up, indulging anticipations of being . . . forgiven by the governor.'

But that boat soon turns around and you are left there on the beach, clothes torn, faces browned and hollow, stomachs empty. But don't forget something, William. You still have hope. A man can always hope.

—

David Collins is fuming. The man is like a dog at a bone. All of these escapes . . . why, it's a slight against his own character. He is still astonished that men he has treated so fairly would choose to flagrantly thumb their noses at him and leave the settlement. It's blatant ingratitude – that's what it is. And now the frustration of the last few months – indeed, the past 20 years of a life filled with disappointment – begins to spill over.

It's time for another notice to the settlement. 'How is it possible that strong hardy men who were always able to consume even more than the liberal allowance of provisions which is issued to them, can exist in a country where nowhere affords a supply to the traveller?' Collins asks.

'The lieutenant governor can by no means account for this strange desertion of the people; were they ill-treated, scantily-fed, badly clothed or wrought beyond their ability, he should attribute it to these causes. But as the reverse is the case he is at a loss to discover the motive.' And with that Collins issues a warning to those who may be thinking about helping others to escape. 'It is his fixed determination to punish them with greater severity than he would the infatuated wretches themselves. He is concerned that the several prisoners who are now absent must be left to perish, as by McAllenan's account they are beyond the reach of every effort he might make to recall them to their duty.'

Collins will hear no more about the absconders. You're dead to him – you, Pye and Taylor. Collins has a new colony to establish. In Sydney, the NSW Governor has agreed he should head south to Van Diemen's Land and now he must supervise the loading of the *Ocean* with the remaining provisions before it slips anchor at the end of January.

Marmon, barely alive, will make it back to camp just before the ship leaves. He will slowly recover from his bout of scurvy and receive a conditional pardon in 1816.

Collins will never see his wife or England again. When the *Ocean* arrives in Van Diemen's Land and everyone disembarks after a short journey up the Derwent River, he will name the new settlement Hobart Town – a nod to the good Lord Hobart himself back in London.

But his melancholy will only deepen. Hobart will experience years of famine and borderline existence. A tired Collins will be criticised by his superiors, his judgement questioned. Barbed reports will arrive in London. Some of the most wounding will come from the acid pen of William Bligh, the fourth Governor of NSW, who will spend time in Hobart in exile after the Rum Rebellion in Sydney in 1808.

The vindictive and temper-prone Bligh already knows too much about rebellions – his epic journey in a small rowboat after the mutiny on the *Bounty* is already the stuff of legend. He will complain to Lord Castlereagh, the secretary of state for foreign affairs, that Collins' habit of walking the streets of Hobart with his latest mistress, Margaret Eddington, is unbecoming of a man charged with the welfare of a young colony, '. . . a moral and civil point of view as great an insult as could be offered'.

Hopes of a return to England and his despairing wife will fade. Collins will father two children with Eddington, a 16-year-old when Collins first takes her into his bed.

Two years later, recovering from a cold, he will take a sip from a cup of tea before falling back into his chair, one arm outstretched, as though warding off that evil genius that had been pursuing him for much of his life.

He will die destitute, just a month after turning 54. Back in London Maria will discover that her handsome husband, who fathered four children to other women, owed almost 300 pounds.

Those who attend his funeral will never forget one of the largest ever seen in these new colonies, filled with pomp and circumstance and solemn speeches about the greatness of the man. It will also come at great cost – almost 500 pounds, a fee that will leave the mandarins in London grumbling that the man was now a strain on the coffers in death, as he was in life.

And then, as so often in life, David Collins will be forgotten.

More than a century later well-meaning officials will begin digging in an unmarked grave to have his coffin removed and given a more decent burial place. They will prise the lid open and be astonished at what they find; inside the coffin of Huon pine are sheets of lead and dried twigs and leaves. Within that, another casket, a second one of sturdy pine. And there, lying inside it to the astonishment of those gathered around, will be a tall, handsome man, perfectly preserved in his red dress uniform with a sword by his side.

There will barely be a blemish on his face, not a grey hair to be seen. All those embalming herbs, all that lead, all that Huon pine, will have awarded a small and belated victory to a man who spent his life desperately craving attention and recognition.

As for you, William Buckley.

You will be remembered for what comes next.

PART II

WILLIAM ENTERS A NEW WORLD

11

'A SPECIES OF MADNESS'

'The whole affair was, in fact, a species of madness,' you will reminisce five decades later when you are an old man with a faltering memory, shaking your head at the sheer absurdity of the scheme.

To think you could have made it to Sydney. You travelled in the wrong direction for a start. But even then, even if through some sheer fluke you had made it to Port Jackson, then what? The irons would have been slapped back on your ankles and another of those sadistic guards would have smiled and then built up a sweat flaying your back. After that? Years on a chain gang, clearing land for others to profit from. Or, more than likely, sent on a ship to join David Collins on another of his ill-fated ventures. At least the pair of you could have kept one another company in your misery.

Now where do you find yourself? Your companions, starving and bitter and remorseful, turned back to try to rejoin the settlement at Sullivan Bay before it departed for Van Diemen's Land. They had tried to convince you to join them. But that was never going to happen. Did you have anything to say to them?

'I turned a deaf ear, being determined to endure every kind of suffering rather than again surrender my liberty.'

Stubborn bastard. Better this meagre diet of shellfish than a return to hard biscuits and salted pork. But how good would a meal like that taste right now? You have been wandering for weeks and nothing in life has tested you like this. The physical pain – the hunger cravings and muscle aches and dehydration – are one thing. But alone in this country, the silence broken only by the odd bird call or the wretched howling of dingoes at night . . . that has been something else. Makes a man think about what he has lost and left behind. A day seems to go on endlessly, a week in a blur of foraging for food and water – and avoiding those natives.

The day after your fellow absconders left you, you came across more than a hundred of these Aboriginals. They apparently had seen you, too, and began making their way toward you. Well, that caused you to panic and you ran straight to a nearby river and dived in. Problem was, you were carrying a fire stick – probably a smouldering remnant from your last campfire – and its warm embers that had helped make those bitter, salty shellfish more edible were immediately extinguished. By the time you reached the other side of the river they had pulled back and you had made your way to a beach, covering yourself with leaves and boughs as night descended.

It rained. Cold and wet, you barely slept. As soon as the sun rose the next morning you continued moving south, the trek becoming more hopeless by the hour. You forded saltwater streams, climbed rocky outcrops, doing your best to stay on the coast and near its sandy beaches rather than move inland with all its unknowns. All that water around you and none of it drinkable. The best you could do was to cup your hands and reach into the boughs of trees where a little melted dew might be on offer.

This went on for how long? Days? Weeks? How exhausted can a man become before he just curls up and surrenders? The very act of climbing over more rocky outcrops came close to defeating you. And then came a little luck. A small well – clearly dug by human hands – provided fresh water. Not long after, next to a small stream that ran into the ocean, the glowing leftovers of a small scrub fire lit a few days before. One of the trees had still been smoking, enough to make a new fire stick.

Food, fire, fresh water. But just when things were starting to look up, sores began breaking out all over your body, matching the weeping blisters on the soles of your feet. It was then that you knew this escape, this constant running, and then walking . . . and now little more than pathetic hobbling . . . had to stop. It was time to rest.

So here you are, perched at the top of a massive rock you will one day call Nooraki, sheltered by an outcrop of land, looking out to sea. You have built a shack of sorts out of dried seaweed and old tree limbs. Some builder you turned out to be. Old Master Wyatt would shake his head in disgust if he saw this pathetic shelter. Nearby, a stream of fresh water tumbles into the ocean. There are wild berries to be picked and a weed called pig face that tastes like insipid watermelon. But it's enough. Your body is healing. The sores are fading and the blisters are now callouses. Your beard has thickened and your hair tumbles over your shoulders and down your back. You stink, actually. But you're starting to think that perhaps this isn't all that bad. The solitude is sometimes overwhelming but the tranquillity almost makes up for it.

And then one day the serenity is broken. For the first time in many months you hear the sound of human voices.

—

You're a stubborn bastard. Where would we be without them? Stubbornness is what brought you to this place and that very same trait drove this land's original inhabitants, too. Their journey started just as far away – but much longer ago. Let's go back a few hundred thousand years to one of the first group of Homo sapiens. They seem content sitting around a fire somewhere in eastern Africa. They have just picked clean the bones of an antelope and as night descends they scratch their full and slightly hairy bellies, yawn and prepare to sleep.

Tomorrow they have plans to travel north. Just a few miles at first. But it will be the first steps on a journey that, over tens of thousands of years, will see them spread around the globe in a relentless march unmatched by any other species.

Hard to imagine them succeeding without vast quantities of pig-headedness. Over the coming centuries, as the continents grind against one another, as the seas rise and fall, they will encounter so many obstacles. There will be dangerous creatures preying on them, other hominid species like Neanderthals competing against them, as well as massive climactic changes thrown at them – from insufferable heat to frigid ice ages. Good thing a little doggedness and intransigence is hard wired into their DNA. Without it they might sprint back to that little campfire and just hang around waiting to become extinct from hunger and sheer boredom. Hunger – you know that too now. And boredom as well.

12

'THEY HAVE SEEN
A GHOST'

The voices belong to three Aboriginal men. They stand on the escarp-
ment, spears in hand, possum skins covering their shoulders. Your
first instinct is to creep into a crevice and try to hide, but they have
already seen you and are now shouting. You can only assume they are
asking you to surrender and, with nowhere to go, you step out and
approach them.

Well, at least what happens next takes you into familiar territory.
'They gazed on me with wonder: my size probably attracting their
attention,' you will later recall.

Not just your size, although that has been enough to surprise
strangers for years. It's your skin. Despite the tan from months in
the sun it's unlikely they have seen anyone like you before. They
seize your hands and then strike their breasts and begin singing and
wailing. And then they begin to inspect this hut of yours, this ragged
shanty of old limbs and seaweed. One of the men dives into the sea
and comes out shortly after with a crayfish that is thrown on to a
hastily made fire. Once cooked it is shared equally.

You remain cautious. Nothing in life has prepared you for something like this. When this cordial greeting and sharing of food is
over the three beckon you to follow them and you do, leaving the

beach and moving inland where you finally arrive at two small huts and spend the night. After a sleepless evening the three men indicate they want to continue moving inland but now the stubbornness in you – or is it fear? – returns. You refuse. One of them points to your worn-out stockings, stained and ridden with holes and loose threads. He wants them, forcing another refusal.

'After sundry striking of the breasts and stamping with the feet they were content to leave me unmolested,' is how you will later put it. But that man is fixated with those stockings. He returns shortly with a woven basket filled with wild berries and tries to exchange it for them and once again you refuse to hand them over. Isn't this how so many first encounters between different cultures begin badly? Not with the rattling of sabres and firing of guns, but over the small things – a misinterpreted wave of the hand or a well-meant offering that instead causes offence. Or a pair of lousy, worn-out, stinking stockings you should have discarded weeks ago . . .

When the man departs again and disappears, you decide to leave, too. Not a good decision, not one of your finest moments. For the next few days you wander through the bush, hopelessly lost among those gnarled eucalypts shedding layers of bark like flayed skin. It's cold and begins to rain and the only shelter to be found is inside a hollow tree. You can light a fire here, keep warm and stay hidden. Now you're starting to think straight . . .

'My fire attracted the notice of wild dogs and oposums, whose horrid howls and noises were such as to render sleep impossible. The cries of the latter were like the shrieks of children, appearing to be at times over me and at others close to my ear.'

This is where all notion of time stops. How many days pass before we find you back in your glorious seaweed hut on the beach? How many weeks watching your clothes fray, the holes in those stockings growing larger? Even worse, as you sit there on that rock looking out over the ocean, searching for the hint of a calico sail on the horizon, the loneliness and despair returns.

Perhaps there is time to make it back to Sullivan Bay – wherever it might be, given your sense of direction has been turned upside down. Perhaps that morose David Collins will still be there, still waiting for you and damned if you wouldn't sink to your knees at the very sight of him and kiss the ground and tear off your shirt and enjoy every bloody lash they unleashed on you.

Off you go then. Broken and beaten, still clinging to that fantasy of staging a miraculous return. You can only manage short distances at a time before exhaustion sets in. You reach a stream you will one day call Dooangawn. Near it is a mound of earth and embedded in it, a spear. You pull it from the ground and use it as a walking stick. But it can barely hold you up; starvation has weakened you to the point where even walking exhausts you and, trying to cross a river spilling into the sea, the high tide almost washes you away.

Crawl into the bush. That's it. Sleep the night. Next morning you must find food. Anything will do – a handful of berries, the root of a small plant. And while you are foraging in vain, two women will see you. This is it.

'These women went in search of their husbands with the intelligence that they had seen a very tall white man. Presently they all came upon me unawares and, seizing me by the arms and hands began beating their breasts, and mine . . . the women assisted me to walk, the men shouting hideous noises and tearing their hair.'

Who can blame them? They have seen a ghost.

—

There was a stubborn bastard on the *Calcutta* with you who you never knew – *Teredo navalis*. It's a bivalve mollusc but don't be fooled by that. It looks like a worm. It has a thin reddish body with two small chalky plates at its front end that grind away at anything in its path, tenaciously forming a burrow, never stopping in its quest to probe deeper.

Damn thing is almost indestructible. If anything deserves the Latin for stubborn bastard – *pertinax bastardis* – surely it is this little wriggler. It can survive for six weeks without oxygen as it bores its way through every obstacle, a very handy attribute given that hundreds of them are now chewing their way through the hull of the *Cinque Ports*, an old pirate ship that has seen better days and will not be seeing many more.

It is the Year of Our Lord, 1704 – exactly a century before a starving convict on the run begins to realise he may shortly die because of his stubbornness. The master of the *Cinque Ports* is Alexander Selkirk, a Scotsman as headstrong as the worms burrowing below him – creatures that have been the bane of wooden ships for centuries. Selkirk has been complaining to his skipper, an arrogant, 21-year-old upper-class twit by the name of Thomas Stradling, that the ship is riddled with the things and needs to undergo immediate repair. The crew has been pumping out water from the holds day and night and they are exhausted. Scurvy and fever have claimed the lives of a dozen men, including the previous captain. Supplies of meat and grain are now infested with cockroaches and rat droppings.

—

Say what you like about pirates, but don't say they are indecisive. Stradling has had enough of Selkirk's complaints and when the Scotsman refuses to quieten down, Stradling abandons him on Más a Tierra, a small, uninhabited island in the Juan Fernandez Archipelago off the coast of Chile. Left with a musket that will soon run out of gunpowder, a cooking pot, a Bible and some bedclothes, Selkirk's first few months alone are the hardest. More than once he will glance at his gun thinking it might quickly end his misery. At night rats chew on his clothes and nibble his feet. He will catch fish but because they 'occasion'd a Looseness' in his bowels, prefers to stick with the local crayfish and the wild goats. You know that feeling from those damned shellfish.

Time passes and Selkirk changes. His spirits soar. Years of hunting make him lean and fast – so quick he can pursue those goats and run them down through the jagged crags that hug the island's mountain-side. The soles of his feet harden. He tames a herd of cats to keep the rats at bay. But it is his mind that begins to run free, taking delight in the simple pleasures of reading his Bible, humming songs to himself, observing the wildlife and climbing to his 'lookout', a point 1800 feet above the island.

When Selkirk is rescued almost four and a half years later he has been transformed. Not only does the scurvy-afflicted crew of the *Duke* discover a man of outstanding physical prowess but they are also captivated by his tranquil nature. He had not surrendered to the scurrying of the rats, the cries of other beasts in the night, even the voices in his own head. The man had triumphed and overcome everyone's fear – loneliness – because he was headstrong and uncompromising and unwilling to surrender.

The skipper of the *Duke*, Woodes Rogers, is astounded and moved to write that: 'One may see that solitude and retirement from the world is not such an insufferable state of life as most men imagine, especially when people are fairly called or thrown into it unavoidably, as this man was.'

A heavily bearded Selkirk, clad in skins roughly sewn together, welcomes his rescuers with a hearty goat soup. At first he finds it hard to relate his story, having 'so much forgot his language for want of use, that we could scarce understand him, for he seemed to speak his words by halves'. But it soon tumbles out and Rogers is so impressed he immediately appoints Selkirk his second mate.

A decade later the English writer and satirist, Daniel Defoe, is said to be so inspired by Selkirk's experiences he uses them to form the basis of a novel about a man shipwrecked for 28 years on an isolated island, constantly under siege from cannibals and mutineers. *Robinson Crusoe* will become the biggest selling and most famous novel in the world.

Defoe's novel will be read by tens of millions of people who will see all sorts of parables in its pages. Even those poor, illiterate people on the streets of London and in the rural towns will have heard about its hero, a man who overcomes enormous obstacles with self-belief and tenacity.

These are the qualities that have really shaped history, from primitive man to castaways and even tiny sea worms with a voracious appetite for wood.

Stubborn bastards. Where would we be without them? And in time, a writer will look at you and think he has found his own Robinson Crusoe.

13

WILLIAM HAS A NEW FAMILY.
AND A NEW NAME

Even ghosts grow hungry and you are by far the biggest ghost these people have seen. They have taken you to one of their huts – a *mia mia* – and you sit there scoffing a pulp they have made for you from gum and water, served in a bark bowl.

You're learning much already. You have a new name. *Murrangurk*, they call you – a spirit raised from the dead. It will become your name for the next 30 years and as you ponder this they hand you several large witchetty grubs that you also swallow greedily. This food is good. To think that just a day ago the thought of salt pork and slop was enough to bring a tear to your eye.

You are still scared. For the past few hours there has been a great deal of commotion outside the *mia mia* but you are too weak to even consider running again. By the time night arrives there is a large fire – a *wiyn* – burning outside and Murrangurk's presence is required. A celebration is underway. Naked women carrying their possum-skin clothing surround you as two men lead you toward the fire.

'I expected to be thrown into the flames, but the women having seated themselves by the fire, the men joined the assemblage armed with clubs more than two feet long, having painted themselves with pipe clay, which abounds on the banks of the lake. They had run streaks of it round the eyes, one down each cheek, others along the forehead down to the tip of the nose, other streaks meeting at the chin, others from the middle of the body down each leg; so that altogether they made a most horrifying appearance standing around and about the blazing night fire.

'The women kept their rugs rolled tight up after which they stretched them between the knees, each forming a sort of drum. These they beat with their hands as if keeping time with one of the men who was seated in front of them singing. Presently the men came up in a kind of closed column, they also beating time with their sticks by knocking them one against the other, making altogether a frightful noise.

'The man seated in front appeared to be the leader of the orchestra or master of the band – indeed . . . the master of ceremonies generally. He marched the whole mob, men and women, boys and girls, backwards and forwards at his pleasure, directing the singing and dancing with the greatest decision and air of authority.'

Are you joining in? This is a corroboree, a sacred ritual and one of the first a white man has seen in this part of the land. All that marching backwards and forwards. Perhaps it reminds you of a song you learned just a few years ago . . .

The grand old Duke of York,
He had ten thousand men.
He marched them up to the top of the hill,
And he marched them down again . . .

—

Time you learned something about these people. For a start they are unlike so many of the planet's other Indigenous people. They are the oldest continuous culture in the world. They have been connected to the same land for so long, their cultural memory has no recollection of any other place. It's why their lives are so inextricably bound to the country; for tens of thousands of years they have endured endless, dust-laden summers and crippling Ice Ages. They have seen volcanoes vomiting ash and lava. They have roamed grasslands and forests alongside powerful, flesh-eating marsupial lions and kangaroos bigger than men. They have hunted Diprotodons the size of hippopotamuses and stalked five-metre long snakes.

But like every other living thing on this ancient land they, too, have come from somewhere else.

That stubborn group of Homo sapiens sitting around that fire in Africa so many years ago? The Sahara desert was a lot different then. It was a lush and fertile valley that helped propel early humans forward on their march into Europe and then on into Asia. Then, 20,000 years later, sea levels began dropping as the polar caps grew; in some places the oceans retreated by up to 100 metres. This quickly began changing the face of the planet. A land bridge formed between Tasmania and the south-eastern regions of Australia and, as the continent's land mass increased by almost a third, its northernmost point became linked to what is now Papua New Guinea. The changes were dramatic; the Gulf of Carpentaria was transformed into one of the world's largest freshwater lakes while hundreds of new islands began to form a necklace in the seas above.

The Neanderthals and Denisovans – two of just many of humanity's cousins – began to die out. Homo sapiens continued their march, island-hopping in basic craft, probably in many cases simply clinging to floating tree limbs. But getting to Australia required much more than scant and hazy knowledge of a landmass further to the south. Reaching this place involved a sea journey that, for those still in the Stone Age, might as well have been an attempt to go to the moon. Luck – the sailor's oldest tool – would be needed. But so, too, would solid sailing craft and real ingenuity; expertly carved canoes and paddles that could withstand a week or more in deep and turbulent water. It required knowledge of how currents worked, and how the stars above could guide you at night. Most of all it demanded forethought so provisions could be stocked and give this small band of travellers a chance of surviving days or weeks at sea.

They must have been stubborn bastards, too.

Let's call them the Very First Fleet. We will gain a small glimpse of them through 21st-century technology when a team of researchers studying mitochondrial DNA and using sophisticated mapping simulations estimate this first colonising party to have numbered between 100 and 300 people. That's all. They most likely launched from Western Timor or a place known as Rote in the lesser Sunda chain of islands off Indonesia. As a feat of exploration and technology, this final leap from Asia into Australia was comparable to anything that would follow: Admiral Zheng He's fleet of 312 ships and 28,000 crewmen during the Ming Dynasty, Magellan's circumnavigation of the globe in the late Middle Ages, even the Apollo missions to the moon. 'The settling of Australia represents the earliest known maritime diaspora in the world,' the scientists will say.

And once they arrived, they stayed. There may have been a series of landing places but there were no large, successive waves of colonisation, no massive second or third fleets capitalising on the pioneering work of the Very First Fleet. Genetic evidence shows little mixing of the gene pool after that initial landing. But they wasted no time in exploring this new continent. Within a few thousand years they quickly spread out around the east and west coasts, finally meeting up on what will become known as the Nullarbor. And for the next 500 and even 600 centuries – the number keeps growing the more we learn – as the planet once again underwent tumultuous change, as empires elsewhere rose and fell, as other cultures discovered farming and experienced massive population explosions, they remained alone.

It has only been in the last couple of thousand years that the outside world began to flirt with the edge of theirs. It probably began with Indonesian fishermen and Macassan traders from Sulawesi hunting for sea cucumber to trade with the Chinese. They brought with them trinkets and pottery and smallpox and venereal diseases. Much later, between the 10th and 14th centuries, explorers will leave behind a scattering of African coins on an island just off what will become known as the Northern Territory.

And then Europeans began arriving. In 1606 Dutch explorer Willem Janszoon made landfall at the Pennefather River on the western shores of Cape York. The Portuguese and others would follow and you know what, William? They always saw the same thing: a vast, untamed and almost unknowable continent inhabited by 'primitive savages'.

William Dampier – a former pirate who will be on the same ship that rescues Alexander Selkirk – meets the ancestors of the Very First Fleet off the west coast of Australia in 1688 and describes them as the 'miserablist people in the world'. It's a comment that will echo down the centuries, influencing the views of all those who will follow, all those thousands who will begin spilling from their strange ships to begin their own march across this leathered land, a relentless wave of walking white ghosts.

—

You are a ghost – but spirits and ancestors are everywhere; they inhabit the animals and plants and the rocks around you. They help drive the seasons and trigger climactic events that reshape the land. All those reverends and priests are going to shake their heads in the years to come and wonder why you never gave these people instruction about the Good Lord himself. *Why didn't you spread the Lord's word?* Well, you will have an easy answer – you feared for your safety and it was best to stay quiet about Him, because there was little He could do to save you from all those so-called savages.

Truth is, these people already have their own complex belief system, rich in stories about their origins and their place in the universe. For many there is Bunjil, the great eagle-hawk man who brought life into the world. The Boonwurrung people whose land the *Calcutta* arrived upon believe Bunjil had prevented a great flood from wiping out the five main tribes known as the Kulin nation who live around Port Phillip Bay. These five groups, who all share a common base language, had been constantly at war and the sea had grown angry and began to rise. Bunjil agreed to make the waters recede if the Kulin made peace with one another. They agreed to stop fighting and Bunjil then raised his spear, Moses-like, and ordered the sea to retreat, preventing a great flood that would have wiped out the entire Kulin nation.

You have now become part of the Wadawurrung, another language group of the Kulin. Their land runs from the Werribee River down into what will become Geelong and then further south toward the coast. They, in turn, consist of about 25 smaller clans who trade with one another, intermarry and share many of the same burial rites and customs. One of these sub-clans – the Wada wurrung balug of the Barrabool Hills – will be identified as the group with whom you will spend most of your time.

Among the Kulin every individual identifies himself or herself as either *Bunjil* (eagle hawk) or *waa* (crow). The Wadawurrung believe Bunjil – or *Karringalabil*, as some call him – lives at the end of the earth and controls the world by supporting it with props. In the years to come you will watch as word spreads that unless Bunjil is given a supply of tomahawks and rope to keep those props in place, the sky will fall in and the world will come tumbling down. Your people will consider moving to a nearby mountain range to escape the danger. But Armageddon will be prevented when some settlers – whalers and escapees from Van Diemen's Land living in the far southern reaches of the Victorian coast – are robbed of their axes and saws and ropes and the tribes forward them, one by one, until they reach Bunjil.

Everywhere you go the spirits will be with you. Fire comes from the *Waa*, a crow that one day dropped dry grass near a woman digging at an ant hill; it burst into flame, igniting a nearby tree and gave the people fire, and ever since the people have been cautious about eating the flesh of the crow.

———

You don't know all this yet, but you will. The corroboree is enough of an introduction. It lasts for more than three hours and after it you sleep heavily for the first time in weeks. You rise the next morning to discover the clan already on the move, the women gathering roots, the men spearing eels. You try and make yourself useful, gathering wood and fetching water, a novice among the skilled and experienced. A young man from another clan arrives and the following day leads your people through the bush to where another group of Aboriginals are camped. Murrangurk has been brought to a family reunion – his own.

'I was soon afterwards transferred to the charge of a man and woman of the tribe we had come to visit; the man being brother to the [man] who had been killed, from whose grave I had taken the spear; the woman was my new guardian's wife and the young man who had visited us was their son and, consequently, according to their order of thinking, my very respectable and interesting nephew.'

Another corroboree follows and when the celebration is over you taste roasted possum. They call it *barnong* and it is the first real meat to pass your lips since your escape from Sullivan Bay. Your sister-in-law also gives you a possum cloak and so you hand over your tattered and stained convict jacket, cementing the new relationship.

But all is not well. The next day a fight breaks out and your new family will pull you aside and watch with you as a battle commences. 'One man was speared through the thigh and removed into the bush where the spear was drawn. A woman of the tribe to which I had become attached was also speared under the arm and she died immediately.'

When peace is restored you watch as a large fire is made and the woman's body thrown on top of it. Once it is reduced to ashes the embers are raked over and the stick she used to dig roots is placed at the head of the remains. And then, with that done, you set off with your new family.

—

These people, William. Or is it Murrangurk now? What do you see? You will be struck by how healthy they appear. They have beautiful white teeth – nothing like that batch of convicts on the *Calcutta* and on the prison hulks, where a rare smile from those blackened gums was enough to make you look away. No sugar, you see – not until the white men begin hauling large sacks of it off their boats and into your camps. The only real sweetness will be the occasional raid you will make on beehives. Their bodies are lean, too, thanks to a diet large on fish speared and netted in the tidal flats and estuaries of what will become known as the Bellarine Peninsula. You are going to eat plenty of fish – *kuwiyn* – as well as *barnabil* (oyster) and many eels (*buniya*).

And this new family of yours, they are not without vanity, either. You will never forget their absolute distaste for grey hair; the women constantly plucking their own and those belonging to their men until 'old Father Time got the better of them'.

'The tribes are divided into families . . . or rather composed of them – each tribe comprising from twenty to sixty of them,' you will remember. 'They acknowledge no particular chief as being superior to the rest: but he who is most skillful and useful to the general community is looked upon with the greatest esteem and is considered to be entitled to more wives than any of the others.'

Word of your arrival among the Wadawurrung is already spreading throughout the lands of the Kulin and further north. In central Victoria the Morpor people of Spring Creek hear about you from their elder, Weeratt Kuynut ('eel spear'). Weeratt is one of those rare men whose presence is tolerated in almost all parts of the land. Once a fierce warrior, he becomes a messenger in his later years, travelling through fiercely defended territories and becoming such a trusted figure that he will be called upon to referee disputes and act as a neutral observer when great battles are staged.

In years to come Weeratt will say Murrangurk 'died and jumped up whitefellow' to become a man treated with consideration and respect, an *arweet* or *ngurungaeta* whose counsel will be called upon to settle disputes or to decide if a tribe or clan goes to war.

'I had seen a race of children grow up into women and men and many of the old people die away,' you will write about your last few years among them, 'and by my harmless and peaceable manner amongst them, had acquired great influence in settling their disputes. Numbers of murderous fights I had prevented by my interference, which was received by them as well meant.' There will be many times when you approach the warring parties before a battle and they will allow you to take away their spears and waddies and boomerangs. A true *arweet*. 'My visits were always welcomed and they kindly and often supplied me with a portion of the provisions they had.'

A peacemaker. As a walking dead man you take no part in the battles. And sometimes that is the hardest place to be.

14

TALES OF CANNIBALISM

Caught in the crossfire of other men's egos and disputes – that's always the way it goes, isn't it? It's one of the reasons you will finally turn to John Morgan in the years to come to help you put together your side of the story. *The Life and Adventures of William Buckley* will be published in 1852, and it will be one of the very few accounts of your 32 years living with Aboriginals.

The book will be a product of its times – a labyrinth of excessive punctuation and tortuous prose, so typical of 19th-century literature. Its chronology will be maddeningly uncertain – perhaps understandable given the time it covers and the memory lapses you will inevitably suffer – and it will give us few insights into your state of mind beyond the superficial. It will frustrate many readers and bears comparison with another man – Neil Armstrong – who also went where no-one else had gone. You may find this hard to believe but Armstrong became the first man to walk on the moon and when he returned he just didn't know how to provide an adoring public with the sort of profound insights they expected. The man who had been the first to leave his home planet and walk on an alien world was a taciturn engineer with a passion for the mechanical, not the mystical.

But your book will need to be written. You will need the money. So, too, will John Morgan.

Your first meeting with Morgan – at least a decade before the book is published – must be one of those rare encounters of kindred souls; two men who have lived much of their lives on the fringes, never quite winning the acceptance of those around them. How could Morgan resist the opportunity to write your story? His very own Robinson Crusoe, a man who survived decades wandering through a savage land filled with cannibals! A man, now standing at his door, just waiting to give John Morgan the opportunity he has been due for so long – the chance to make his name as the new Daniel Defoe . . .

Come in, Mr Buckley. May I call you William? Please, take a seat. Rest those big feet on my desk, by any means . . . whatever makes you comfortable. Now tell me all about it . . .

Morgan is a newspaper editor who has been battling bankruptcy for years. Born near Portsmouth in 1792 he had seen action while serving with the Royal Marines in Spain and had moved to Perth in the late 1820s as a government storekeeper. There, he issued credit notes to those who were starving because of a shortage of supplies. The notes were never honoured and he would go on to spend more than 20 years dodging the British Treasury who hold him liable for the debts.

Morgan moves to Van Diemen's Land, finds works as a police magistrate and as a farmer before trying his hand at journalism as the founding editor of the *Hobart Town Advertiser*. Here, finally, he finds his true voice, an outlet for his deep dislike of British Tories and rampant government excesses. He condemns the state of the local hospital as nothing but a 'slave ship on shore'. He pleads for higher standards for lawyers and judges and calls for an end to capital punishment.

John Morgan is the workingman's friend. If he lived a century later he might have been bequeathed the ultimate Australian tribute – the title of shit stirrer. He sees threats to the liberty of common people everywhere. In editorials he rails against the 'moral leprosy' of the colonial powers in Hobart and sneers at the Bunyip aristocracy – that collection of settlers, freed convicts and wealthy, upper-class twats from London – who act as if they own the town.

Morgan will grow more resentful as he ages, snubbed by polite society whose acceptance some believe he secretly craves. It probably doesn't help when the Establishment does its best to discredit his – and your – finest work.

Life and Adventures will garner a wide audience, be translated into several languages and eventually lead to an improved pension for you. But it will also leave you in familiar territory – your name and reputation caught between rivals with strong egos and reputations to uphold.

It's the perfect showdown. John Morgan, cranky firebrand who has also served a stint as secretary of the local hotelier's association, up against James Bonwick, a highly religious teetotaller who campaigns against the evils of drink and regards himself as one of the eminent historians of this fledgling nation.

Bonwick has been living in Hobart for the past few years and has seen you 'slowly pacing along the middle of the road with his eyes vacantly fixed upon some object before him, never turning his head to either side or saluting a passer by. He seemed as one not belonging to our world.'

It clearly never occurs to Bonwick that he might approach you himself, perhaps ask you a few gentle questions. Instead he remains on the other side of the road, nervously watching you, no doubt intimidated by your huge figure and those vacant eyes. Perhaps you saw him – a serious looking man with one of those strange beards where the chin is completely shaved, leaving a ring of whiskers from ear to ear like a lion's mane. No wonder you kept walking . . .

'Not being divested of curiosity we often endeavoured to gain from some of his acquaintances a little narrative of that savage life but utterly failed in doing so,' Bonwick will write. 'Several newspaper folk tried repeatedly to worm a little out of him through the steamy vapour of the punch bowl; but though his eyes might glisten a trifle his tongue was sealed.'

So clearly Bonwick, a colourful writer from the James Hingston Tuckey School of Prose, had his own plans to write about your life but Morgan beat him to it. It's a pity because Bonwick, despite his paid-up membership of the temperance movement, is in some ways a man ahead of his times. Born in Surrey and taken under the wing of a Baptist minister in his late teens, Bonwick is already disturbed by the fate of his adopted country's original inhabitants. He will write a book, *The Last of the Tasmanians*, that will become a paean to a lost civilisation and its demise at the hands of a ruthless society that pushed it relentlessly toward extinction. He will also spend time on the Ballarat goldfields – not very successfully – and walk away with a scene forever embedded in his memory.

'We saw a party of natives plied with drink by Englishmen until their bestial manners and coarse speech excited the brutal mirth of their cruel temptors,' he will recall. 'Throughout the night the bush was disturbed with the mad yells and quarrels of the poor creatures.'

Bonwick rises early next morning and discovers the cause of the moaning near his tent. Nearby lies a 'wretched man in the mud, with nothing upon him but a shirt thoroughly drenched with a night of cold wintry rain. While his limbs shook with the inclemency of the weather his brow was wet with the sweat of agony.

'In answer to questions he groaned out: "Me killed – Long Tom did it – him drunk – him stab me knife."

'Lifting his shirt we beheld a large gash in his side, out of which part of his bowels were protruding and mingling with the grit of the muddy soil. The doctor arrived and pronounced the case hopeless – the poor fellow must die . . .

'Why should the black race pass away? There was no apparent diminution of physical force, moral power, mental activity. The signs of their decrepitude suddenly fall upon them as the curtain of night in the tropics. With diseased frames, with hopeless feelings, homeless and childless, the present generation will soon glide away from us. Like the leaves of an English autumn they wither and fall; but, alas! There is no spring for them. The Sheoak hangs its mournful, weird-like appendages over their tombs; and on its knotted, leafless strings, the passing breezes play their solemn requiem.'

Tuckey could not have rhapsodised any better. The problem with Bonwick is that he likes to be liked. Unlike Morgan, you won't find the man storming into a room, waving his arms around and not caring whose toes he treads upon. When Bonwick walks into a room he gets straight down on all fours and performs pedicures. There's a deep strain of sycophancy through much of his work. And he can't help showing his jealousy over Morgan beating him to this new country's very own version of Robinson Crusoe.

A few years after *Life and Adventures* is released, Bonwick hits back with his own book: *William Buckley, the Wild White Man and his Port Phillip Black Friends.*

Funny how someone can write a book without consulting the subject, isn't it, William?

Bonwick opens with guns blazing, condemning your book because 'there are weighty reasons of objection to its authenticity . . . all those with whom we have consulted, who knew Buckley both in Port Phillip and Hobart Town, repudiate the book. They all agree in saying that he was so dull and reserved that it was impossible to get any connected or reliable information from him.' And that is just the start of it. Bonwick has a long list of eminent people of the era – just the sort of Establishment figures that make Morgan grind his teeth – ready to dismiss the accuracy and relevancy of *Life and Adventures.*

The problem with all this is that all these prissy white critics who have had their toenails clipped and buffed by Bonwick have no idea what they are talking about. You'll be happy to hear that over the next few decades there will be a greater appreciation of your work. Historians will say that while Morgan has clearly exaggerated here and there – and let's never forget he has written the book for an 1850s readership – many of your experiences with Aboriginals will ring true. Your descriptions of everyday life with the Wadawurrung people and other language clans – sometimes unpalatable – will give 'a truer account of Aboriginal life than any work I have read', according to one prominent historian.

Another historian will dismiss all this talk about you being a simple buffoon. 'In order to exist at all he must have had qualities of shrewdness, courage and endurance of a higher order.'

—

But John Morgan wants you to spice things up a tad. So there must be some unpalatable claims, too. You know what he needs. Tell him about the patriarchal society where a man whose brother is slain is entitled to take his dead brother's wives as his own. If one of the women objects she can face death. We will never quite know how you and Morgan wrote your book. Did the pair of you sit by a log fire during those cold winter evenings, your legs stretched out, cup of tea in your hands, a flickering candle growing shorter by the hour as Morgan scribbles in his notebook? Or did the man employ the 'steamy vapour of the punch bowl', plying you with whiskey in a bid to extract the juiciest morsels from your time with the Wadawurrung?

Morgan never left behind drafts or notes; his impulsiveness usually saw him leaping frenetically from one project to another. But you came through for him because *Life and Adventures* is filled with stories of battles and murderous revenge killings as well as that subject the English obsess about whenever they encounter a new culture – cannibalism.

'They have a brutal aversion to children who happen to be deformed at their birth,' you say in the book. 'I saw the brains of one dashed out at a blow and a boy belonging to the same woman made to eat the mangled remains. The act of cannibalism was accounted for in this way.'

—

These 19th-century colonialists lap it up whenever the subject of eating human flesh arises. And if it serves to underline all those ingrained prejudices about primitivism and the uncivilised, they hardly shrink away when it comes to stories of their own kind devouring one another, either.

Tales of its practice litter seafaring lore. Take the surviving crew members of the *Essex*, sunk by a sperm whale in 1820 in the Pacific, who drift for three months in small boats eating the remains of their dead, a tale that will be popularised 30 years later by Herman Melville in *Moby-Dick*. Or what about the French frigate that runs aground off the coast of north-east Africa in 1816? More than 140 survivors crowd on to a makeshift raft; only 15 survive their two weeks at sea after a horrific journey pitted with daily suicides, murders and cannibalism.

But it is not just mishaps at sea that force early 19th-century Europeans to devour one another. One of the darkest tales to emerge from Australian colonial history takes place two years after the sinking of the *Essex* when a group of seven convicts in Van Diemen's Land escape from the Macquarie Harbour Penal Station.

They had originally planned to make their way to the Derwent River, steal a schooner and either sail home to England or to China, living out their days without chains and the fear of another flogging. Had they succeeded it would have become one of the most remarkable escape stories in history. Instead it becomes one of the most macabre.

Making their way through some of the world's most rugged terrain on the island's west coast, the escaped convicts begin drawing straws using small twigs to see who will be murdered and eaten. According to an account by the only survivor, the first victim is killed by an axe blow and is almost immediately set upon: 'Matthew Travers with a knife also came and cut his throat and bled him; we then dragged him to a distance and cut off his clothes and tore out his inside and cut off his head. Then Matthews Travers and Greenhill put his heart and liver on the fire and eat it before it was right warm; they asked the rest would they have any but they would not have any that night.'

Of course, hunger will eventually get the better of all of them. Days and weeks pass trying to forge their way through near impenetrable mist-clad rainforests. Hemmed in by swollen rivers, frustrated by the lack of animal prey, lacking the knowledge to survive off the land and increasingly suspicious of one another, they continue to kill off the weakest of their pack, assigning equal portions of the flesh. Two escapees are found dying from exposure on the shore of the harbour weeks later, the last of the human remains still stuffed in their clothing.

Eventually it comes down to two – Alexander Pearce, a trouble-prone Irish convict transported for stealing shoes, and a former sailor, Robert Greenhill. For days they eye one another from a distance, perhaps history's most uncomfortable fellow travellers, until Pearce seizes Greenhill's axe one evening while he sleeps and kills him.

Pearce survives, going on to join a small band of bushrangers before being caught several months later. Taken to Hobart in chains, Pearce will be interrogated by the town's acting magistrate, none other than the Reverend Robert 'I sleep where I dine' Knopwood. The reverend cannot bring himself to believe the account – it is too fantastical. He dismisses it as a lie designed to cover for the rest of the escaped felons and sends Pearce back to Macquarie Harbour to be feted by his fellow convicts as the only man to ever make it out of the place and live to talk about it.

A year later he escapes again, this time with Thomas Cox, a young man who demands Pearce take him with him, despite knowing the older man's dietary habits while on the run. Pearce is captured four days later holding a piece of Cox's flesh. He is taken to Hobart and hanged. And then the body of the most celebrated cannibal in Australian history will itself serve another purpose, his skull being sent to the prolific American author and scientist Samuel Morton, who is amassing the greatest collection of human craniums in the world.

So cannibalism is a practice that can be understood, if not forgiven, as a last, desperate act of survival. But its practice as a cultural rite – however circumscribed and unconfirmed among some Aboriginal cultures – is abhorrent to English senses. Colonial journals and memoirs will be obsessively filled with reports of flesh-eating rituals.

It will be one of the first questions asked by the Reverend George Langhorne when he interviews you more than 18 months after you return to white society.

'It is true they are cannibals,' you will tell Langhorne. 'I have seen them eat small portions of the flesh of their adversaries slain in battle. They appear to do this not from any particular partiality for human flesh but from the impression that by eating their adversaries' flesh they would themselves become able warriors.

'Many of them are disgusted with this ceremony and refusing to eat, merely rub their bodies with a small portion of fat as a charm equally efficient [a practice known as 'kidney fatting'].

'They eat also of the flesh of their own children to whom they have been much attached should they die a natural death. When a child dies they place the body in an upright position in a hollow tree and allow it to remain there until perfectly dry when they will carry it about with them.'

It's not hard to picture Morgan sitting by his candle, working late into the night with visions of himself as the antipodean Defoe, laying out with gusto your macabre tales of the battles and their aftermath around Port Phillip. One instance follows the deadly spearing of a 20-year-old member of the tribe in a dispute over a woman: 'When we had settled ourselves down there, some of the men went to the spot where we had left the young man's remains hanging in the tree and brought away the lower part of the body, leaving the upper quarters and head where they found it suspended.

'The usual uproar commenced amongst the women on the arrival of the part of the corpse, lamentation succeeding lamentation, burning with fire sticks and all the rest of it, until at length the mangled remains were roasted between heated stones, shared out and greedily devoured by these savages. Again I was pressed to join in this horrid repast but I hope I need not say that I refused, with indignation and disgust.'

After that, you will be determined to return to living on your own. It's something you will do frequently, particularly at the Karaaf just to the west of what, more than a century later, will become the coastal town of Breamlea. You have built a hut just where the river runs into the sea and not only is there plenty of food – an unending supply of eels (*buniya*) and fish (*kuwiyn*) and duck (*bernarr*) and yam daisy (*murnong*) – but the low, flat land will give you a perfect lookout to see any approaching clans. However, these moments craving solitude never last long. Within days or weeks you will see their outline on the horizon and before long you are on the move with them again, back into a world where you will encounter for Morgan plenty more episodes of gothic horror, Herculean bravado and near-death experiences.

And, of course, a mandatory touch of romance.

15

THE ONES WHO CAME BEFORE YOU

How often does it start with gifts and lies? One of the first encounters between Port Phillip's original inhabitants and white men takes place just a year and a half before the *Calcutta* sails into the bay. The *Lady Nelson* is an 80-ton brig sent from Port Jackson to explore the still unknown lands to the south. She is an odd-looking ship constructed to work shallow waterways, commissioned 'for the purpose of prosecuting the discovery and survey of the unknown parts of the coast of New Holland'. As a result she sits low in the water, in part because of four extra brass guns fitted shortly before her departure in early 1800. On her way to the colony she had sailed out of Dead Man's Dock and into the Thames and so strange did she look sailors on nearby ships ridiculed her as 'his majesty's tinderbox'.

But despite her looks the *Lady Nelson* proves to be a rugged and reliable explorer. She has already mapped much of Bass Strait and its islands and acting lieutenant John Murray, a Scotsman who had been the mate on her original voyage to Sydney, has now been ordered to return and investigate the large bay and its surrounding country.

It does not take long for the first encounter between Europeans and the Kulin people to go wrong. In early 1802, a month after its first attempt fails, the *Lady Nelson* manages to navigate the turbulent rip at the mouth of the bay and Murray finds himself in a 'fine harbor of large extent'. On one of his first nights Murray sees fires burning on nearby land and decides to send a small boat and crew toward shore in hope of making contact.

They take gifts of white dress shirts, wrapped with a fib. 'I sent the launch with Mr Bowen and four hands armed to see if any natives were here,' Murray will write in his journal. '. . . before the boat was halfway on shore we had the satisfaction of seeing 18 or 20 men and boys come out of the wood and seat themselves down on a green bank waiting the approach of our boat, with which I sent some shirts and other trifles to give them. The boat accordingly landed in the midst of them and a friendly intercourse took place with dancing on both sides . . .

'They wished much to know what our arms were and their use and did not seem entirely to believe Mr Bowen that they were only walking sticks.'

The next day Murray sends ashore one of the youngest members of his crew, a boy called Brabyn, to win the confidence of some of the younger members of the tribe. From the deck of the *Lady Nelson*, Murray watches Brabyn give the young men handkerchiefs and dress them in shirts and trousers. He is soon joined on land by more of Murray's crew.

And then things turn ugly.

Brabyn turns and looks toward a clump of trees and sees a man 'in the very act of throwing a spear'. Behind him a large group of warriors suddenly appear, also with spears poised.

'The boy immediately cried out to Mr Bowen – who was at that very time in the act of serving out bread to all the party he was sitting among – that he would be speared. But before the words were out of his mouth a spear of the most dangerous kind was thrown at and did not escape Moss by a yard . . . in an instant the whole of the treacherous body that Mr Bowen and four of our people were sitting in the midst of opened out to the right and left.'

It is an old-fashioned ambush. There are screams and shouts as long spears hurtle toward the *Lady Nelson*'s men. One of the crew fires a gun but this only creates a small panic among the warriors.

And so, says Murray, 'our party was obliged to teach them by fatal experience the effect of our walking sticks.

'The first fire made them run and one received two balls between his shoulders . . . the second fire they all set off with astonishing speed and most likely one received a mortal wound. Before another piece was fired Mr Bowen laid hold of one of their number and held on till three of our people came up and also grappled him: strange to tell he made such violent struggles as to get away from all. Now did the contents of the officer's piece bring him up, although one ball passed through his arm and the other in his side.

'He was traced a good distance by his blood . . . thus did treachery and unprovoked attack meet with its just punishment and at the same time taught us a useful lesson to be more cautious in future.'

Murray considers the natives around this bay to be similar in size and height to those he has seen in Sydney: '. . . their understanding better though for they easily made out our signs when it answered their purposes or inclination. When it did not they could be dull enough. They were all clothed in opossum skins . . . I concluded they live entirely inland and if we may judge from the number of their fires and other marks this part of the country is not thin of inhabitants.'

Chastened by the encounter, Murray continues the expedition around the bay, avoiding further contact. Three weeks later the *Lady Nelson* prepares to sail back home. But first, in the time-honoured tradition, Murray assembles the crew on deck at eight in the morning on the 8th of March in the Year of Our Lord, 1802, and hoists the colours of the kingdom of Great Britain.

'. . . under a discharge of three volleys of small arms and artillery the port was taken possession of in the name of his sacred majesty George the Third of Great Britain and Ireland, King etc etc . . .'

Murray adds one more important note: 'Served double allowance of grog'.

—

Collisions between cultures are nothing new. It has been happening throughout millennia, from the time when those stubborn Homo sapiens first came face to face with the Neanderthals, through to Columbus' arrival in the new world and his subsequent brutalisation of the local people. By the late 18th and early 19th century, encounters between Indigenous people and outsiders have become an even more lop-sided equation; gunpowder against sticks and stones, supported by even heavier artillery of smallpox and venereal microbes.

The chasm between Australia's Aboriginals and the British will be vast and almost without common ground. On one side of this gulf: the Dreaming, a universe where time flows in many directions, where tribes of hunter-gatherers live within a land imbued with sorcery and mysticism and the unmistakable signs of their ancestors. On the other: the Enlightenment, with its tribes of scientific rationalists wielding measuring instruments and mathematical formulae and an unchallengeable belief in the superiority of civilised man.

These two disparate worlds will scrape against one another for the first time in 1770 as the *Endeavour* under the command of Lieutenant James Cook sails along the east coast of Australia on the final leg of its history-making three-year voyage of discovery through the Pacific.

Cook is sailing with a set of 'hints' or instructions handed to him by James Douglas, the Earl of Morton and president of the Royal Society, which has supplied much of the funding for the voyage. It includes advice to 'exercise the utmost patience and forbearance with respect to the natives of the several lands where the ship may touch . . . to have it still in view that shedding the blood of those people is a crime of the highest nature – they are all human creatures, the work of the same omnipotent Author, equally under his care with the most polished European, perhaps less offensive, more entitled to his favour'.

The Earl also provides advice that, even centuries later, will be remarkable for its time: 'They are the natural and in the strictest sense of the word, the legal possessors of the several regions they inhabit.

No European nation has a right to occupy any part of their country, or settle among them without their voluntary consent.'

So much for the 'hints'. The *Endeavour* has just sailed around New Zealand after visiting Tahiti to record the 1769 transit of Venus across the sun. After dropping anchor near a river on its north island, an encounter with the local Maori had ended with the killing of a warrior with spirals of 'tattaou' on his cheeks and nose. The first Australian Aboriginal tribe Cook encounters will be the Gweagal people and that meeting will set the tone for all future conflict – a rock thrown at the English, who have not sought permission to enter tribal land, is immediately answered by musket fire that strikes a Gweagal man on his legs.

This is a time when Europeans, confronting a new era of machines and technology, cling to a romantic fantasy of naked brutes uncorrupted by modern civilisation, the 'Noble Savage' who lives in harmony with the land and whose soul is untainted by material ambition and the accumulation of wealth. The closest the crew of the *Endeavour* has come to finding this pure breed of man was in Tahiti. What specimens they turned out to be: graceful and lithe and ever so lusty, their libidos no doubt driven by the tropical heat and their Garden of Eden surrounds. At the urging of his young botanist, Joseph Banks, Cook had taken on board a man called Tupaia, said to be the most gifted of all Tahitian navigators. If these white-skinned men and their marvellous ship fascinated Tupaia, he felt in no way inferior.

He was . . . well . . . *noble*.

'He was a shrewd, sensible, ingenious man,' Cook writes in his journal, 'but proud and obstinate which often made his situation on board both disagreeable to himself and those about him.'

Tupaia proves invaluable as an interpreter and diplomat during the journey around New Zealand. But he is as mystified by Australia's Aboriginals as the white men. Unlike the Maori, whose songs, traditions and language share Pacific ties with the Tahitians, Tupaia finds Australia's Aboriginals almost as unknowable as the rest of the *Endeavour*'s crew.

From the deck of the *Endeavour*, Banks watches an old woman and three children emerge from the woods and make their way toward several huts near the beach: 'She carried several pieces of stick and the children also had their little burthens; when she came to the house three more younger children came out of one of them to meet her. She often looked at the ship but expressed neither surprise nor concern.'

Banks is flummoxed. He is a man of science, a true son of the Enlightenment, a collector and identifier of new species, a rational fellow constantly in awe at how the good Lord has clothed nature in such a complex manner. His role in life is to uncover God's signature, to show how His hand has forged this world. Surely this sense of wonder, this air of inquisitiveness, is a trait of all civilised people. Yet these Aboriginals seem to be lacking as much in curiosity as they are in clothing – 'the women did not copy our mother Eve even in the fig leaf'.

But the watchers are being watched. The English do not know that their arrival is already being recorded, not in journals or written form, but in an oral tradition that has existed for more than 50,000 years, long before the first modern humans had ever reached Britain. Stories are already being passed from clan to clan about the arrival of a 'big bird' filled with small scampering creatures crawling all over its body; other tales tell of a large canoe carrying the spirits of ancestors, white figures they will call *Murrangurk* or *wawu-ngay*.

The gulf between the two worlds will be too large for any shared understanding. 'We thence concluded not much in favour of our future friends,' writes Banks, a sentiment mirrored throughout the next century in the journals and reports of explorers and early settlers on the Australian frontier. To them, the Aboriginals are indifferent and even lazy, preferring to lie about rather than be industrious and tend to the land.

The land. The Australian soil, more than language and customs, will become the starkest difference between the two cultures. To the British, this new world will bring to mind a saying that becomes popular in London society in the early 1800s. The Prince of Wales is one of the first to employ it: 'Girls are not to my taste,' he will say. 'I don't like lamb, but mutton dressed as lamb!'

From the deck of the *Endeavour* the eastern coastline offers a tranquil vista that reminds many of the patchwork quilts of fields and cultivated lands back home. 'The woods are free from underwood of every kind and the trees are at such a distance from one another that the whole country, or at least a great part of it, might be cultivated without being obliged to cut down a single tree,' writes Cook in May 1770.

Moving north he sees little to dampen his enthusiasm, noting in August that 'the mountains or hills are chequered with woods and lawns'.

Banks, never one to avoid a clumsy metaphor, will write that 'the country tho in general well enough clothed, appeared in some places bare. It resembled in my imagination the back of a lean cow, covered in general with long hair, but nevertheless where her scraggy hip bones have stuck out further than they ought, accidental rubs and knocks have entirely bared them of their share of covering.'

The view from the *Endeavour* is largely optimistic. But the British will soon learn that this fertile coast is simply a green curtain disguising a dry and arid heartland. It is mutton dressed up as lamb, an ancient crone with some hurriedly applied make-up. Within days of the arrival of the First Fleet, Englishmen are stunned to discover that much of it will defy the plough; the unyielding clays and sandy soils are enough to make the most stubborn bastard cry. It will be a difficult lesson to learn: the earth did not yield to brute force; you had to find a way to live and work within its limits. And those limits are severe. Even the four predictable seasons back home that English farmers could rely on arriving almost to the day defy prediction.

When the *Calcutta* arrives in Port Phillip on the cusp of a new summer its passengers are astonished by the severe and abrupt changes in the weather; days of unrelenting heat driven by dry northerly winds broken within minutes by bursts of bone-chilling Antarctic air and squalls of icy rain. It was so typical of the luck of David Collins that he chose to enter Port Phillip Bay and turn right to find poor sandy soils and little water. Had he simply gone left by pushing to the west and further north he would have found more water and some of the most fertile land in the world, enriched 40 million years earlier by constant volcanic eruptions.

But that was the story of this unpredictable country. Water becomes such a lottery that a man, moving inland in some places, will find that annual rainfall can drop by an inch for every mile he travels. And so the British quickly conclude that Australia's Aboriginals remain locked in a Stone Age with little hope of progressing toward an agricultural state for a very simple reason; they are far too primitive and managing this land requires a sophistication far beyond their means.

A view that you, William, quickly discover is mistaken.

16

WILLIAM ADOPTS A BLIND BOY – AND FINDS LOVE

Ahem. A delicate matter has come to our attention, and we need to deal with it. You have been spending more of your time on your own at the Karaaf, that shallow, slow-moving stream that begins in the Barrabool Hills a few miles away and lazily makes its way toward the coastal sand dunes next to the ocean. You have your hut and plenty of fish and the isolation you desperately crave whenever life with the Wadawurrung gets too hectic. Truth is, these people are not that different to the white ones you left behind, are they? Same old jealousies and petty disputes. And talk . . . they love to talk. You not being that mad about words means the Karaaf has become your fortress of solitude. But that doesn't mean you don't get lonely . . .

Sex, William. That's what needs to be discussed.

The months and years are passing and you're still a young man and, well, we know you enjoyed scenes of 'riotous dissipation' during your years as a soldier. It's the reason you're here now. And you surely know that in the years to come there will be an army of armchair psychologists analysing your life and how you manage to survive against such insanely long odds.

But surely this one beats them all. It comes from an historian writing more than a century later.

'One of the possible reasons for his survival is that he could have been under-sexed and, accordingly, did not participate in the continual warfare caused by the pursuing of women.'

Under-sexed? Say what you like about William Buckley but don't say this man munching fish and roots at the Karaaf has sworn a lifelong vow of celibacy. For a start there will be several accounts of settlers coming across Aboriginal children with pale skin in the years to come. A grown daughter of yours will be pointed out one day – 'an exceedingly tall and handsome young woman of lighter hue and European countenance' – while other claims will surface of you fathering several children. The Reverend George Langhorne will write that: 'Buckley says he did not live with any black woman but I have doubted from the circumstances which came under my notice the truth of this assertion, and also I think it probable he had children.'

This is where you get caught telling fibs – and fibs to a man of God, no less. That interview with Langhorne takes place in early 1837. We know that 15 years later you publish *Life and Adventures*, and in it you include a couple of admissions of dalliances with women.

The first begins when you are visited at your hut by a clan that so admires the life you have made for yourself they invite themselves to stay. Very soon they decide you need a wife.

You will recall you have no say in the matter when you are given to a 20-year-old widow, 'tolerably good-looking, after a fashion, and apparently very mild tempered'. Morgan will note that there are none of the trappings of an English wedding – no fees to pay a piper for music, no ceremony or the added costs for a dress and a celebratory feast.

Instead the pair of you simply adjourn to your hut. You remain together for several months until you discover that your 'dearly beloved played me most abominably false . . . one evening when we were alone in our hut, enjoying our domestic felicity, several men came in and took her away from me by force; she, however, going very willingly'.

She moves in with another man and for this slight, this show of disrespect, you are urged by your clan to take revenge. But there is no need for that; she is soon speared by the man 'with whom she had been coqueting and to who she had also played most falsely'.

Another fight will ensue – there are so many it is hard to keep track of them – 'in which many heads were broken . . . I took no part in these, excepting assuming the defensive and threatening them with punishment if they interfered with me, being now quite as expert as any of them with the spear and boomerang.'

And that, as far as you and Morgan are concerned, is almost the end of the matter. By the 1850s the curtain of Victorian prurience has been lowered; dear readers are to be protected from lurid accounts of sexual escapades and conquests lest their blushing lead to heart palpitations and impure thoughts.

The other intimate encounter you hint at takes place decades into your life with the Wadawurrung and is the most intriguing. For some time you say you have been caring for the daughter and blind boy of your brother-in-law who has been slain in another dispute. You have grown attached to them, taking them on your frequent fishing and hunting expeditions, instructing them in the things their father might have taught them. Children seem to warm to you; during your first years with the Wadawurrung they often slept with you in your hut, listening to your tales about the great battles fought by the English against Napoleon. Easier to talk with children, is it not? So less demanding.

The blind boy becomes your shadow, completely reliant on you for food and warmth. It is an unusual relationship for the time. Children with disabilities are rare; not only are they believed to be cursed but anything that slows the movement of a family clan is seen as a hindrance. But when a young man from another clan staying with you falls ill and dies, his family blames the blind boy who had been sleeping in the same hut. Sorcery and bad luck doing their work once more. The family of the dead boy kills your blind child in retribution. Heartbroken, you give up the boy's sister to her intended husband and then depart, once more, for the Karaaf and another stint of solitude.

But it always ends the same, that desperate need to be alone quickly turning to despondency. One day you are 'unexpectedly joined' by a young woman who has fled while her clan is engaged in a battle with rivals. She stays with you 'for a long time'. At one stage you kill a seal for the two of you: 'We found the flesh very good eating and my female friend enjoyed the repast with great gusto; greasing herself all over with the fat after we had made the most of the carcass, which might well be compared to bacon.'

The pair of you move along the coast during a cold winter, taking shelter in caves and rock crevices, always searching for food. The relationship seems to be a lengthy one. By now your memory of English has faded and you are fluent in the Wadawurrung language. Do you engage in small talk with her, the kind you will always shy away from in the white world? It's something we want to imagine; the pair of you huddled and smiling beneath a kangaroo skin rug by a small fire, bellies warm and full, the faint sound of waves crashing nearby, the sky above a carpet of glittering gems. Surely you deserve a little happiness, someone to love and care for. But just when we picture you caressing her tenderly and she gazing into your hazel eyes, almost hidden beneath those deep-set and overhanging eyebrows, the scene goes to black. You and Morgan yank that curtain down again by abruptly saying 'my amiable young lady friend' decides to return to her clan. That's it. Nothing more, except further tales of carnage and mayhem.

It will not be until the early 1880s that the name emerges of a woman who could have been your wife. It will come to us courtesy of a Scotsman, James Dawson, a pastoralist who works his way out of bankruptcy on the Victorian goldfields and settles in the state's western district. History will remember him as an amateur ethnographer and one of the greatest critics of the way in which Australia's Aboriginals have been treated.

Dawson's unfashionable passion for Aboriginal rights will become legendary. He's a blunt man who is not afraid to take on the Establishment. On one occasion he will attack an influential Melbourne newspaper editor with an umbrella for not printing allegations about the mistreatment of Aboriginals.

Dawson will publish a weighty tome entitled *Australian Aborigines: the languages and customs of several tribes of Aborigines in the western district of Victoria, Australia.* In that book he will include a report from William Goodall, the superintendent of an Aboriginal station at Framlingham.

Goodall will say: 'There is, at the Aboriginal Station at Framlingham, a native woman named Purranmurnin Tallarwurnin, who was the wife of the white man Buckley at the time he was found by the first settlers in Victoria.

'She belonged originally to the Buninyong tribe and was about fifteen years old when she became acquainted with Buckley.'

This already makes sense. Mt Buninyong is an extinct volcano just south of the town of Ballarat in Victoria's Central Highlands and the Keyeet balug clan of the Wadawurrung has long occupied its surrounding land.

Purranmurnin Tallarwurnin's account matches with many of your memories. It supports your claim that as the years pass you learn you have less to fear from the Aboriginal people and even become indifferent when a new group approaches you. One story appears to be set by the Barwon River, a favourite haunting place of yours where the water flows through a series of rock pools and small waterfalls, a place that will be dubbed 'Buckley's Falls' in the years to come.

'One of the natives discovered immense footprints in the sand hummocks near the River Barwon and concluded that they had been made by some unknown gigantic native – a stranger, and therefore an enemy,' reports Goodall's summary of what Purranmurnin has told him. 'He set off at once on the track and soon discovered a strange-looking being lying down on a small hillock, sunning himself after a bath in the sea.

'A brief survey, cautiously made, was sufficient. The native hurried back to the camp and told the rest of the tribe what he had seen.

They at once collected all the men in the neighbourhood, formed a cordon and warily closed in on him.'

When the naked Buckley sees this cordon he takes little notice. 'They were very much alarmed. At length one of the party finding courage addressed him as *muurnong guurk* (meaning that they supposed him to be one who had been killed and come to life again), and asked his name.

'You Kondak Barwon?' (*Are you the sap of the tree of Barwon?*)

'Buckley replied by a prolonged grunt and an inclination of the head, signifying yes . . . they were highly gratified and he and they soon became friends.'

—

That historian who suggested you might be under-sexed – that you did not participate 'in the continual warfare caused by the pursuing of women'.

Could be they got something right.

Your book with Morgan barely manages to proceed for a few pages without recording another violent episode caused by disputes over the possession of women. At first you struggle to comprehend the meaning behind so much of the bloodshed you encounter, 'but afterwards understood that they were occasioned by the women having been taken away from one tribe by another; which was of frequent occurrence. At other times they were caused by the women willingly leaving their husbands, and joining other men, which the natives consider very bad.'

In this staunchly patriarchal culture the women might be chattels to be passed from clan to clan for marriage, to be treated roughly and even violently. But it does not stop them from joining the heat of battle. There's a clash you will always recall – a very large tribe you call the Waarengbadawa (possibly the Wongerrer balug people from the Wardy Yalloak River). Their warriors are smeared with red and white clay and 'by far the most hideous looking savages I had seen'.

When the major battle begins, you, Murrangurk, are ordered to stay in the background. Dead men do not take part in wars, apparently. They are just the end result. Outnumbered, your people take on their opponents and the battlefield begins to resemble that deep abyss in Greek mythology – Tartarus, the dungeon used by the Titans to torture their prisoners.

'I had seen skirmishing and fighting in Holland; and knew . . . of what is done when men are knocking one another about with powder and shot . . . but the scene now before me was much more frightful . . . Men and women were fighting furiously and indiscriminately, covered with blood.' The Waarengbadawa retreat after a few hours and that night a group of your warriors, probably from the Bengalat balug clan with whom you spend much of your time, launch an ambush against the Waarengbadawa.

'The enemy fled, leaving their war implements in the hands of their assailants and their wounded to be beaten to death by boomerangs . . . the bodies of the dead they mutilated in a shocking manner, cutting the arms and legs off with flints, shells and tomahawks.'

Now this is the sort of material John Morgan craves. None of that romantic nonsense, please. Bad enough the colonial reader should even dare imagine a white man having a black woman as his 'female friend'. It's easy to picture Morgan sitting there by the fire, nodding impatiently as you tell him about your relationships and dalliances. Torrid battles between painted savages is what he really wants to hear about.

Now that's all good. But back to that battle . . . what happened when the successful warriors of your tribe returned to camp?

'When the women saw them returning, they also raised great shouts, dancing about in savage ecstasy. The bodies [of the vanquished] were thrown upon the ground and beaten about with sticks – in fact, they all seemed to be perfectly mad with excitement; the men cut flesh off the bones and stones were heated for baking it; after which, they greased their children with it, all over. The bones were broken to pieces with tomahawks and given to the dogs, or put on the boughs of trees for the birds of prey hovering over the horrid scene.'

These words come to us almost 70 years after James Cook and Joseph Banks, standing on the deck of the *Endeavour*, make their first observations of this land's long-time inhabitants. Banks is unimpressed and even Cook will say they live like wild beasts.

But there is something that catches Cook's eye, something that suggests he can see further and deeper than just about anyone else over the coming century. 'They may appear to some to be the most wretched people upon earth,' he will write in his journal, '. . . but in reality they are far more happier [sic] than we Europeans, being wholly unacquainted not only with the superfluous but with the necessary conveniences so much sought after in Europe; they are happy in not knowing the use of them.

'They live in a tranquility which is not disturbed by the inequality of condition. The earth and sea of their own accord furnishes them with all things necessary for life. They covet not magnificent houses, house-hold stuff etc . . . they seemed to set no value upon anything we gave them, nor would they ever part with anything of their own for any one article we could offer them.'

17

WORDS AND THINGS

'Snake.'
Kadak?
'Goanna.'
Djulin?
'Welcome to Wadawurrung country.'
Kim-barne Wadawurrung Tabayl?

Never were a great student, were you? But the clans are patient with you. After all, you have died and jumped up whitefella. Your taste buds, your language, your bush skills – all must be relearned. But you have plenty of time and over the years it comes to you – how to speak, how to throw a 12-foot-long spear with great accuracy, how to skin a kangaroo or possum with a sharpened mussel shell, how to take that skin and stretch it before leaving it to dry in the sun, how to take the sinews and prepare them so they can be used to sew the skins together for rugs.

There are beehives high in the trees to be plundered for honey, nutritious roots to be dug from the ground and wombats – *ngurr-ngurr* – to be pulled from their deep burrows (you're far too large to crawl through their tunnels – that is the job of small children). You learn to become a mimic, luring wildlife with their calls and whistles, and are taught the art of camouflage and patience, standing or even lying motionless for hours in order to trap goannas.

Sometimes, when larger groups come together, they will hunt as a pack, forming an immense circle more than a mile in diameter, each man a couple of hundred yards apart. The circle will gradually contract, driving game like kangaroos and rats and possums into the centre, where they will be speared and clubbed.

Even the insects provide much needed protein. Within minutes you will be able to gather handfuls of those almond-flavoured witchetty grubs, the larvae of moths that can be eaten raw or roasted. To the east of Port Phillip, hundreds of clans will journey to the alps in late spring and early summer to smoke out millions of Bogong moths clinging to rock walls and crevices, a protein feast that, when dried, will last a group for months.

All those white historians in future years will never understand just how deep you go, how much of your old self you leave behind. You learn how to sharpen the head of your tomahawk, your *kallallingurk*, grinding its black stone head with rough granite until you can fell a tree with just a few swings. These black heads of the *kallallingurk* come from a special quarry you call Karkeen many miles north of the coast where you live. In the language of the Woiwurrung people on whose land it sits it is known as *Wil-im-ee Moor-ring* – 'the axe-place'. Over the next couple of centuries it will become a protected site near the modern-day Lancefield, a window into an industrial trading hub that for thousands of years supplies the heads of *kallallingurk* deep into Victoria's south-west and into the southern reaches of New South Wales. This quarry of volcanic greenstone has flaking floors and a large rock that has served as an anvil for centuries. Surrounding it are several hundred mining pits – many several yards deep.

When Cook and Banks stand on the deck of the *Endeavour*, when David Collins takes one last miserable glance at Port Phillip as he heads to Van Diemen's Land, when the white wave of settlers and convicts begin their march further inland – they will see and imagine none of this. Suggestions that your people have a deep and intrinsic tie to the land – that there is a strong sense of ownership as well as complex forms of commerce and industry – will be dismissed as flights of fancy. Aboriginals are idle wanderers. Nothing more. A prominent newspaper will describe them as having 'bestowed no labour on the land' and to whom 'this country was to them a common'.

—

Burning eucalypt. It is an unmistakable smell, uniquely Australian, and on one afternoon in 1802 its acrid odour begins to fill the nostrils of the son of a French naval officer. Francis Barrallier is an explorer, surveyor and future soldier who has just returned from a journey on the *Lady Nelson* to the southern reaches of the continent. He is now attempting one of the first crossings of the Blue Mountains and is quite proud to have just heard the word *coo-ee* ('come here'), a shout used by the Dharug people. Accompanied by several Aboriginal guides and a handful of convicts, Barrallier can smell and see bush-fires in the distance. One of his guides, Bungin, tells him the fires have been purposely lit by 'a chief called Canambaigle with his tribe who were hunting, and had on that very day set the country on fire'. A month later he sees 'the country a mass of flames towards the north east, at about five miles from us, near the mountains. Gogy told me it was Goondel, who with his party was hunting bandicoots, lizards, snakes, kangaroo rats etc.'

Barrallier is one of the first white men to realise one of the greatest tools of the Aboriginal. These fires he sees are controlled burns, not the intense conflagrations that will rip through the Australian bush in centuries to come, feeding off endless ground fuel ignored for years by the descendants of European settlers, growing so fierce they will burn for weeks. These are fires that might begin with a man crouching low to the earth. He might spy a group of white ants carrying their eggs out of a creek and placing them on higher ground. Rain, surely, is coming. So with a handful of fire sticks he will begin burning small patches, sometimes along the crest of a hill, keeping it contained and only allowing it to flare when he is certain a deluge is near.

The reason Cook and Banks had seen so much grass inter-spersed with woodlands is that Aboriginals had constantly applied a blowtorch to the land. This is also something you come to learn, William. Setting fire to much of the country every few years promotes grassland that draws more grazing animals like kangaroos. A small blaze restricted to just a few trees can drive sought-after prey into clearer territory, making it easy to hunt them down. The ash enriches the soil, encouraging the growth of new plant life. Native trees and plants like the eucalyptus grow more exposed to disease and insects without regular burning. Hot flames also weaken hard seeds like those of kangaroo grass, another food source that can be ground and turned into bread.

This knowledge has been handed down over millennia. Australia's Aboriginals have encountered few of the outside forces that have influenced and reshaped other Indigenous cultures. Until now there has been no turning point like the one experienced by some of the North American Indians. The introduction of the mustang by Spanish conquistadors in the early 16th century into the arid mesas of Mexico resulted in an astonishingly swift transformation of the Indians of the plains. The Spanish horse was small and light, bred to travel long distances without requiring water, and able to scrounge grass from the most miserly terrain. Within a few decades the Comanche went from being a sedentary tribe to the greatest horse riders since the Mongols, able to unleash 20 arrows in the time it took to fire a single shot from a musket and reload.

But Australia's people have encountered few of these outside forces, instead honing their own unique tools and weapons like the boomerang, a remarkably accurate instrument in experienced hands that is the culmination of experimentation over tens of thousands of years.

It is the same with agriculture. The Europeans will see no animals roaming behind tidy fencing, no crops sown in orderly rows. But the land has been cultivated and fertilised by countless generations. Early explorers will come across fields with huge stacks of millet, intricately arranged so the seeds drop to the middle of the stack to be easily collected and ground into flour for bread. They will find dams and re-routed waterways and wells as deep as three men. In the southern lands there will be swamps enlarged by human hands and elaborate weirs to trap fish and eels. Some of the channels will cover acres of land. Hair and grass are woven into intricate baskets while the always available stringy bark is turned into exceedingly strong rope.

Large nets hundreds of yards long trap ducks and other low-flying birds. In some places traditional hunter-and-gatherer tribes become sedentary, building large huts with stonewalls that can each house dozens of people. Aboriginal canoes, so often derided by white men as nothing but crude bark contraptions, serve their purpose. They can be created within hours and used for fishing expeditions, the hunter standing calmly and motionless with spear in hand. Once the canoe has served its purpose it can simply be discarded or left on the bank for future use.

The land is not as harsh and uncompromising as the white men believe. Food is plentiful, from wild raspberries and nasturtium leaves to dozens of other edible fruits and plants. One of the most popular is the yam daisy – you know it well. It is a Wadawurrung staple, a dandelion flower whose tuber-like root tastes a little of coconut and can be roasted or eaten raw.

Suffering from congestion? A vapour bath can be constructed quickly by creating a small fire in a hole in the ground, covering it with eucalyptus leaves and pouring water over it. With a possum rug placed over their head, the sickly can breathe the steam until wet with perspiration. Rheumatism is treated with an infusion of bark from the blackwood tree; joint pain cured by wrapping the affected area with fresh eel skin; eucalyptus gum stuffed into tooth cavities to treat toothache.

The people travel great distances throughout the territories they claim as their own, the sky a navigational aid and a calendar keeping tabs on the passing of the seasons. To some, if Canopus, the second brightest star in the sky, hangs just over the horizon at dawn, the time has come to collect the emu's large, protein-filled eggs; for others, when the star cluster Pleiades is low in the eastern sky just before daybreak, it is time for clans to gather to provide wives outside their marriage group, and celebrate with a corroboree.

And all around are the spirits. They inhabit the animals and plants, drive the seasons and cause the earth to move and the sky to darken. You are now so embedded in Aboriginal culture, you see all this, even the mythical Bunyip. You catch a glimpse of its back as it moves through the waters of Lake Modewarre 'which appeared to be covered with feathers of a dusky grey colour. It seemed to be about the size of a full grown calf . . . the creatures only appear when the weather is very calm and the water smooth.' And being the stubborn bastard that you are, you unsuccessfully try to spear one on several occasions but decide not to tell anyone: 'If I had succeeded in killing, or even wounding one, my own life would probably have paid the forfeit, they considering the animal . . . something supernatural.' What are we to make of this? You are not so far from Cheshire, after all. The mystical blends with reality.

Death is rarely natural in this world so layered with meaning. You won't forget the time you travel with a clan when one of its highly regarded men dies after being bitten by a poisonous snake. To you it is one of those unfortunate accidents. Could happen to anyone – particularly men with enormous feet like yours. But every action has a cause and an explanation. The dead man's body is placed in the branches of a tall tree 'with all the honours suited to his value'.

Not long after this you return to your small family group, your so-called brother-in-law and his wife and their children. In the distance you suddenly see a group of about 60 men painting their faces with clay and ochre preparing for battle. 'We hoped our defenceless position would induce them to treat us mercifully,' you recall. But there is no such luck. After a face-off across a river where they furiously shake their spears, the invaders cross the water and begin attacking. This is the battle where your brother-in-law is speared, his wife and one of his sons killed.

'The savages then came back to where I was supporting my wounded friend; who, seeing them approaching, sprung up, even in the last agonies of death, and speared the nearest assailant in the arm. My friend was, of course, dispatched immediately with spears and boomerangs . . . strange to say not one raised his hand against me; had I done so against them I must have been sacrificed instantly; for what could I do, being only one against so many?'

Turns out that the attack is revenge for the death of the man bitten by the snake. The hostile clan believes it was no snakebite; your brother-in-law had caused his death through sorcery.

'They have all sorts of fancies of this kind and it is frequently the case that they take a man's kidneys out after death, tie them up in something and carry them round the neck as a sort of protection and valuable charm.'

—

The death of your family members has a resounding effect on you. You are no longer a young man. You have been with these people on and off for more than 25 years. These are the people who laughed at your first faltering attempts to learn their language, who encouraged you to do better, to become of them.

If your arithmetic is roughly correct, you are now close to 50, a lifespan that makes you an ageing man in the oldest land in the world. And you have seen enough.

'I am not ashamed to say that for several hours my tears flowed in torrents and that for a long time I wept unceasingly . . . of all my sufferings in the wilderness there was nothing equal to the agony I now endured.'

This grief – and fear you may be hunted down by the rival clan – triggers a decision to go out once more on your own. First, you return to the site of the battle and scrape together the ash and bones of your family, burying them as best you can. Then you leave for your hut near the sea where fish are abundant. You have long forgotten the English language; even the events that led you here are beginning to fade.

You stare out at the ocean for a glimpse of a ship. Feeling sorry for yourself? As always, you will be able to depend on John Morgan to find the words.

'It is related in the fabulous history of Robinson Crusoe that he was fortunate enough to save a Bible from the wreck of his ship and by that means consoled and benefitted himself. But I, the real Crusoe, for so many years amongst savages in the then unknown forests and wilds of the vast Australian continent, had no such help to mind.

'I beg the humane reader to reflect on this circumstance with feelings of kindly sympathy – for mine was, in truth, a sad existence . . .'

No need to feel lonely. There are some people who know how you feel.

18

YOU ARE NOT ROBINSON CRUSOE

You're not the only one. Hard to believe but there have been – and will be – others just like you, people torn from everything they know and thrust into strange new worlds. Most will never survive for as long as you do, or become so deeply immersed. But some will come close.

Take James Murrells. He will find himself involved in one of the most poignant and harrowing shipwreck tales in Australian history. Murrells is a boy from Essex who goes to sea at a young age, working his way around the world until he finds himself in Sydney in 1846. He signs on as a crewman on the *Peruvian* that departs for China in February. A week into the journey a violent storm maroons the ship on rocks at the southern tip of the Great Barrier Reef. As waves crash over the boat the crew hastily put together a makeshift raft using the *Peruvian*'s mast and side timber. Twenty-one survivors then set off with little food and water in the hope of reaching shore.

They drift for more than a month. People begin dying at the end of the first week, their bodies dumped overboard. The remaining survivors watch their supplies dwindle. Their cache of preserved meat runs out first and, determined not to resort to cannibalism, those who remain must rely on what they can catch.

Murrells – just like you – will one day sit down with a writer (in this case, Queensland journalist and government printer Edmund Gregory) and relate his story. 'Seagulls were caught and their blood was eagerly drunk and the raw flesh eaten with gusto,' he will recall.

But the birds are not enough to sustain those who remain alive. The death toll begins to mount. 'The sucking baby of Mrs Wilmott was the next to succumb; shortly afterwards the other little girl, and next to her Mrs Wilmott herself. Her husband stripped of her what clothing she had on, all but a nightdress, and appealed to us to turn our heads when he threw her overboard and he trusted we would not look at her.

'She however remained floating in company with us longer than the others; she was in sight about 20 minutes . . . And now they dropped off one after another rapidly, but I myself became so exhausted that I forget the order of their names.

'We next began to think about how we should obtain food. Our only fishing line had been broken and carried away by a big fish . . . there were plenty of sharks about, some of which we tried to catch. The captain devised a plan to snare them with a running bowline knot which we managed as follows: we cut off a leg of one of the men who died, lashed it at the end of an oar for a bait, and on the end of another oar we set the snare, so that the fish must go through the snare to get at the bait. Presently one came which we fortunately captured and killed with the carpenter's axe. We cut his head off and flayed him.'

In the days that follow more sharks are taken but it does little to stem the flow of deaths. By the time the raft finally reaches land 42 days later, just south of present-day Townsville, only seven remain.

Murrells is eventually the last man standing and is taken in by the Bindal clan of the Birri Gubba, who live in the region surrounding Mt Elliott.

Like you, he is filled with visions of being placed in a pot and eaten by cannibals during one of his first meetings with the locals: 'They were powerful-looking men and seemed to be sitting in state;

they did not move when we came up. Great fear seized hold of me, for I thought they were chiefs; and when they came to lead me up to them to satisfy their curiosity I thought it could be for no other purpose than to be killed, cooked and eaten . . . they looked at me and observing me shake with fear they warmed their hands at the fire, rubbed them over my face and body to reassure me, seeing which I took heart again.'

Murrells is immersed in local Aboriginal lore and culture. He masters eight dialects. He learns how to hunt, becoming an expert at snaring birds and fish. He attends corroborees and initiation ceremonies. Time drifts. Months become years. One day when he approaches a hut occupied by three armed kangaroo hunters he calls out: 'Do not shoot me, I am . . . British . . .'

He is astonished to discover 17 years have passed.

His return to white civilisation is difficult, too. Here is Edmund Gregory in a revised 1896 edition of his original pamphlet detailing Murrells' return to white society: 'From Port Denison Murrells was passed on to Rockhampton by the captain of one of the steamers, where he stayed a short time, and while there the inhabitants also made a subscription for him. From thence he went on to Brisbane in a similar manner. In each of these places he was besieged by those curious to see the man who lived such a strange and eventful life.

'He was, however, very shy, especially at first, and was not very communicative; this arose mainly from his inability to express himself readily. The knowledge of his own language came back to him very slowly, and it was very troublesome for him to understand what was said to him, and harder still for him to make himself understood . . .'

He becomes an interpreter as the relationship between the aggressive pastoralists sweeping through North Queensland and the local tribes grows ever more fractious. And he becomes a man far ahead of his time, a staunch advocate for Aboriginal land rights, suffering harsh criticism for taking such a stand.

But those years in the bush take their toll. 'Long exposure to the tropical sun and all weathers had left its marks on him and tanned his skin. He was rather short and thick set, his eyes were sunken and he had a rather wide mouth. His teeth were nearly worn down to the gums and no wonder, they were his only knife for years. He had suffered much from rheumatism . . . he had large rheumatic swellings on various parts of his body . . . which he said he believed would ultimately have some connection with his death.'

Murrells dies at 41, his tales of the rich and complex nature of Aboriginal life largely ignored, even by his biographer. 'The Aboriginals among whom James Murrells had been living are described by him as being physically superior as to general appearance to any others he had seen in the southern parts of the colony,' writes Gregory. 'Nevertheless they are treacherous, jealous and exceedingly cunning . . . They are not black – they are more of the colour of half-castes. When born they are nearly white but when they are three days old the gins squeeze out their own milk on them and rub it and powdered charcoal into their skins to make them black and shiny. They have sunken eyes, broad flat noses (which are made so by pressure by their mothers in infancy), and very broad mouths.'

—

John Wilson is one of the first Englishmen to be initiated into Indigenous culture. A First Fleet convict sentenced to seven years' transportation for stealing cloth, he joins the Dharug people along the Hawkesbury River after serving his sentence. Settlers view him with disdain, none more so than that melancholic and increasingly depressed judge advocate of the Sydney colony, David Collins.

Wilson, Collins writes in his diary, chooses to live with the local tribe because of his 'idle wandering disposition . . . no good consequence was likely to ensue from it; and it was by no means improbable that at some future time, if disgusted with the white people, he would join the blacks and assist them in committing depredations, or make use of their assistance to punish or revenge his own injuries'.

Say what you like about David Collins, but don't say he cannot sense an unhappy ending.

Wilson, initiated into the clan by having parts of his torso scarified, is reportedly murdered by Aboriginals in 1800 after trying to take an Indigenous woman against her will. Collins is perfunctory in his summary of the outcome: '. . . her friends took an opportunity, when he was not in a condition to defend himself, to drive a spear through his body, which ended his career for this time and left them to expect his return at some future period in the shape of another white man.'

There are many other episodes; the wildly differing accounts of Eliza Fraser's six-week stint with the Badtjala people after being shipwrecked off what will become known as Fraser Island; another shipwrecked woman, Barbara Thompson, and her four years living with Islanders and Aboriginal people in Queensland's far north. And there are tales of many other convicts, including James Davis and David Bracefell, who escape from the harsh Moreton Bay penal settlement and live with the locals on and off for many years.

But it is Narcisse Pelletier whose story, like Murrells', bears such a striking resemblance to the life of William Buckley. It begins, like so many other Robinson Crusoe-style accounts of castaways confronting tribes of savages, with a shipwreck. Pelletier is a 14-year-old cabin boy who joins the *Saint Paul* in Marseilles in 1857. It stops in Hong Kong, where it collects more than 300 Chinese labourers destined for the Australian goldfields.

The ship strikes a reef off Rossel Island. About a dozen of the crew ultimately escape in a small boat and spend 12 days adrift on the Coral Sea before landing on the eastern side of Cape York Peninsula. Exhausted and left alone by the others, the young Frenchman meets three Aboriginal women who quickly summon their men. Many years later Pelletier's experiences will be recorded by a French author, Constant Merland, who describes the boy's first encounter with a clan group now known as the Wanthala.

'When they were close to him Pelletier tried to make them understand that he was abandoned and that he was dying of hunger and thirst. The two savages were brothers-in-law. The man who was soon to become his adoptive father was not moved by feelings of compassion alone; he also placed certain conditions on his assistance. Pelletier was holding a small tin cup. He asked him for it and, having received it, he passed it to his brother-in-law. Understanding that this was a powerful means of winning them over, Pelletier also offered them his white handkerchief. From this moment the alliance was made: it was never to be broken.'

Again, there is an initial fear of cannibalism. The next morning Pelletier wakes to find himself alone. 'Had they left with the intention of enlisting their friends, killing him, sharing the spoils and perhaps using his body to make a great feast?'

Turns out they have only gone to fetch him a breakfast of local fruit. Pelletier will spend the next 17 years living with the clan. He has an earlobe pierced and extended with a wooden plug; his chest and an upper arm are covered in cicatrices – adornment scars sometimes used as a form of storytelling.

In April 1875 a group of pearlers discover Pelletier and at gunpoint take him aboard their boat. Within a month he is reluctantly placed on board the *Brisbane* which sails down the east coast for Sydney and his eventual repatriation in France.

Lieutenant John Ottley, an English passenger on the *Brisbane*, is the only person on board fluent in French. 'When he was put aboard our ship he had to all intents and purposes forgotten his own mother tongue,' Ottley will recall almost a half century later. 'It is true he remembered his name and this gave a clue to his nationality but beyond this almost the only intelligible thing he could say was "*je ne sais pas*"(I don't know).'

Ottley begins to speak with the young Frenchman, coaxing him until his language skills improve. But Pelletier is clearly uncomfortable on the ship among white people. 'We were somewhat surprised to find that though he had gone about stark naked for so many years yet he seemed to feel the cold very much when wearing clothes. He frequently shivered on deck when we were under steam and invariably took refuge on the lee side of the smoke stack . . . he certainly was never comfortable in his clothes and I fancy he often wished to get rid of them.

'At times I found him a serious nuisance owing to the fact that he had no notion of private property and seemed to think that we ought to hold things in common. Coming down to my cabin he used calmly to annex anything that struck his fancy and shewed his annoyance when I took things from him and locked them up in my trunks.'

The similarities with Murrells and Pelletier are striking. Do they ring a chord with you, William? Pelletier is reluctant to give any details about the intimate customs and beliefs of the clan he has lived with for so long. And, of course, the usual 19th century obsession with the contents of the native dinner plate is never far from the moustache-quivering lips of these inquiring gentlemen.

Cannibals, young man. Do these savages eat the flesh of men?

'To this Pelletier gave very vague replies that left us under the impression that he knew more than he chose to confess.

'He appeared to have lost all conception of the deity or of religion in any shape or form. Eventually I managed to make him remember the existence of his parish priest and to admit that he had been confirmed but all this meant nothing to him and were mere words without any meaning. In short his early life and all that it meant had apparently been completely wiped off the slate of his memory.'

Pelletier returns to France and is reunited with his family, who have long believed him to be dead. The population of his home town, Saint-Gilles-du-Gard, turns out to welcome him home with an enormous bonfire. He becomes a celebrity across France, the young boy who grew up among the *sauvages*. But he finds great difficulty in adjusting back to white civilisation. At one stage, concerned over his detachment and an apparent desire to return to his former life in Queensland, his family summons an exorcist. He later becomes an object of ridicule; taunted as *le sauvage*. He goes on to marry and dies childless at the age of 50, a recluse who spends his days staring wistfully out to sea.

WILLIAM BUCKLEY,
THE WILD WHITE MAN.

'. . . *with eyes fixed on some distant object* . . .' A portrait of William Buckley in his final years in Hobart. Drawn by Nicholas Chevalier and engraved by Frederick Grosse. The image is based on an oil painting by Ludwig Becker. (State Library of Victoria)

'*. . . still grimly hanging on to life, still sucking the last of the marrow from those medieval bones.*' The 1200-year-old oak tree in Marton, Cheshire – Buckley's birthplace. Its bark was used by locals to ward off illness and warts. (John Beresford)

'*. . . unforgettable scenes of carnage.*' The British-Russian invasion of North Holland in 1799 in which Buckley was injured. More than 12,000 men died and 25 ships were lost in a devastating blow to the English. (Painting by J. A. Langendijk)

'No hint of the madness to come . . .
[or] foam forming in the corner of his
mouth.' King George III in his early
20s following his coronation in 1760.
His 59-year reign spanned one of the
most turbulent eras in British history.
(Painting by Allan Ramsay)

'I was considered the
thief and though
innocent sentenced
to transportation for life.'
The *Sussex Weekly Advertiser*
report of William
Buckley's death sentence,
and subsequent reprieve,
on 9 August 1802.

but their appearance would neverthelefs have
given additional zeft to the entertainment.

At our Affizes, which ended on Tuefday
laft, ten prifoners were tried, four of whom
were capitally convicted, and received fentence
of death, viz

John Wells, alias Lancafter, aged 25, for
ftealing a wether fheep, the property of his
Grace the Duke of Richmond.

Andrew Jones, aged 20, for a highway
robbery, on the perfon of Richard Brown.

William Buckley and William Marmon, the
former aged 20, and the latter 25, for bur-
glarioufly entering the fhop of Mr. Cave, of
Warnham, and ftealing therein two pieces of
Irifh linen.

William Hall, aged 32, for felonioufly
ftealing, in the dwelling houfe of Jofeph
Fielder, of Speldhurft in Kent, a white linen
waiftcoat, and other property.——And William Shaw, aged 25, for forcibly entering the
dwelling houfe of Mary Minns, and felonioufly ftealing therein about five pounds of cheefe
and a cotton handkerchief, were fentenced to
feven years Tranfportation each.

Edward Bridger, for Manflaughter, was fined one fhilling and difcharged.

The following three, Margaret Harris,
Charles Davey, and William Hobs, were difcharged by proclamation.

Wills, Jones, Buckley and Norman, were
all reprieved before the Judges left the town.

At the above Affizes, about 21 caufes were
entered for trial, the greateft number of which
were, on the recommendation of the Judge,

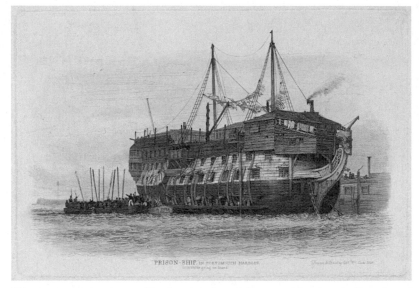

'Floating wrecks housing nothing but despair and disease . . .' A prison hulk anchored in Portsmouth Harbour, similar to one in which Buckley was imprisoned. Decommissioned ships like these were used to house the overflow from England's prisons and were rife with cholera, typhus and violence. (National Library of Australia)

'. . . a world less than half a soccer field, held together by nail and rope and more than a little of, yes, hope.' Extract from a prison hulk log book confirming the pending transfer of Buckley and William Marmon to HMS *Calcutta* (their names are fifth and sixth from the bottom). (Public Record Office, London)

'. . . it took more than 2000 wagonloads of oak dragged all the way from the forests of Sussex to put her together.' HMS *Calcutta* was a 56-gun ship originally built for the East India Company. She carried more than 500 passengers, including 308 convicts, to Port Phillip in 1803. (Painting by Antoine Roux)

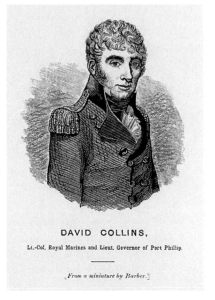

DAVID COLLINS,

Lt.-Col. Royal Marines and Lieut. Governor of Port Phillip.

From a miniature by Barber.

'Good-looking man this Collins, tall and broad shouldered . . . no wonder so many women find him attractive.'
David Collins was appointed Lieutenant-Governor of the Port Phillip settlement. Shortly after Buckley's escape, he moved most of the settlers and remaining convicts to Van Diemen's Land and what would become Hobart Town.

'. . . the gnarled, wind-whipped sandstone cliffs where Buckley's Cave sits beneath the lighthouse.' The barricaded entrance to the cave at Point Lonsdale in Victoria, said to have sheltered Buckley during the three decades following his escape from Sullivan Bay, near Sorrento. (Museums Victoria)

'A favourite haunting place of yours where water flows through rock pools and small waterfalls . . .' Buckley's Falls in what is now Highton in Geelong. Buckley knew this place as Woorongo and said it provided him with regular catches of eels. John Wedge dubbed it 'Buckley's Falls' while touring the region with him in mid-1835. (Georgia Linnell)

'We find Buckley to be a most valuable man to us . . . he is a complete terror to the natives.' The iconic moment William Buckley approaches John Batman's Indented Head settlement in 1835, as imagined in this wood engraving by O. R. Campbell and S. Calvert in 1869. (National Portrait Gallery)

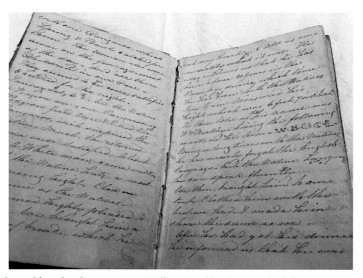

'He then told us that his name was William Buckley, having the following marks on his arm – W.B and marks like a crab, half-moon and small man.' William Todd's original diary from 1835 recording Buckley's arrival at the Batman camp. (State Library of Victoria)

'A rogue, thief, cheat and liar, a murderer of blacks and the vilest man I have ever known.' A rare portrait of John Batman, explorer, pastoralist and one of the co-founders of Melbourne. In later life a disease believed to be syphilis left him with a disfigured nose and unable to walk. (State Library of Victoria)

'You intended to obtain undue influence over the mind of Buckley and through him over the minds of the natives.' In this painting by H. L. van den Houten in 1878, John Batman (red shirt) is wrongly depicted as greeting Buckley at Indented Head. Batman was already back in Van Diemen's Land boasting of his treaty with the Kulin people. (State Library of Victoria)

WILLIAM BUCKLEY.

ABOVE LEFT: '. . . a white man, of immense size, covered with an opossum-skin rug, and his hair and beard spread out as large as a bushel measure.' Buckley became adept in the use of the spear and other weapons during his time with the Wadawurrung and became a favourite of 19th-century artists. (Museums Victoria)

ABOVE RIGHT: '. . . four of Buckley's clubs of various shapes rudely ornamented.' Some of the Aboriginal artefacts on display in the Saffron Walden museum in Essex. Many of them were donated by John Helder Wedge as souvenirs of his time in Port Phillip in the years after 1835. (Saffron Walden Museum)

LEFT: 'There is no calculating on the mischief that might ensue by the hostile feelings he would . . . instill into the breasts of the natives.' Surveyor John Helder Wedge met Buckley in 1835 and helped secure his pardon from the British government. (Tasmanian Archives)

William Buckley

'There's that snub nose and low bushy eyebrows hanging above hazel eyes.' The first known sketch of Buckley, made by John Helder Wedge in 1835 just a few weeks after he made his presence known to the Batman camp. His beard has already been shaved and his hair cut. (State Library of Victoria)

'A mindless lump of matter.' John Pascoe Fawkner, photographed in 1863 six years before his death, became a strident critic of Buckley and claimed his loyalties lay with the Aboriginal people of Port Phillip. (State Library of Victoria)

'He is chief of a tribe and possesses the most complete control over his people – Buckley will be our mainspring.' Dressed in a dark coat and hat (far left), Buckley is shown talking to a group of Kulin people near the Yarra River in 1837. Painting by Joseph Anderson Panton. (State Library of Victoria)

'Hard and all knowing – the look of a man rarely racked with self-doubt or uncertainty.' Foster 'Flogger' Fyans, who had brutally repressed a prisoner uprising on Norfolk Island, journeyed by foot from Melbourne to Geelong with Buckley and called him a 'monster of a man'. (State Library of NSW)

'You have all this place, no good have children . . . me tumble down and die very soon now.' Derrimut, an *arweet* of the Boonwurrung people, painted by Benjamin Duterau during his visit to Van Diemen's Land with John Fawkner in 1837. (State Library of NSW)

'In an almost impregnable castle on the sea coast dwelt a terrific giant named Hacho . . .' An advertisement in *the Austral-Asiatic Review* in Hobart on 16 January 1838, promoting Buckley's on-stage appearance as the Giant Hacho. He quickly withdrew from the production.

'His balding head softened by a chubby face and fleshy chin . . .' Sir John Franklin, Lieutenant-Governor of Van Diemen's Land, who gave Buckley his first job on the island in 1837.

'It is . . . an unusual union.' The register of marriages in Hobart records the wedding of Buckley and Julia Eagers in early 1840. Buckley is about 58, more than 30 years older than Julia, a native of Cork in Ireland. (Tasmanian Archives and Heritage Office)

301 607	St John's church Newtown September 6 1853	William Jackson and Mary Ann Higgins	30 19	Labourer

Married in the Parish Church according to the Rites and Ceremonies of the United Church of England and Ireland.

This Marriage was solemnized between us, *William Jackson / Mary Ann Higgins*   In the Presence of us, *William Buckley his mark / Julia Buckley her mark*

302 608	St John's church Newtown October 3 1853	George Bellamy & Mary Wilson	32 33	Gardener

'. . . *you press the quill on the page just a little too long; the ink runs . . .*' Buckley leaves a smudged 'X' as he and Julia witness the marriage of Julia's daughter, Mary Ann, to 30-year-old William Jackson. (Tasmanian Archives and Heritage Office)

'*If you kill one white man white fellow will shoot you down like kangaroo . . .*' William Barak, last of the *ngurungaeta* of the Wurundjeri-willam clan who, as a young boy, watched and listened as Buckley warned Indigenous people not to trespass on white men's territory. (State Library of Victoria)

NOTICE.

The Life and Adventures of

WILLIAM BUCKLEY,

THE ANGLO PORT PHILLIPIAN CHIEF.

IN ONE VOLUME, BOARDS, 7s. 6d.

THE individual whose extraordinary adventures the Editor of his Life undertakes truthfully to relate from the rough memoranda before him, was thirty-two years a wanderer in the wilds of the unsettled country about Port Phillip, now the Colony of Victoria. By the Natives near the coast of that part of the Australian Continent, he was adopted as a principal Chief; his commanding height (six feet five inches), and other circumstances, having given him, in their opinion, the pre-eminence over others. On the arrival of the first party of emigrants from Van Diemen's Land, an opportunity was afforded him of resuming his former habits, language, and associations; and some time after, he arrived in this Island. That William Buckley, by his influence, was most useful to the enterprising individuals who first settled at Port Phillip, cannot be doubted; and, at this eventful period in the history of the Australian Colonies, it is considered probable, that the hardships he endured, and the services he rendered, may be generously borne in mind, and an account of his life be favourably received. It may be proper to add, that the publication of the " LIFE OF BUCKLEY " was contemplated several years since; but being then fully occupied by the local Government, he could not arrange his recollection of time, and events, so as to furnish faithful material to work upon. He is, however, at present unemployed, and it is therefore hoped the object may be accomplished in about three months, provided those who have taken charge of the subscription lists are kind enough to give them the attention respectfully requested.

The Work will be embellished with lithographed views, maps, &c. of particular localities, &c. The names of Subscribers will be published in an Appendix.

JOHN MORGAN.

Hobart Town, March 1, 1851.

Copies already ordered in this Colony—100.

Lists have been forwarded to Melbourne and Geelong; and others are with MR. DOWLING, of Launceston, and MR. ROLWEGAN, Stationer, Collins-street, Hobart Town.

J. M.

'The money from the book sales must be invaluable . . .' An advertisement in April 1851 in Hobart's *Britannia and Trades' Advocate* spruiking the forthcoming book co-authored by John Morgan about Buckley's experiences in Port Phillip.

'All your life you have managed to find a way out, but there is no grand escape this time . . .' 'Buckley's Rest', a small park off Sandy Bay Road in Hobart that commemorates Buckley's burial place. The lush grove is on the site of the old St George's burial ground in Battery Point.

'There is no mistaking the hanging brow and the pair of haunting eyes. They stare impassively back . . . the look of an ageing man who has seen far more than he can ever tell.' Portrait of Buckley believed to be painted by Ludwig Becker.
(State Library of Victoria)

It ends like this so often. Far from grateful for having been rescued and restored to civilised life, these people trapped between black and white worlds pine for the days when they were free to roam, unshackled from the expectations and restraints of industrialised society.

Your years among the Wadawurrung are coming to an end. You don't know it yet as you sit there by the ocean, staring out to sea just like Pelletier will in his final days. But this three-decade journey is almost over. You say you have had enough of this life, that if an opportunity to live among white people ever presents itself you will not hesitate to take it.

Be careful what you wish for.

19

THE DECISIVE MOMENT

Beyond the south-west coast of Victoria lies a treacherous stretch of water, a seething oceanic mass that sweeps in from the coldest depths of the Antarctic to pummel the fragile coast. The first man to successfully circumnavigate Australia, Matthew Flinders, will say he has 'seldom seen a more fearful section of coastline'. In 1802 John Murray ventures into the area in the *Lady Nelson* before going back to explore Port Phillip. Caught in a storm, he records in his journal: 'I shall only observe that I never experienced such a length of bad weather at any time of the year, or in any country since I sailed the seas.'

Below this constantly turbulent surface lie scores of shipwrecks and the bones of countless sailors, testament to the sea's abrupt mood swings and deceptive waters. Its fury and force – driven by the world's largest current carrying 130 million cubic metres of water per second along a 20,000-kilometre path – is best seen from the cliffs near the Port Campbell National Park. There, just offshore, stand a series of jagged limestone stacks known as the Apostles. Only eight remain but more will be created in the next few centuries as the constant waves and swell continue to eat away at the steep, crumbling cliffs.

A little further north-east the coast turns inland and becomes slightly more protected. But only just. Days without wind or a strong salty breeze are a rarity. It was here almost three decades ago that you spent those first months and years forlornly scanning the waters where the Southern Ocean meets Bass Strait, looking for a ship that might pluck you from a land that each day seemed to contain another hidden horror.

But that was then. As the years passed you became more confident in this new realm and less sure about white outsiders. 'I never supposed I should be comfortable among my own countrymen again,' you will tell the Reverend Langhorne. But in recent years there has been an increasing number of those countrymen moving into Aboriginal land. Small groups of ex-convicts have been forging a living stripping wattle trees of their bark and sending them back to England to be used in the leather tanneries. A fledgling whaling industry is also gaining momentum in the waters around Portland at the southern tip of western Victoria. Whalers, sealers and ex-convicts – often one and the same – are hard men. Some of them have been eking out a living on the islands of Bass Strait for years. 'They are complete savages, living in bark huts like the natives, not cultivating anything but living entirely on kangaroos, emus and small porcupines,' reports the *Sydney Gazette* in 1817, before adding: '. . . they smell like foxes'.

They trade sealskins for tobacco and alcohol and are well known for kidnapping native women, often treating them brutally.

—

We know you have been reluctant to make contact with white people for a long time. The woman who will claim to be your wife, Purranmurnin Tallarwurnin, says ships – possibly whaling vessels – are sometimes seen visiting the coast to obtain water and wood and that 'Buckley never sought to make himself known to any of them'. But it's a different story when word spreads that a ship has been wrecked on the coast 'and all hands perished . . . Buckley and his tribe secured a large quantity of blankets, axes and other articles which he taught them how to use.'

Just like the Southern Ocean's relentless battering of the Victorian coastline, you can sense the coming cultural collision; a foaming, unstoppable white wave rushing to meet an ancient world. You are now in your early 50s, an age when most men begin to prefer the comforts of the familiar rather than the challenges of the unknown. For a long time your constant companions have been an old man, his wife and their children. You travel together as a small group, sometimes falling in with a larger clan, but most times keeping to yourselves, moving with the seasons. But among the Wadawurrung, fresh stories about new ghosts in their giant canoes are increasing.

A *koorong*, or ship, has been seen anchored in the bay just off the land of the Bengalat balug people that will be later known as Indented Head. Its sailors, watched unseen from the shore, lower a smaller boat into the water and begin rowing it up a nearby river. Once it is out of view, three men of the clan swim across and clamber aboard the main boat, quickly taking sails, rope and glass bottles before returning to the bush. The returning crew, discovering the theft, fire guns at the shore and move their ship further into the bay.

You hear about this incident and are implored by the Aboriginal men to return with them to act as a decoy in the hope of stealing more items. You discourage them, warning them of the consequences. 'I did all possible to divert their attention, telling them that if they went to where the ship was they would again be fired upon and all killed.'

But you are fascinated. Memories are stirring. You visit the area on your own and, becoming 'almost nervously wild with desire to make myself known to those on board' make a large fire on the beach, hoping to attract their attention. You can see the crew on deck. You want to shout but no longer remember what words to use. Frustrated, you wave your spear and arms and continue doing this through the night and into the next day.

The only response you receive is laughter. It is easy to picture this scene. From across the water an immensely large and hairy figure clad in kangaroo and possum skin stands next to a fire, gesticulating wildly, his shouts unintelligible. The men on the boat smirk and shake their heads at this primitive. Is he trying to attract their attention or lure them to their deaths? Or is it merely another of the strange rituals these black men practise? The boat remains anchored for a few more days before sailing away and you never learn the purpose of the ship or the intentions of its crew. But the Bengalat bulag have other tales of these white men coming on to their land. They have not forgotten a scene from a long time before; two white men taken ashore by a larger group of men, tied to trees and then shot, their limp bodies left to rot.

Suddenly there are more signs of outsiders visiting the bay. In your travels you find a whaling boat partly buried in sand on the beach and a makeshift sail made out of three blankets. You cut up the blankets and divide them equally among some of your people. They tell you that a few days earlier two white men, cold and bruised, had made their way inland. Befriended and fed with fish and kangaroo until they regained their strength, 'the natives then tried to make them understand there was a white man . . . amongst them and that they would go in search of me; but the poor fellows could not be made to comprehend their meaning and went away by themselves.'

You later hear that the pair, probably castaways from a larger vessel, are murdered while crossing the Yarra River.

But this white wave . . . it is coming, growing stronger and more certain.

—

Months later. A large cask is lying partly buried on a beach. You dig away in the sand, hoping to extract the iron hoops encasing the barrel, the metal a valuable item for trade. Smashing open the cask you taste the liquid inside. After 30 years of drinking nothing but water, the flavour 'appeared to be horribly offensive and the smell equally so'. It is not strong enough to be a spirit like whiskey or brandy and is probably wine or beer. You let the contents drain into the sand – just in case 'the natives take a fancy to it' – and then hand out the iron hoops to people who have shown you kindness.

'These presents added greatly to the influence I had already acquired over them . . . I began to fancy they were gradually becoming more docile and civilised.'

You are out one day gathering roots with the old man, your closest friend and constant companion, when two young men approach, waving spears adorned with coloured handkerchiefs. The pair say they have just met a group of white and black men at a camp on the shore of Bengalat balug land. It seems they have been left behind by a ship and have built themselves two white huts. They have plenty of provisions including tomahawks and blankets and have already made offerings of knives and scissors to the local clan.

A plan is afoot. The two men are looking for help; they need more numbers in order to return and kill the white men for their possessions. It is at this moment that you begin to feel a sensation that will gnaw at you for years to come; the frustration of a man trapped between two cultures. Your first instinct is to warn these white men about an impending attack and save them. But issuing such a warning . . . will that not also be an act of treachery toward your own people?

So you decide you must see these newcomers for yourself. You walk for a day and much of the next until, suddenly, you see a Union Jack hoisted on a long pole. It is cold and windy; heavy skies overhead have turned the water of Port Phillip just off Indented Head a dirty grey.

How do you feel? Your emotions must be raging. You had stood not far from this place more than three decades before, a young man racked by hunger pains, self-doubt and fear. But even then pride had won out. You had not turned back like your companions, but turned your own back on a life of captivity.

Now you have another choice to make. You can stay hidden from these white men and continue living a life of freedom, to choose where you want to go and what to do. Or you can finally stop being a stubborn bastard, approach them and take a chance they will not return you to a life in irons deep in the bowels of a creaking ship.

What's it going to be? These white men are sitting with several Aboriginal companions around their tents. One of them, fetching a pail of water, looks up and sees you. He points you out to the others.

Now there is no choice. You pick up your spears and your club – your *waddy* – and start walking toward them on this winter's day, 6 July 1835.

20

COMING IN

William Todd has been growing frustrated over the past few days and, if truth be told, a little nervous. He can't quite put his finger on it but in this place heavy with the scent of wood smoke and eucalyptus, he can sense something else in the cold air, a vaguely menacing threat.

For the past two weeks the number of Aboriginals coming to the camp on the edge of Port Phillip Bay has been growing and no amount of pleading – let alone bribing with food and trinkets – has managed to get them to leave. Just two days earlier he had cooked up a large batch of damper bread – 60 pounds of valuable flour he'd used – and they consumed it all. And that had followed a batch of 100 pounds a week earlier. There seems to be no end to their appetite, nor any inclination to leave.

Todd and the rest of the crew have done everything they can to encourage them to go. Two mornings ago everyone went without breakfast to try and show them they had run out of food. But if men like Joe the Marine, Pigeon, Bullet – some of the Sydney Aboriginals hired by Todd's master – cannot persuade them to go, then what chance has he?

The locals seem to be having a fine old time, singing each night, staging corroborees, encouraging their children to stay with the white men. They have laughed and smiled and all the while set about stealing everything of value. Axes have gone missing and food supplies are running dangerously low; the 90 square yards of freshly turned earth Todd and others have just sown will not be producing any onions, turnips and carrots for months. They have caught fish and the odd kangaroo. But if this keeps up – if this small encampment of eight men continues to be expected to feed a village – then Todd is starting to wonder what will happen when the food runs out.

Each night he takes out his brown calf leather journal and dutifully records the day's events, a diary the man he serves, John Batman, has asked him to keep. The past month has been extraordinary, even for those accustomed to life with Batman. The voyage from Van Diemen's Land had been hard enough; strong winds and heavy seas pushing them back for a fortnight each time they tried to cross Bass Strait. And then, after making their way into Port Phillip Bay, came that historic day when Batman signed his treaty with representatives of several tribes, leasing more than 600,000 acres of the best grazing land anyone had seen. And the price? An annual rental of 40 blankets, 30 axes, 100 knives and some handkerchiefs and flour! Had anyone ever struck a deal like it?

Batman, intoxicated by this triumph, has returned to Launceston to replenish supplies and inform his partners and backers about the deal. His own journal flows with praise for this new country. Everywhere he has looked Batman has seen endless pastures and grass-filled plains. On the Keilor Plains he spies 'the most beautiful sheep pasturage I ever saw in my life. I am sure I can see 50,000 acres of land in one direction and not 50 trees.'

A few days after this, on Saturday 6 June, Batman and his crew had fallen in with a family of local Aboriginals and, after shaking hands, 'and my giving them tomahawks, knives &c – they took us with them about a mile back where we found huts, women and children. After some time and full explanation, I found eight Chiefs amongst them who possessed the whole of the country near Port Phillip – three brothers, all of the same name, are the principal chiefs, and two of them men of six feet high and very good looking; the other not so tall but stouter. The other five chiefs were fine men – and after a full explanation of what my object was, I purchased two large tracts of Land from them about 600,000 Acres more or less and delivered over to them, Blankets Knives, looking Glasses, Tomahawks, Beads Scissors, flour &c &c.'

Batman has met with elders of the Wurundjeri and Boonwurrung people, including the towering Billibellary, a *ngurungaeta* of the Wurundjeri-willam clan. Controversy will swirl around this 'treaty' for centuries. It will be the only formal document ever offered by Europeans to Aboriginal people and many will doubt if the eight Aboriginal men who leave their mark on it fully understand they are signing away ancient tribal lands, believing instead that it forms part of a *tanderrum* – a ceremony allowing safe passage to visitors travelling through their territory.

No-one will even be sure of the exact location where the signing takes place. But Batman notes that nearby there is a river that strikes him as being 'the place for a village'. And then, mission accomplished, he leaves to spread the good news back in Van Diemen's Land, leaving his Sydney Aboriginals and servants – Todd, Alec Thompson and Jim Gumm – to form a supply depot at Indented Head, just a few miles north of the entrance to the bay.

As usual Batman has left explicit instructions, too. The men are to go straight to work erecting a hut, making a garden, establishing a rapport with the local tribes and 'to put off any person or persons that may trespass on this land I have purchased from the natives'.

Well, giving orders like that might be one thing. But with more than 60 Aboriginals gathering around the camp, what sort of persuasion might one employ to get them to leave?

You can sense the growing alarm and exasperation in Todd's journal. An educated Irishman, his handwriting is neat and even, sloping gently to the right. Monday 29 June begins well: 'Three hands gone kangarooing; as usual returned with a large forester [a big grey kangaroo]. Natives still with us. Find it very difficult to get them to leave us, they having taken such a particular liking to the bread. We are obliged to use none ourselves, on account of their distressing us, they being of such a greedy disposition that they would take it all from us. Stopped all night. Watching as usual.'

The next day brings no change. 'Tried all we could to get them to leave us, but find it impossible. Three hands obliged to go again kangarooing . . . returned home with two kangaroos. Remained all night quiet and well satisfied, but seem to have no idea of leaving us, which makes us exceedingly uncomfortable, not being able to get a meal of victuals in comfort, and always obliged for our own safety to keep watch.'

On 4 July everyone is woken at four in the morning after hearing cries and whistles. 'At daylight . . . sent two men to see who it was but they returned home without seeing them, which we imagined was no more than to frighten us. We told them we would not be afraid of 100 of them . . .'

Two days later, nothing has changed. Early in the morning Pigeon goes hunting with the natives and with two shots kills two kangaroos 'which surprised the natives much. They returned home well satisfied.'

And then, early in the afternoon on this cold day, the Union Jack fluttering overhead from a makeshift flagpole, a dead man walks into camp, out of the bush and in from the past, and takes a seat next to their fire.

—

Twenty years living among white people as William Buckley and you always struggled to find the right words. Thirty years living as Murrangurk and now you have none at all.

You open your mouth to say something and . . . nothing comes out. Sitting there with your spears and waddy between your legs, a crowd gathering, staring in disbelief, and not a single word comes to mind. Ridiculous, isn't it? For one of the first times in your life you have so much to say but no way to say it.

You point to the tattoo on your arm – those faded initials, 'W.B'. Perhaps that might help. But they keep staring and you can tell what they are thinking; this man with his long matted hair and thick beard and animal skin cloak, this mute who keeps moving his lips without uttering a sound, is clearly . . . *one of us*. Tanned and wild and more than a little intimidating, but he is *one of us*. One of them reaches for that fast disappearing damper and hands you a piece. You take it, turning it over in your hands and a word slowly forms from the fog in that head of yours.

'Bread?'

It's as if a spell is broken. Over the next few hours more words will come back to you. But it's your size, your overwhelming presence, they find most compelling. Jim Gumm, a pardoned convict, will measure your height at close to six feet and seven inches and that night Todd has much to write in his journal.

'He seemed highly pleased to see us. We brought him a piece of bread which he eat very heartily and told us immediately what it was. He also informed us that he has been above 20 years in the country, during which time he has been with the natives . . . He then told us that his name was William Buckley, having the following marks on his arm – W.B and marks like a crab, half-moon, and small man. Being a long time with the natives he has nearly forgot the English language, but the native language he can speak fluently. We then brought him to our tent, clothed him with the best we had and made him share the same as we.'

But even with fragments of English returning, and with so much to tell these men, you remain cautious. After 32 years of living free, the last thing you want is to return to His Majesty's custody. Best not disclose your whole story; not yet, anyway.

Todd: 'After he had got his dinner he informed us that he was a soldier in the King's Own, and a native of Macclesfield in Cheshire and was wrecked off Port Phillip Heads. The vessel's name he has forgot, but she had come from England with transports and was bound for Van Diemen's Land, being the first vessel that brought prisoners out for there. She struck on a rock and all hands perished with the exception of him and three others, who swam ashore, one of which was the captain of the vessel, who could not swim.'

Not a bad story, William. So much for all those critics in future years who will complain you are a simple dolt lacking any sort of imagination. If only they were here now, the flames of the camp fire flickering and casting shadows across your bearded face as you hold your audience in thrall. Not a bad feeling, is it? Just hours out of the bush and here you are spinning stories like a man on a stage, something you would never have dreamed of doing in the past.

That skipper of the boat, the one you were saying could not swim? What did you do when the ship capsized? Why, you placed the captain across those big shoulders of yours and in the pitch black of a swirling sea, began swimming toward land alongside a couple of other survivors.

It isn't hard to imagine William Todd in his tent late in the night, candle burning, shaking his head at this incredible tale of courage and strength, making sure he gets down every detail. Folks back home will choke on their whiskey when he tells them this one.

'He was 24 hours swimming before he reached the shore. When they got to the shore they were completely exhausted, with the exception of the captain, whose life Buckley saved. Shortly after, the captain left them, and proceeded where we cannot tell, not having seen or heard of him ever since. The other two died after a few days and Buckley was left to himself to the mercy of those savages, expecting every hour to meet with them and be put to death.'

Who do you think you are? Daniel Defoe? You tell them in your faltering English how you lived off mussels and roots and spent 40 days wandering on your own – *oh, you're Moses now* – before you fall in with a local mob of Aboriginals 'and has remained with them ever since, never having seen a white man and has only seen two vessels since he has been here. He is quite rejoiced to see his own native people once more, never having expected to meet with any.'

At 8 pm, Todd reports that a group of natives 'came running down to our hut and told me that there was a mob of blacks coming down to kill both us and them. Prayed for our protection and made signals for us to shoot them if they came close . . .

'Buckley cried out "We shoot them. I'll shoot them."

'After they were quiet Buckley explained everything to them. It was most astonishing to see how amazed and pleased they were . . .'

—

You have told Todd and Gumm you want to remain with them, at least until John Batman returns on his chartered schooner *Rebecca*. Part of you wants to meet this man. But you are also trying to buy some time. In the next few days more warriors will arrive as word spreads of the plunder to be had by the shores of the bay. You might be able to stave off an attack by telling them that if they wait, a new ship carrying more riches will soon arrive.

It's a tense time. One of the clans spreads a rumour that a vessel has just been seen entering the bay, a false claim Todd notes is for the purpose 'of getting us all down to the water side so they might plunder the hut. But they found their plan of no avail . . . Buckley has again told the natives in their own language that we have no more provisions for them and they must retire in the bush until such time as the vessel arrives. They consented and retired for the night well pleased.

'We find Buckley to be a most valuable man to us. He seems to get more attached to us every day. Always keeping a sharp lookout, he is a complete terror to the natives.'

A week later, Todd writes that you have overheard one of the Aboriginals saying 'that they should wait for an opportunity to get one of us going for water so that they should spear us. He desired us to be on our guard and keep sentry day and night. We told him we should act according to his wish.

'He then exclaimed "I shall lose my own life before I'll see one of you hurted."'

If they didn't quite trust you before this, they do now. In *Life and Adventures*, you take up the story: 'I told the white men to be on their guard. Arming myself with a gun I threatened in strong language the life of the first native who raised a hostile hand against the strangers, telling them that on the arrival of the vessel they should have presents in abundance. This pacified them and they turned their thoughts from mischief to fishing and hunting.'

This is how it really starts, isn't it? This is where you will find yourself at the impact point between those two colliding worlds. For the past couple of weeks you have managed to delicately move between them, keeping this uneasy peace. But it will never be easy again.

There is no doubt in your mind any longer that you will remain with these white men. Your English is slowly returning – it will take a long time before you are fully fluent again – and the longer you spend with them makes you think it might be time to end all these years of wandering.

But it's not as though you are not perplexed and more than a little suspicious about the motives of these men. They have told you about this deal Batman has struck with the people of the Kulin nation. Todd and the rest of them say they were there the day the deed was signed.

It doesn't make sense. Who are these chiefs who have signed away hunting lands? What man, what warrior, would even dare contemplate giving up his ancestral home?

It's a point that will remain a sore one many years later. 'They have no chiefs claiming or possessing any superior right over the soil,' you will say. 'I therefore looked upon the land dealing as another hoax of the white man to possess the inheritance of the uncivilised natives of the forest, whose tread on the vast Australian continent will very soon be no more heard . . .'

Say what you like about William Buckley. But don't say an old convict cannot smell a sham from a mile away.

PART III

WILLIAM BRIDGES
TWO WORLDS

21

THE PRESS BREAKS THE NEWS

Finally, a decent story. William Lushington Goodwin has been waiting for something like this to cross his desk. He has been editor of the *Cornwall Chronicle* for only a few months and damned if he is not going to turn his little newspaper into the talk of Launceston and, indeed, right across Van Diemen's Land.

This new report – an incredible tale about a giant white man who has been discovered after living among the savages in Port Phillip for three decades – is just the thing he can use to liven up his pages. Launceston, huddled around the junction of the Tamar River at the northern end of the island, is a town of little more than 5000 people, a third of them convicts. Revelations in the *Chronicle* that a cow has been impounded, or the local vet has just changed premises, have hardly been the stuff to force locals to extract a shilling from their tight pockets.

Goodwin may be driven by curiosity but outrage is his closest companion. He comes from a sailing family and arrived here after skippering a convict ship from London filled with a mutinous crew and more than a hundred boisterous and despicable female prisoners. But it has not taken him long to find his legs as a cantankerous editor shouldered with the responsibility of protecting civilisation.

Everywhere he looks the colony is awash in muck and scandal, its progress trapped by the iron grip of authoritarian government and a toadying class only interested in profit.

Why, he's a man just like John Morgan. 'Liberty with danger is to be preferred to slavery with security,' wrote the Roman historian Sallust, words that so stir Goodwin's fighting spirit that he plasters them across the front page of his paper each week.

But it is not only the fight for freedom that drives Goodwin. He worries that the courage, indeed the *manliness*, that helped forge this great British Empire is also disappearing. 'We are fast becoming priest-ridden and effeminate,' he will rail in an editorial. He yearns for the old days when hardened men could right the wrongs of the world with sheer physical strength and determination.

Men, actually . . . like William Lushington Goodwin.

Five years earlier as captain of the 353-ton *Kains*, Goodwin had steered his convict ship loaded with 120 female prisoners on a slow and tumultuous eight-month voyage from Plymouth to New South Wales. Trouble began within days. The ship's surgeon, Thrasycles Clarke, was horrified to discover that their human cargo was filled with 'immoral and abandoned' women, '. . . some of them by nature and habit were cleanly while others were filthy to the 90th degree'.

But it was the crew that would prove to be the most difficult. One of the *Kains*' able seamen, 20-year-old Charles Picknell, was shocked that just 200 miles out from England, Captain Goodwin 'began to ill use us'.

Goodwin, hearing whispers of a mutiny, had six crew placed in irons and tied up on the poop deck – the highest point of the ship. He left them there for two days with guns trained on them. But he was only getting started. Next he had a young apprentice hauled on deck, tied to the rigging and flogged with 72 lashes for making a complaint about the weight of a barrel of wine. Wrote Picknell in his diary: 'Guard over him, swords, daggers, Captain struck several, women crying.'

There would be several deaths during the voyage, including a number of the convicts' young children. There would be a close-run encounter with a pirate ship, more floggings, desertions and maggot-infested food. Scurvy would afflict some of the crew and Goodwin would spend much of his time eyeing off the supposed mutineers and confining his chief mate below decks for repeated drunkenness. Another attempted uprising in Cape Town saw Goodwin attack and beat four hapless mutineers with a mallet before putting them ashore in a jail cell. But they finally made it and William Lushington Goodwin knew in his bones that only his discipline and toughness, his *preparedness* to do the hard thing, had got them through.

Yet here they are, this colony in Van Diemen's Land barely a generation old, and just about everywhere Goodwin looks he sees softness and a growing complacency. Thank the Lord that good men like the local pastoralist and explorer John Batman can still be found. Like every other newspaper editor Goodwin has been detailing Batman's exploits for the past few months, breathlessly highlighting his foray across the dangerous waters of Bass Strait and – defying the warnings of those government dolts! – seizing millions of acres of prime grazing land.

Brave man, Batman. You want to know about *manliness*? Look no further. He has provided the newspapers of Van Diemen's Land with plenty of fodder with his adventures down the years, hunting and capturing bushrangers and Aboriginals alike. But apart from his recent expedition – and thank the Lord for his good sense and intelligence, for what else did Batman do when he arrived back in Launceston but stride straight from the port to the *Chronicle*'s office to brief Goodwin on his Port Phillip discovery – the pickings when it comes to interesting news have been slim.

This story, however, has captivated Goodwin and will surely have everyone talking. He may only have fallen into this journalism caper by accident a few years earlier but Goodwin is a man who relishes the unexpected. His top lip is masked by a fashionably thick moustache, his chin heavily bearded. But you can still imagine a broad smile breaking through those whiskers, maybe even a little warmth creeping into those cold, deep-set eyes.

He has come across a report in one of the Hobart Town papers. They are not to be trusted, of course. One of them, he will sneer, is clearly 'the paid organ of the government'. He loathes them almost as much as his cross-town rival, 'our dictatorial contemporary', the *Launceston Advertiser*. But this article is worth plundering. For a start, it adds another chapter to the ongoing saga and adventures of John Batman. But even more, it details a discovery so extraordinary it could not have been dreamed up by even the drunkest fabulist down at the bar of the Cornwall Hotel.

Dated Saturday 5 September, the front page of the *Cornwall Chronicle* is worth a shilling in itself.

'A most extraordinary discovery has taken place at Port Phillip,' begins the story. 'Some of Mr Batman's men were one morning much frightened at the approach of a white man, of immense size, covered with an opossum-skin rug, and his hair and beard spread out as large as a bushel measure. He advanced with a number of spears in one hand and a waddy in the other. The first impression of Mr Batman's men was that this giant would put one of them under each arm and walk away with them. The man showing signs of peace, their fears subsided and they spoke to him. At first, he could not understand one word that was said and it took a few days before he could make them understand who he was and what he had been. His story is very remarkable.

'This man's name is William Buckley, he was formerly a private in the 4th, or King's Own, he was transported to New South Wales and accompanied Governor Collins in the year 1804 to the settlement of Port Phillip. Whilst the new colony was being established Buckley with three others absconded and when the settlement was abandoned they were left there, supposed to have died in the bush.'

In case the readers start thinking this astonishing report is nothing but a hoax, the article says Buckley's story has been confirmed after a couple of Batman's men sounded out one of the original settlers who was part of David Collins' Port Phillip expedition.

'The question was put, whether any of the party remained after the settlement was broken up. [He] immediately said that four men were left, one of whom he particularly recollected because he was much taller . . . and his name was Wm Buckley.

'It appears Buckley has never seen a white man for upwards of thirty years. He has been living on friendly terms with the natives and has been considered as a chief . . . curiosity induced Mr Batman's party to measure this Goliath, his height is six feet five inches and seven eights; he measures around the chest three feet nine inches, the calf of his legs and the thick parts of his arms are eighteen inches in circumference. By all accounts he is a model for a "Hercules" – he is more active than any of the blacks and can throw a spear to an astonishing distance . . .

'This man may be made most useful to the new settlement; and, we trust, every precaution will be taken to conciliate the blacks and bring them by degrees to industrious habits through the medium of this man.'

Surely this is a story to get Goodwin's readers talking. A spear-throwing wild white man, in from the bush, his hulking frame making even Batman, himself a tall and powerfully built fellow, look small in comparison. And now the prospect of the two of them working alongside one another, guarding each other's backs as Batman and his intrepid band of explorers forge onwards into one of the greatest acreages God ever set forth on this earth? Surely this is enough to restore Goodwin's faith in the qualities of *manliness* and courage.

But William Lushington Goodwin isn't quite finished yet. This edition of the *Chronicle* might be his best yet. Buried in the column next to the story about Buckley's miraculous survival is a letter signed, simply, 'A. Mariner'.

It can only be Goodwin himself. The writer wants it known that his attention a few nights earlier was drawn to the ship *Kains*, now just a shadow of its old self, its hulk sitting in a specially designed dock attached to a wharf at the end of Charles Street. The ship Goodwin had almost single-handedly steered around the world in the face of so many obstacles was now nothing more than a hollow shell leased by the Customs department to store alcoholic spirits and liqueurs.

In the middle of 1831, having unloaded his cargo and crew in Sydney, Goodwin had set out for Launceston in the *Kains*, only to encounter horrendous weather. Two men and two horses were lost and Goodwin had to return to Port Jackson to repair broken masts. Still, it was just a hiccup compared to what he had endured over the previous 12 months. He was soon making his way down the east coast again and came painfully close to Launceston, only to find himself becalmed in the Tamar. The *Kains* then struck a rock and had to be beached before ultimately being turned into a novelty store.

'A. Mariner' is alarmed for he has seen a man running across the old ship's deck at night lighting the lamps with a flaming torch in his hand. Do people not understand that the *Kains* is now a veritable bomb, filled with all sorts of flammable spirits set to ignite from the slightest careless spark?

The *Kains* may have been transformed but so, too, has William Lushington Goodwin. The hardened and crusty sea captain has turned himself into a true newspaper editor with a flare for the unusual and an instinct for scaring the daylights out of his readers.

'... should the *Kains* take fire with the prevailing wind at NW the whole town of Launceston must fall sacrifice to the devouring element ... and should the flames be directed that way who can tell where they will stop and who ... could arrest their progress?'

You can sense that the warmth in those deep-set eyes of Goodwin has turned cold, his smile buried once more beneath a mask of whiskers and sternness. The ruthless man of the sea is never far from the surface and his disdain will resonate through the pages of the *Chronicle* almost two centuries later.

'Oh when,' he writes, 'shall we have a change of men and measures in this fine but mismanaged island?'

22

JOHN BATMAN – HERO, HUNTER, MURDERER

Early evening at the Cornwall Hotel in Launceston, the air thick with pipe smoke and sour whiskey breath. There are men in waistcoats and hats murmuring in the corner; others with sweat-stained shirts huddled in small groups. It's as if the essence of Van Diemen's Land has been distilled into this one room, a place where William Goodwin could stand quietly and just soak it all in and forget everything he'd ever said about this island turning soft and effeminate. He might even feel the urge to shout the bar because despite the tobacco haze and body odour, what you can inhale above all else is *manliness*. This is what life on a real frontier should look and feel like; settlers and freed men alike, wealthy and poor, all of them schemers and dreamers, real men of action, cradling their drinks in coarse, chapped hands, even the quietest among them listening intently and joining the conversation.

And there is only one topic for discussion on this night.

John Batman. Just when you think the man has peaked, just when it seems he has finally achieved his crowning glory by negotiating a treaty with the blacks of Port Phillip, he comes up with something else. What was it he had shouted just a few weeks ago when he'd stormed through the hotel doors, arms raised victoriously in the air, after returning from his journey across the Strait?

'I'm the greatest landowner in the world,' he'd announced, and there wasn't a man in the bar who could argue with that. Surely this son of a convict, effectively run out of Sydney, had no need anymore to prove himself as an equal among men. It was true that some of the men who formed the Port Phillip Association that Batman led – wealthy pastoralists, former politicians and surveyors who had provided the patronage and funds to bring such an outlandish idea to fruition – saw their man as a blunt instrument. But who among them could disagree that he had delivered everything he had promised? More than 600,000 acres, prime grazing lands leased from the local tribes for a pittance!

Not only that but he'd seized the land in defiance of government orders. Now that surely had to win the respect of even his greatest critics. And let's not forget there are a few of them scattered around this island. That painter and neighbour of Batman's over at Mt Ben Lomond – John Glover – he's no admirer. How will he sum up the man? 'A rogue, thief, cheat and liar, a murderer of blacks and the vilest man I have ever known.'

Well, every man has his faults and Glover is an *artist*, let us not forget. A painter of landscapes, an old man who ponces around the countryside with brush and easel by his side, delighting in the 'remarkable peculiarity of the trees'. He might be well known back in London but is anyone speaking in admiring tones in the bar tonight about his use of subtle colours and delicate tones?

No, all anyone wants to hear about is Batman and the news of this giant striding in from the bush. See what happens? No-one mentions your name for 32 years and now it's all they talk about. The news is stunning: a towering white man, dressed in skins who has lived with the savages since before the founding of Van Diemen's Land? If true, and if this Hercules now stands by Batman's side, advising him and helping him deal with the always troublesome natives, then who can stop Batman?

Everyone wants a piece of Port Phillip now. There are millions more acres to be grabbed. The reports of a land just waiting to be plundered are almost as endless as the grassy plains Batman and his party have described. The best sheep country God ever put on this earth. Even that short, slightly stooped and pasty faced man who built this hotel, wants in.

Johnny Fawkner.

Little Johnny Fawkner. William, you were warned about that 10-year-old boy who spent six months clambering about on the *Calcutta* all those years ago, watching everyone, eavesdropping on conversations, the sort of kid you could always find lurking in a corner.

Well, not much has changed. Hasn't grown much, has he? Fawkner had been in the Cornwall Hotel on that night back in June, doing what he does best, listening and making mental notes, as Batman boasted about how he had found the perfect place for a village; a deep river that would supply endless fresh water and the pasture land . . . why, the man was in raptures. The plains were so level and lush 'a horse might run away with a gig for twenty miles on end without fear of upsetting from irregularity of the ground'.

In fact, Fawkner should already be in Port Phillip, seeing it all for himself right now, if it were not for the small matter of some debts a group of local creditors had . . . err . . . requested he attend to. He was even on board his schooner – the *Enterprize*, the boat taking him and his settling party to this promised land – when he'd been forced to disembark and trudge back home to go through his finances. He might have been burning with embarrassment that day – and little Johnny has known more than his share of humiliation over the years – but don't think such a trifling matter like this is going to stop him. The *Enterprize*, without Fawkner, has already negotiated the rip guarding Port Phillip Bay and has made it all the way to the Yarra River. In just a few weeks, his debts sorted out, Fawkner will join its crew and help start a new settlement.

He'll go to war with Batman, of course. To Fawkner, Port Phillip promises more than just land and wealth. There are legacies to be won across Bass Strait, reputations that might endure down the ages, opportunities to rewrite history and even wipe away the stains of his past. And if you happen to be a Batman ally, then he'll go to war with you, too.

Fawkner has a vague memory of a big man called Buckley. A convict at the settlement at Sullivan Bay, wasn't he? Another prisoner on the *Calcutta*, just like little Johnny's father. There are some things from your childhood you never forget and the Fawkner family's six-month journey from England to New Holland is something he has never wiped from his memory – or wanted to. Men are all the same to Fawkner. Big or small, doesn't matter. You just have to find their weak point. If Johnny has shown a skill over the past three decades it is his ability to persevere, to put up with ridicule and humiliation, to bide his time until an opportunity presents itself and then ruthlessly press home his advantage.

But all that will come later. There are more urgent issues occupying the thoughts of the dreamers and schemers in the Cornwall Hotel on this night. Questions that rise far above the pipe smoke. How quickly can I get to Port Phillip? How much for a berth to get me across Bass Strait? Is this story of a possum-skin clad Goliath actually true?

And just who does John Batman think he is?

—

James Bonwick has the 19th century version of a man-crush. If you didn't know the man was a rabid teetotaller you would think he was in the throes of a bender. But he's just drunk on admiration and awe. The historian who will write William Buckley off as a guileless oaf is infatuated with John Batman. Forget any notions of Bonwick giving the man a pedicure; he's too busy stooping to kiss the man's feet.

Batman, he will say, 'was a youth of considerable intelligence and vigour, with a merry eye, a handsome face and a flattering tongue to please the other sex'. A flattering tongue, indeed. It won't be the only appendage of Batman's to get him into trouble.

Batman was born in 1801 in Parramatta, just a baker's dozen years after the founding of Sydney. His father, William Bateman (he dropped the 'e' from the surname in 1810), had been transported for 14 years for stealing. By the time John had reached the age of 15 he was apprenticed to a Sydney blacksmith, James Flavell, himself a former convict. But his career lasted barely a year. Flavell and one of his assistants, William Tripp, were arrested for burglary in 1816 and young John gave evidence against his employer.

The judge was in no mood for leniency, the *Sydney Gazette* reporting his finding that Flavell, a long-time resident of the colony with a lucrative business, was an 'almost unexampled case it had been unhappily brought to proof that it was scarcely possible for human depravity more to debase the human character than he had done'. Flavell and Tripp were hanged on 15 November, the *Gazette* noting that 'we feel gratified ... that the unfortunate men conducted themselves in their last moments in a becoming manner, and died penitently'.

For the next few years Batman took on an assortment of roles around Sydney before trouble struck. A resident of the local orphans' home, Elizabeth Richardson, named John as the father of her unborn child. The committee of the institution launched an investigation and suggested Batman marry the girl. He refused and so the committee asked for a donation of 50 pounds to cover her expenses. John's father intervened – the fee was eventually whittled down by half – and within days of the scandal being settled, John and his younger brother, Henry, were on a ship bound for Van Diemen's Land.

The John Batman Cheer Squad – a collection of sycophantic historians and admirers of real *manliness* – tend to either ignore this episode in his life, gloss over it or explain it away as a youthful indiscretion. Why, who could expect young John to stay around and support a child when he had an empire to forge?

Even as late as the 1970s, C. P. Billot, who writes a detailed biography of the man, will excuse his behaviour: 'All his life John Batman was a highly sensual man and Sydney would have provided a most exciting and fruitful soil for the sowing of wild oats. Can it be doubted, then, that this handsome, powerful young man was a hit with the ladies of the city? And in a community where these highly desirable ladies would be closely guarded by often violent husbands or fathers, can it be wondered at if the young, virile Batman had to leave Sydney in a hurry as a result of a too-ardent temperament expressing itself in a too-casual manner?'

In Launceston, Henry becomes a wheelwright and a drunk; John, ever the restless spirit, takes to the land, immersing himself in bush-craft. He begins amassing land around the slopes of Ben Lomond, beginning with a grant of 500 acres that will eventually grow to 7000 acres. And it is here, in the northern reaches of Van Diemen's Land, that Batman's reputation as a man who *gets the job done* begins. What he does next is almost enough to force Bonwick to break his vow of abstinence and raise a glass to the man who will reshape the southern half of the continent. Instead, he reaches for even higher notes of rhapsody: 'I learned that this man of nerve, of powerful frame and daring courage, had the manners of a gentleman, the simplicity of a child, the tenderness of a woman.'

Why, they also happen to be the very qualities supposedly possessed by the man Batman sets out to capture, the 'gentleman bushranger' Matthew Brady, an escaped convict whose exploits have been infuriating the authorities in Hobart Town, particularly the Lieutenant-Governor George Arthur. With his high forehead and pinched face, Arthur is a zealous reformer propelled by a deep streak of evangelicalism. But he is also thin-skinned, an autocrat whose patience has been stretched to its limits by Brady's ability to avoid the law.

If a growing guerilla war with the dwindling Aboriginal tribes is occupying more and more of Arthur's time, the bushranger problem is surely one of those issues that can be dealt with quickly. For years absconding convicts have been taking to the bush, plundering local settlements and committing crimes against the poor and the Indigenous people. To Arthur their continued presence is an embarrassment, a corruption of everything a penal colony should be. But without a structured police force the bushrangers have been allowed to roam with little fear of being caught. Convicts have been offered a free pardon if they can infiltrate Brady's gang and turn him in. But even a bounty of 100 guineas or 300 acres of land has not been enough; Brady's gang, with their leader's reputation for being courteous to women and only using violence in self-defence, are, if not quietly admired by many, at least appreciated by a population more accustomed to the ruthless violence of such men.

Who – except the humourless Arthur – could not appreciate the cheek shown by Brady when he nails a notice to the door of the Royal Oak Inn in Crossmarch.

'It has caused Matthew Brady much concern that such a person as Sir George Arthur is at large. Twenty gallons of rum will be given to any person that can deliver this person to me.'

But Brady's two years on the run are drawing to a close by early 1826. A posse led by Batman captures a former member of Brady's gang, Thomas Jeffries, without a fight and hauls him off to the Launceston lock-up to be interrogated. It's a scene straight from the Wild West; Jeffries behind bars, quickly turning informant and giving critical information on the whereabouts of Brady's gang while three-quarters of the town gather outside forming a lynch mob. Brady is apoplectic when he hears the news that Jeffries has been ratting him out and has to be talked out of attacking the Launceston lock-up, seizing Jeffries and flogging him to death.

Like others, Brady is not just offended by Jeffries' treachery. There is much more to the man to be loathed than that. Jeffries will forever be remembered as one of the cruellest psychopaths in Australian history. A convict with a history of violent sex offences, he had enjoyed his work as a flogger at Launceston's jail before escaping with three other prisoners. On the run he had killed and eaten one of his fellow escapers, kidnapped a woman and horrifically murdered her baby. Days later he shot a constable in the head. There was no-one in the colony, even George Arthur, who could disagree with Brady's assessment of Jeffries as a 'sub-human monster'.

But Jeffries had at least provided information on the rough where-abouts of Brady. The Great Western Tiers in the Central Highlands of Van Diemen's Land are perfect bushranger territory; steep gullies and jagged cliffs broken by open plains gave a man countless places to hide. It is here just weeks after the capture of Jeffries that Batman finds a weakened Brady, limping and supported by a makeshift walking stick. It's a classic moment, undoubtedly honed and polished by the John Batman Cheer Squad, that loyal band of brothers eager to embrace their heroic figure.

According to Charles White in his first volume of *History of Australian Bushranging*, Brady sees Batman first, throws down his walking stick and aims his rifle at his pursuer. What follows is a con-versation straight from a 20th century comic book.

'Are you a soldier, officer?' shouts Brady.

'I'm no soldier, Brady,' says Batman. 'I'm John Batman; surrender, there is no chance for you.'

Brady ponders this for a moment before realising the game is up. Batman is the better man, a hero whose 'powerful frame and daring courage' are clearly too much for the bushranger.

'You are right, Batman,' says Brady. 'My time is come; I will yield to you because you are a brave man.'

In early May Brady and Jeffries are hanged in Hobart, Brady indignant he should be executed on the same gallows as the monster who sold him out. It is a triumph for Batman, whose standing has risen greatly, particularly in the eyes of George Arthur. When the Lieutenant-Governor requires a trusted hand for the next major problem that crosses his desk, he will turn to the man with a well-earned reputation for *getting the job done*.

—

Batman is a man you will always respect. Not in the way that Bonwick and that grovelling crowd of historians will, but your loyalty to the man will never fade. After all, it is Batman who takes you in, who will help you win your freedom. And let's not forget that one of his daughters will make you your first fresh shirt in more than 30 years (and won't everyone talk about how much cloth had to be used just to make it fit . . .).

But if you had known the truth about Batman's encounters with some of Tasmania's Aboriginals, would you feel the same way about the man?

If you knew about Batman's role in their ultimate extermination, if you had been told about the roving parties and the rewards sought by Batman for his part in what will become a mass 'ethnic-cleansing' campaign, perhaps it might stifle that sense of admiration.

Certainly you will never be aware of an article that appears in the *Launceston Advertiser* on Monday, 24 August 1829. Like dozens of other briefings of local newspaper editors in the years to come, Batman's fingerprints are all over it:

'We learn from good authority that Mr John Batman is to be employed for some time as conductor of a party of 10 Crown prisoners, part of whom are to receive emancipation and part tickets of leave if they behave well. Their task is to capture all the Aborigines or as many as they possibly can.

'We understand that some of the Aborigines from NSW to the number of five or six with their gins [wives] are to be invited from Sydney to join in this highly useful undertaking. No possible means could ensure the desired effect better than the use of Sydney blacks, their dexterity in the use of the spear, their quickness in guarding themselves from any spear wounds by means of their shield (made of the iron bark tree), their keen sight, both for tracking and discovering living objects . . . render them the most desirable auxiliaries.

'Mr J. Batman is very well fitted for this office, from his knowledge of the bush from his early habits, and from his great capability of enduring fatigue and privation . . . we trust he will be successful and we doubt not that Lieut. Governor Arthur will reward his services in his usual generous manner.'

Arthur has promised Batman a grant of 2000 acres if he agrees to 12 months of 'zealous service' as part of a plan to remove Aboriginal people from the mainland of Van Diemen's Land to an island in Bass Strait. It is the culmination of what will be dubbed the Black War, an escalating guerilla conflict fought between two cultures over land and resources. For years settlers and freed convicts have been encroaching on traditional Aboriginal hunting grounds, depleting stocks of kangaroos and demanding the government protect their rights. Despite his evangelicalism and a history of sympathising with Indigenous cultures, Arthur, who is amassing his own personal fortune on the side by dabbling in land purchases and lending money, has formed the view it is time for the Aborigines to be removed.

And in the north-east of the island there is one man who can be relied upon. Batman is soon roaming the country and diligently reporting on his progress. His September report explains how, in 'pursuit of the Aborigines who have been committing so many outrages in this district', he follows tracks that lead him and his roving party to a group of between 60 and 70 Aboriginal men, women and children.

'I immediately ordered the men to lay down; we could hear the natives conversing distinctly, we then crept into a thick scrub and remained there until after sunset . . . and made towards them with the greatest caution.'

By 11 pm Batman's party has crept to within metres of this family clan, intending to 'rush upon them before they could arise from the ground'. It is a curious plan when you break it down – a dozen armed and burly men creeping through the bush late at night and then springing from their hideout to . . . gather up more than five dozen people without shots being fired? Perhaps Batman hopes his Sydney Aboriginals – Pigeon, Joe the Marine and Old Bull – might open a conversation and convince the clan to surrender peacefully. But those men are said to have little time for their brethren on this island, and struggle to speak their dialect as well. It's all moot, anyway. According to Batman, one of his men fumbles, knocking his musket against another man. The noise sets off the dogs in the Aboriginal camp and suddenly chaos erupts.

'The natives arose from the ground and were in the act of running into a thick scrub, when I ordered the men to fire upon them . . . we only captured that night one woman and a male child about two years old.

'Next morning we found one man very badly wounded in the ankle and knee, shortly after we found another, 10 buckshot had entered his body. He was alive but very bad, there were a great number of traces of blood in various directions and learnt from those we took that 10 men were wounded in the body, which they gave us to understand were dead or would die, and two women in the same state had crawled away besides a number that was shot in the legs.

'We shot 21 dogs and obtained a great number of spears, waddies, blankets, rugs, knives, a tomahawk, a shingle wrench etc etc.

'On Friday morning we left the place for my farm with the two men, woman and child, but found it impossible that the two former could walk . . . after trying them by every means in my power for some time, found I could not get them on I was obliged to shoot them.'

The chill that accompanies that final, abrupt sentence, made that much colder by its matter-of-fact nature, is enough to make even George Arthur wince, even at a time when his declaration of martial law effectively allows the slaughter of Aboriginal people. More than a dozen deaths are attributed to the Batman massacre – a group of armed men firing on the backs of dozens of panicked men, women and children attempting to flee into the bush. After considering the report, Arthur will take pen in hand and scribble that Batman has 'much slaughter to account for'. In the years to come repeated attempts will be made to soften Batman's reputation for dealing with Aboriginals; many historians will write about how he takes Rolepana, the young boy he captures during the attack, into his own home (he will eventually accompany the family to Port Phillip); how he always seems at ease among the native people and how the Sydney Aboriginals will remain loyal to him right to his dying day.

'Looked at alone, even in the mildest form, these measures are revolting,' will write John West about the colony's policy of removing Aboriginals from the mainland. But to West, who will be regarded as one of the founding fathers of Australian historical writing, Batman deserves to be singled out for praise for 'mingling humanity with severity, of perceiving human affections in the creatures he was commissioned to resist . . . he certainly began in the midst of conflict and bloodshed, to try the softer influences of conciliation and charity'.

Just how large is this John Batman Cheer Squad? It's standing room only. But there's always a place for a new member. So please squeeze together so Henry Melville, who writes one of the first histories of the Van Diemen's Land colony, can have his say about Batman's roving party: 'They proceeded, not with the sword, but with the olive branch.'

Truth is, Batman's roving party – and dozens more like it across Van Diemen's Land – are regarded as failures. The following year Arthur unleashes the biggest military operation ever seen in the colonies. More than 2000 colonists and soldiers will form an extraordinary cordon hundreds of miles across, advancing toward the island's southeast corner in an attempt to drive the last of the Aboriginal people out of the settled districts. Dubbed the Black Line, it is an extraordinary offensive costing almost half of Van Diemen Land's annual expenditure. It also fails miserably, with two Aboriginals captured and another two killed.

Eventually several hundred Aboriginals are sent to Flinders Island where, huddled against the cold winds that endlessly batter Bass Strait, large numbers of them will die from disease, malnutrition and a collective depression after being torn from their home lands.

When his 12-month commission with the roving party comes to an end, Batman writes to the authorities requesting his 2000-acre bounty and recommends pardons and rewards for the convicts and Sydney Aboriginals who accompanied him. And then he offers a little advice on future dealings with the Indigenous people.

'It certainly would be most desirable to be upon friendly terms with them, and if possible reconcile them, before further coercive measures be taken but this, I fear much, will not be effected. Generally it is the natives that are in the middle of this island and on the east coast that have committed so many murders ... and in my opinion nothing but severe steps for a time will effect a reconciliation.'

23

THE BACK-ROOM BOYS

If John Batman never tells you about those dark days hunting Aboriginals, William, does he at least admit to you he is dying?

The man with the flattering tongue and the merry eye has been led astray once too often and now it is a race between the syphilis raging through his body and the amounts of mercury being used to treat it to see which will claim him first. All that energy – that ability to endure fatigue and privation – is already draining from him; in the next couple of years the bacterial infection festering inside will become apparent to all when it begins eating away at his nose.

What about the Port Phillip Association that Batman leads? They are little more than trespassers on Crown land – the area around Port Phillip has already been proclaimed the territory of New South Wales in complete disregard of its original inhabitants. But if the authorities in Sydney and London have made it clear they are not supportive of a colony being established by lawless squatters caught up in a frenzy of land seizures, it has hardly stemmed the flow of ships heading across Bass Strait.

Grab the land and deal with the consequences later – that's what being a bold man on the frontier is all about. Besides, there are many who suspect that back in Hobart Town Lieutenant-Governor George Arthur is quietly supporting their move – and may even be a silent investor. And even Batman, competitive and driven though he may be, is welcoming the news that others like little Johnny Fawkner are making their way to the mainland. There will be comfort in numbers.

You probably know none of this. But what you are beginning to understand after just a few weeks of living at the depot at Indented Head is that, rather than being at the mercy of these settlers because of your convict background, your knowledge of the land and your reputation among the Wadawurrung is giving you influence you never dreamed possible.

Look at the way they lean in and listen when you talk in faltering English about the land and how it provides food for all; how they hang on every word when you describe some of the Aboriginal customs. This Todd, he's a good listener, is he not? Conscientious. A diligent note-taker. But you won't be seeing him for much longer because there's something else about Batman you definitely don't know. It's as if the man is cursed, that if you grow too close to him fate's black hand will ensure a miserable outcome. Todd will be one of many whose lives will end in tragedy. He will soon return to Van Diemen's Land (there's a suggestion he may fall out with John's brother, Henry) and become an invalid. And then one day years later he will be admitted to hospital, singing to himself and 'relating imaginary exploits' before stuffing part of his shirt down his throat and choking himself to death.

It takes three weeks before you feel confident enough to admit to Todd and the others you have lied about your past. There never was a ship skipper who you slung over your shoulders before swimming to shore. Todd will note that you did not tell them the truth at first because 'he was very much frightened of us, & he thought if he had told us the truth we should have shot him'.

When the *Rebecca* returns to the camp carrying Henry Batman and his wife and family – along with a man called John Helder Wedge – you suddenly find you have another audience to entertain and hold spellbound with your physical presence and stories.

If Batman is the chief executive and public face of the Port Phillip Association, answerable to a board of investors and pastoralists far wealthier than himself, then Wedge is chief operations officer. An Englishman close to Batman who has been in Van Diemen's Land for a decade, Wedge has just resigned his role as a government surveyor because this venture offers far more potential.

Wedge is one of the very few characters turning 1835 into such a pivotal year in Australian history whose image will endure photographically. In one he stares at the camera, hair parted down the middle and falling each side to just below the ears, a slightly bemused look on his face, looking every inch the dapper gentleman explorer so many of the era fancy themselves to be. An expertly tied cravat – the fashionable neckwear of the era – sits around a freshly laundered shirt. In his right hand he clasps a large hat, perhaps the one he once wore while climbing Ben Lomond with Batman. It is not hard to imagine his ever-present journal to the side, just out of view, pressed flowers drying between pages of notes about undulating fields and latitudes and longitudes. Wedge is far more literate than Batman and to him will fall the responsibility of attempting to achieve your free pardon.

But one of the first things he does when arriving at Indented Head is sketch you. It is four weeks after you walked out of the bush and you look nothing like the way you will be depicted by artists in the years to come. Gone is the bearded wild white man, hair down to the shoulders, spear in hand. Drawn from the side, your hair has been cut, beard shaved and the only notable feature is that sharp, upturned nose. It is a crude drawing; as a surveyor Wedge is all about boundaries and straight lines, not the meandering subtleties of the human face. He performs better when he sketches the Indented Head depot; two basic sod huts, a tent next to them, surrounded by sloping open ground and scattered gum trees.

Wedge's mission is to map the territory Batman has secured from the Kulin 'chiefs' and ensure each member of the Association knows how much land he has been allotted. But before he sets off – grateful to have you by his side leading the way – Wedge writes to the authorities in Hobart seeking a pardon for a man he already knows will prove invaluable to the Association.

The petition is a lengthy document detailing your history and how you saved the lives of Batman's party at Indented Head. Apart from noting the extraordinary amount of time that has passed since that escape from the Sullivan Bay settlement, Wedge also plays the fear and loathing card. It's a move you might normally associate with a William Lushington Goodwin or a John Morgan, not a mild-mannered surveyor. Wedge wants it known that if a pardon is denied, this huge white man next to him might very well retaliate by unleashing the dogs of war.

'I beg most earnestly to recommend this petition to the favourable consideration of His Excellency the Lieutenant-Governor,' writes Wedge, 'and in doing so, I feel that I scarcely need advert to the danger that would ensue to the lives of those who may in future reside here, by his being driven to despair by the refusal of his petition, which would probably induce him to join the natives again.'

Wedge feels no need to resort to subtleties. He is dealing with the Colonial Secretary, John Montagu, who reports directly to George Arthur, the man who instigated martial law and personally took charge of the Black Line.

'There is no calculating on the mischief that might ensue by the hostile feelings that he would have it in his power to instill into the breasts of the natives.'

Letter dispatched to Hobart Town, you and Wedge embark on a week-long tour of the area. Each day he is reminded how critical a role you will play in the months and years to come. It's almost as if you are showing off to the man. You impress him with your knowledge of the local customs. You guide him across the land, pointing out its features and sources of water. The following year the Royal Geographic Society in London will publish Wedge's *Narrative of an Excursion amongst the Natives of Port Phillip on the South Coast of New Holland*. It is in this, along with his field notes, that you are suddenly transformed from a curiosity to an indispensable aide.

You guide Wedge to one of your favourite haunts, that place on the Barwon River you know as Woorongo 'where I had caught a vast quantity of eels'. Well, Wedge is having none of that. He renames Woorongo 'Buckley's Falls' – and who are you to disagree? You take him to your old hut on the Karaaf River, where ducks and geese are shot in the presence of local Aboriginals 'to entertain great dread of the use of fire arms. I was authorised to tell those I met with that if they would go to the settlement presents would be made to them of blankets, knives etc, and many promised to visit us.'

You are also quick to provide Wedge with an assessment of the various characters of the Wadawurrung. There is the head of one family, Murradonnanuke, who, you tell Wedge, 'is more to be dreaded on account of his treachery than any of the other chiefs'. Wedge is quickly satisfied that most of the Aboriginals are not dangerous 'although I learnt from Buckley that in the treatment of each other they were treacherous . . .

'To command their respect I found it was necessary to make them fully understand that it was in our power not only to minister to their wants and comforts, but amply to avenge any outrage. In impressing them with this idea Buckley was of great use to us by making known to them the ample means we had of furnishing them with food, blankets . . . and explaining the object we had in view in settling amongst them, and our desire to be on friendly terms with them.'

But that question everyone wants to know . . . you've been waiting for Wedge to ask it. Sure enough, it doesn't take long. 'I learnt from Buckley that they were cannibals,' writes Wedge, '. . . but they do not seem to indulge in this horrible propensity except when the tribes are at war with each other when the bodies of those who are killed are roasted and their bones are infallibly picked by the teeth of their enemy . . .'

On one occasion Wedge is bemused 'although it was no fun to the four women concerned' – when Murradonnanuke punishes his wives for not fetching enough food for him by throwing fire sticks at them 'in the most furious manner'.

A week after returning to Indented Head, Henry Batman pulls you aside and tells you a letter has arrived from Hobart Town with news you are to be pardoned. The letter is from John Batman, who says he has just met with Lieutenant-Governor Arthur, who will move to have the pardon confirmed through Sydney and London as quickly as possible.

A free man, after all these years? To never look over your shoulder again? It's enough to make even a man like you break into Tuckey-style prose: '. . . whose heart, bounding from so many long years of solitude and captivity into freedom could, or can, beat like mine?' you and Morgan will write.

Wedge, the author of the pardon request, is also relieved, delighting in your happiness. 'Nothing,' writes Wedge, 'could exceed the joy he evinced at once more feeling himself a free man, received again within the pale of civilised society.' But below the bonhomie, something sticks in Wedge's craw. In the battle for land and wealth, egos bump hard against one another. He senses the hand of Batman taking all the credit and writes to him immediately.

'I could not shut my eyes or be deaf to the remarks you made respecting Buckley's obtaining his pardon through your influence with the Lieutenant-Governor,' Wedge tells Batman. 'A very few minutes after your brother had perused your letter he remarked to Buckley that it was very fortunate that you happened to be in Hobart Town at the time the memorial arrived there, that you had waited on the Governor and obtained his free pardon, etc, giving him to understand that it was through your influence alone that Col. Arthur conceded to the prayer of the petitioner . . . I cannot do otherwise than suppose that what he stated was your instructions . . .

'If the pardon was through your influence, every credit is due to you for it, and no-one would feel under greater obligation to you than myself. If, on the other hand . . . I do not think it fair toward others . . . for it certainly looks as though you intended to get the whole credit for yourself, and by which to obtain an undue influence over the mind of Buckley and through him over the minds of the natives.'

—

Those natives. Wedge knows all about dealing with Aboriginals – probably far more than he will ever tell you. The man is a collector and very soon a large array of Aboriginal artefacts bearing his name will sit in a museum near his home in the market town of Saffron Walden in Essex. There will be spears and clubs and boomerangs, souvenirs from the Black War and Wedge's first months in Port Phillip. Among them, according to notes made by the museum in 1844, will be 'four of Buckley's clubs of various shapes rudely ornamented'. They will be described as being solid and heavy – invaluable relics of your time with the Wadawurrung and testament to how deeply embedded you had been in their culture.

But weapons, dried flowers and insects were not the only additions to the John Helder Wedge collection. In 1828 he had been surveying a lease for the Van Diemen's Company in the island's remote north-west, territory of the Peerapper people who were now fighting back against the white predators stealing their land and killing their warriors. Wedge's party had opened fire on a group of Aboriginal men and then watched as one of them dived into the ocean to escape. Exhausted by the rough swell, he was soon washed ashore and revealed to be a boy no more than 10 years old. Here was another addition to the Wedge collection. The surveyor had the boy's hands tied for three days as they continued on their march into unknown territory.

The bachelor Wedge made the boy, Wheete, his 'constant companion', showing him off at dinner parties as yet another curiosity he had unearthed in his travels. He was heartbroken when the boy died two years later from a chest infection but it was not the end of his experimentation with Aboriginal children under his 'care'. He would eventually – and unusually – take five of them under his wing. Like Batman, several historians will portray Wedge as a noble humanitarian. The man himself will say he took Wheete into his home 'for I always dissented from the prevailing opinion that, however kindly treated even if taken in their infancy, they would be treacherous and take the first opportunity to return [to] their tribes again'.

But there will always be some who will feel uncomfortable about John Helder Wedge and his collection of the living and the dead.

—

In early 1836 Charles Darwin visits Hobart Town after a stint in Sydney as his five-year voyage around the world on the *Beagle* draws to a close. If the journey of the *Endeavour* half a century earlier had been the trigger for Britain's foray into New Holland, Darwin's experiences in Australia and elsewhere are already laying the ground for an idea that will transform humanity's understanding of how life evolved on earth.

Still in his mid-20s, balding and with large mutton chop sideburns, Darwin had been fortunate to secure a berth as the *Beagle*'s resident gentleman naturalist because the ship's captain, the temperamental Robert FitzRoy, did not like his nose. FitzRoy is an admirer of 18th-century Swiss philosopher Johann Kaspar Lavater, an influential figure in the field of physiognomy, a method of assessing a person's character and personality traits by their physical appearance. FitzRoy had seen in Darwin's large and fleshy nose the telltale signs of someone with a weak constitution who would find the perils of a long sea journey too difficult to handle.

He has not been that wrong. Darwin walked away from medical studies because he disliked the sight of blood and was horrified by the butchery of the era's surgeons. On the *Beagle* he has endured extreme seasickness and constant stomach complaints. But on land Darwin has overcome these ailments – and FitzRoy's doubts – through sheer perseverance and an insatiable curiosity. By the time he arrives in Hobart Town he is already something of a celebrity back in London. A selection of his geological letters has been published and circulated by his old botany professor, and the scientific establishment is already beginning to take notice of the young naturalist.

In Van Diemen's Land Darwin climbs Mt Wellington – 'a severe day's work' – and is paraded in front of the Bunyip aristocracy, all of them dressed in their finest. He remains on the island for 10 days and as the *Beagle* begins her voyage home, the naturalist has plenty of time to reflect on his experiences in the new colonies.

'The Aborigines have been removed to an island in Bass's Straits, so that Van Diemen's Land enjoys the great advantage of being free from a native population,' he will write in his book *The Voyage of the Beagle*. 'This most cruel step seems to have been quite unavoidable, as the only means of stopping a fearful succession of robberies, burnings, and murders, committed by the blacks; and which sooner or later would have ended in their utter destruction. I fear there is no doubt that this train of evil and its consequences originated in the infamous conduct of some of our countrymen.'

Darwin had already seen the impact of white culture on Australia's Aboriginals during his couple of weeks in New South Wales. There, he reported, 'The number of Aborigines is rapidly decreasing. In my whole ride, with the exception of some boys brought up by Englishmen, I saw only one other party. This decrease, no doubt, must be partly owing to the introduction of spirits, to European diseases (even the milder ones of which, such as the measles, prove very destructive), and to the gradual extinction of the wild animals . . . Besides these several evident causes of destruction, there appears to be some more mysterious agency generally at work. Wherever the European has trod, death seems to pursue the Aboriginal.'

But the man whose theory of natural selection will trigger a scientific and cultural revolution – and horrify FitzRoy who will see it as a slap to the face of God – is largely unimpressed with his experiences in Australia. 'Farewell, Australia!' he writes, 'you are a rising child, and doubtless some day will reign a great princess in the South; but you are too great and ambitious for affection, yet not great enough for respect. I leave your shores without sorrow or regret.'

What has stuck in Darwin's craw is the culture of the place. Forget about his still embryonic theory about the survival of the fittest; what he has seen in this young colony is the survival of the fattest; he who accumulates the most land and places the greatest number of sheep on it will emerge triumphant.

'The whole population, poor and rich, are bent on acquiring wealth,' writes Darwin. 'The subject of wool & sheep grazing amongst the higher orders is of preponderant interest.'

—

It's a safe bet you have no idea just what sort of stir you have created. The world is now being notified of your existence. Ink wells are running dry and quills worn out with the amount of letters being sent containing your name. John Montagu, the secretary to George Arthur, writes to Wedge on 25 August confirming that Arthur will support the request for a pardon, and that it is 'founded upon a desire to prevent bloodshed, and with a view to remove any inducement on Buckley's part to make common cause with the natives in the commission of any outrages upon the white immigrants, which might lay the foundation of a war of extermination . . . if this man's energies and influences be well directed, the Aborigines may be so thoroughly conciliated as to ensure a lasting amity between them and the present or any future immigrants . . .'

Another, dated 28 August, is sent by Arthur to Lord Glenelg in London, who has been Secretary of State for war and the colonies only since April. Arthur, bowing and scraping and ever mindful of managing up, says he is in no doubt that he has no lawful authority to grant a pardon as a mere Lieutenant-Governor, and while Batman and Wedge and the rest of the Port Phillip Association are nothing but intruders on Crown land, 'I have nevertheless felt it to be my duty at once to grant the prayer of Buckley's petition; from very dear bought experience I know that such a man at the head of a tribe of savages may prove a dangerous foe . . .'

This can only be a reference to the man who became known as Musquito, a man of the Eora people in Port Jackson who, after being sent to Van Diemen's Land, waged a guerilla war against settlers on the east coast before being hanged on flimsy evidence in early 1825. The execution of Musquito is often seen as the trigger for the island's Black War. But Musquito was just one of many Aboriginal resistance leaders.

The most famous had been Pemulwuy, another Eora man of the Bidjigal clan who spent 12 years fighting the British, burning crops and destroying cattle.

Known among his people as a healer who could talk with the spirits of the land, Pemulwuy had been born with a turned left eye. But the deformity hardly held him back; he was regarded as the strongest and the fastest of his clan and more adept with the spear than anyone else. In 1790 he had launched his weapon with great accuracy into the side of Governor Phillip's gamekeeper, John McIntyre. Outraged, the Governor ordered a company of marines to pursue Pemulwuy's group and return with 10 of their heads to be displayed in the settlement. Like all subsequent missions it failed and Pemulwuy's reputation continued to grow, particularly after John 'Black' Caesar, the first Australian bushranger, cracked Pemulwuy's skull during an encounter at Botany Bay.

A few years later he was shot in the head and body but continued to survive, his people now believing he was impregnable to the buckshot fired from the white men's muskets. Various search parties were sent out regularly but all returned empty-handed, their loud and blundering forays into the bush easily avoided by Pemulwuy's people. It was not until 1802 that his decade-long insurgency came to an end. Shot dead, his head was preserved in a jar of spirits and sent to Sir Joseph Banks in London, accompanied by a note from the Governor advising that 'Although a terrible pest to the colony, he was a brave and independent character.'

So it is no surprise that strong fears are held among the members of Batman's Association of an organised resistance by the Port Phillip Aboriginals. They have seen how much damage Aboriginals can create with their tactical use of fire and their ability to stealthily track prey, attack and then vanish back into the landscape. But imagine, suddenly, a general leading these warriors, a white man no less with a history of fighting white men's wars, but one who can also command and turn hundreds of small clans and family units into an organised army . . .

One of the most influential members of the Port Phillip Association is Charles Swanston, a man who knows more than most about native insurgencies. He is one of Hobart Town's most prominent citizens. A member of the Legislative Council, he has just established the Derwent Savings Bank and is well on his way to making a fortune, dabbling in the importation of rum and tea, the exporting of wool. But don't mistake Swanston for a banker with soft hands. Made lieutenant in the private army of the British East India Company at just 16, he fought in several legendary battles and later captured an elusive Marathi leader so despised the British had placed a 10,000 pound bounty on his head. But perhaps his most impressive feat was his arrival in Istanbul after a quick trip back to England. Travelling by horse via Baghdad, Swanston made the 3000-kilometre journey back to India in just 48 days. Two portraits of Swanston seem to capture him best. In one he is a handsome and dapper captain, sideburns trimmed exquisitely and stretching almost to the corners of his mouth. In another, said to have been painted in 1819 as he became captain of the Poona Auxiliary Horse brigade, he holds the reins of a rearing white horse, the dry red plains of India stretching endlessly behind him.

Swanston is a hardened Scot and has kept in close contact with several friends from his time in India, including George Mercer, a fellow Scot who has become one of the Association's investors and a critical advocate for it in London. In July, Swanston writes to Mercer to update him on the Association's progress in Port Phillip and has some concerning news regarding Batman.

Lieutenant-Governor George Arthur has told a confidant of Swanston's that Batman 'had destroyed more natives than any other man, and that he was, consequently, an unfit person to place in charge and in communication with the natives of Port Phillip. On what grounds Col. Arthur has made this statement we are unable to discover. All I can say is this, that Col. Arthur up to this hour treats Mr Batman with confidence.'

A month later, Swanston updates Mercer on the news that has everyone talking: 'The account of Buckley is most curious. To him,

Col. Arthur has sent a free pardon so that now, with his aid, we shall have most complete control over all the natives and will, through his information, be enabled to take possession of the finest tracts. He is chief of a tribe and possesses the most complete control over his people . . .'

Now, William, if John Batman never quite gets around to telling you about his prowess hunting Aboriginals, or the fact that he is dying, then it's a safe bet he never tells you what the Association has in store for you, either. You're going to be their blunt instrument. Charles Darwin is right about these people. They are bent on acquiring wealth and do little but talk about sheep and land and the need to control the natives of Port Phillip.

'No means will be left untried to conciliate and keep them on good terms,' writes Swanston about the Kulin people.

'Buckley will be our mainspring.'

24

AN ENEMY LURKS

John Pascoe Fawkner peers into the grave and shudders. Only six feet deep but the way some folks fear it, damn thing might as well be an endless black staircase descending all the way to hell. Well, let them flinch whenever they step too close to it, let them show the usual reverence and respect.

But not little Johnny.

The grave might send a shiver down his spine like anyone else but for someone whose first instinct is defiance, death's doorstep is just the final obstacle in the endless hurdle race of life. It deserves to be sneered at, stood up to, shown contempt, mocked and . . . well, treated like every other enemy of John Fawkner. And there are plenty of those because Johnny is – always has been – capable of finding enemies everywhere. Even here, by the side of this grave. And certainly down there, deep in that black, yawning pit.

Near Fawkner stand two men he has already decided shall be his lifelong adversaries. John Batman is a full foot taller than Fawkner, but even he is dwarfed by the giant he is using to calm the natives, that buffoon Buckley. These two men will need to be dealt with – along with John's constantly drunk brother, Henry. But gnawing away at Fawkner even more is an enemy he can't quite see at the base of the grave; a mass of worms, writhing and squirming their way through the sodden earth, just waiting to do their work.

This infant colony of what will become Melbourne, not yet a year old, has just suffered its first death. A small crowd has gathered to watch the cedar coffin containing the body of a young boy be lowered into the grave, a pit as dark and infinite as Fawkner's imagination.

Fawkner will take to his diary later this wintery day and recall how the grave's 'wet and cold appearance caused my flesh to revolt at the thoughts of the cold, damp dark doleful depository of the body when the mortal spark has fled. Here is only one grave in a burial ground of ten acres – the first natural death in this new settlement commenced by me on the 31 August, which day my people and horses landed, having been 10 days exploring the river and getting vessel up. One death in just 10 months. Our present population is 179 . . . one consigned to the tomb, how many more would there be committed to the dark house within the next five years, how many will strong drink hurry there prematurely?

'I fear a great many. Well, I hate the grave. Let my mortal remains be placed on a pile of timber and reduced to ashes. This will prevent the loathsome worms from preying upon me.'

Here, distilled in less than 150 words, is the essence of John Fawkner: one watchful eye following the funeral, the other gazing into the future just to make sure history spells his name correctly. To hell with the worms. He will find a way to deprive them of the satisfaction of consuming his remains. To hell with those who want to drink their life away – as the settlement's first publican he might as well profit from their mistakes. And to hell with Batman and that lumbering oaf by his side. Batman might claim to be the founder of this settlement – the arrogant fool has even been referring to it as *Batmania*. But Fawkner is already plotting to make certain 'this new settlement commenced by me' is remembered as *his* idea.

Every utterance, every diary entry, will be made to ensure that when the history of Port Phillip is finally decided, the true Father of a modern democratic metropolis will be revealed as that pioneering genius John Pascoe Fawkner. Many years later, a stooped old man with a persistent cough, he will frequently take the stage before any audience willing to listen to him – from bored students and polite church congregations to private gentlemen's clubs thick with cigar smoke. They will have to strain to hear the man with the wispy white hairs dangling from beneath his hat. But the message will always be the same. '. . . the country is (*cough, cough*) something indebted to me,' he will tell them.

What drives this incessant combativeness? No-one knows for sure but if the Devil suddenly climbed out of the grave at this moment, laughing maniacally and taunting the solemn crowd, little Johnny would be the first to take a swing. His life has been one long fight, a rugged, drawn-out, bare-knuckle battle with the world around him.

Take Christmas Day, 1806. The Fawkners are living in a wooden slab hut on a small farm in Glenorchy. It's just two years after little Johnny was hit hard by scurvy during the early famine years in Hobart Town. Back then his right leg was so swollen for weeks he couldn't walk. The best he could do was press his toes gingerly on the floor, the flesh bruised purple and yellow.

Now 14-year-old Johnny and his younger sister, Betsy, have been left home alone. Their mother has returned to England to claim an inheritance. The old man, a free man now but never too far from the wrong side of the law, has told the kids he has to go to Hobart Town 'on business' – probably code for a days-long drinking binge. It might be Christmas but the kids will just have to look after themselves.

It's a White Christmas typical of this land; ash flakes and embers falling from the sky, whipped by a scalding northerly wind fanning a raging bushfire. The two Fawkner children spend the day watching the nearby flames and breathing in the scorched air heavy with burnt eucalyptus.

They eventually fall asleep on Christmas night when two men – one a former convict from the *Calcutta* – burst in and begin rampaging through the hut demanding valuables. Who can blame them for thinking this will be an easy hold-up? No-one home except a small girl and her pallid, sickly-looking older brother. Who could possibly believe the boy is an outstanding specimen of the species *pertinax bastardis*?

Stubborn little Johnny stands against the wall with Betsy, refusing to give the men anything. The Fawkners don't have much, anyway. But Johnny, ever watchful, notices the bushrangers have left their pistol on the table. As the two men continue searching the hut, Johnny leaps forward and grabs his father's musket, takes aim and . . . it misfires. Say what you like about John Pascoe Fawkner, but don't say he's not quick on his feet. By the time the hapless bandits can grab their pistol, Johnny and Betsy are sprinting into the smouldering bush where they will spend the rest of the night hiding. When they return the next morning most of the food and clothes are gone and the place has been ransacked.

The episode is just another example of how life is always unfair. It's as though Johnny Fawkner decides the only way to balance the ledger is to fight back. By the time he reaches his early 20s he finds himself in deep trouble. He plays a pivotal role in an attempt by several convicts to escape and receives 500 lashes and three years hard labour at Coal River in Newcastle. And who will be one of the magistrates who sentences him? Why, none other than the good Reverend Knopwood.

Of course, Fawkner will never forget to even that ledger. Many years later he will recall the reverend as 'fond of drink and also of women and given to the coarse vulgar propensity of swearing if not blaspheming. He was a remarkable man: he never was known to look any man directly in the face – he carried his head on one side when conversing with anyone and scowled under his very dark eyebrows with a one-sided glance, and if looked at, invariably cast his eyes down, still holding his head at an angle with his body. He had a dark sinister scowl and his head finally settled on one side.'

When Fawkner returns to Van Diemen's Land a few years later trouble is never far away. The year 1819 is a turbulent one. Having opened a bakery he is convicted of selling short-weighted loaves of bread and fined 20 shillings. A few weeks later he is found guilty of stealing roof shingles and is ordered to repay the government by providing it with 1400 of them at no charge. In July he is placed on a good behaviour bond for 12 months on suspicion of being involved in the robbery of a general store by several Crown prisoners.

He has been whipped, jailed and racked by severe illness. All of it seems to fuel the fury inside him. And if those worms in the grave are not to be feared, a huge former convict who lived with the blacks for 30 years is hardly the sort of foe to instil fear in his heart. In the years to come Fawkner will dismiss Buckley as nothing more than a savage, 'a mindless lump of matter'. Given the way Johnny describes most folks, it's almost a compliment. You can even sense the historian and pedicurist to the rich and famous, James Bonwick, wrestling with how best to describe the furnace blazing inside Fawkner. In the end he will suck in his breath and write that Johnny has 'a native energy that made him rise superior to all assaults, endure all sneers, quail at no difficulty, and that thrust him ever foremost in the strife, happy in the war of words and the clash of tongues'.

It is as close as Bonwick will ever come to describing someone as a vindictive bastard. Others will be more than happy to do so. Hamilton Hume, the acclaimed explorer and an old school friend of Batman's, will say in the years to come: 'Fawkner must be a vindictive, vain-glorious and a low bred fellow. His accusations against poor Batman prove him such.'

That's just a little too crude and direct for Bonwick. You can almost see him shrugging his shoulders when he writes of Fawkner: 'Although a public personage with rancorous foes, the temptation to exhibit his private weaknesses is to be resisted as unworthy of the historian, and contemptible in manhood.'

But the temptation to exhibit the private weaknesses of others has never been a problem for Johnny. For the rest of his life he will do his best to criticise Batman and distance himself from the man. Yet the pair will forever remain shackled together; pioneers of a new settlement, sons of convicts . . . and husbands of convict women.

Batman's wife is Eliza Callaghan, a tough Irish woman – 'passionate and sexually attractive in a dark, perhaps even sullen way' – who had been transported for 14 years for forgery. A serial absconder who once spent time in the stocks and was forced to wear an iron collar, Batman had sheltered her after she escaped from her role as servant to the superintendent of police in Launceston and finally gained her a pardon after lobbying the Governor.

Fawkner's story of how he found his wife involves, like a lot of his tales, a stretching of the truth, shaped to suit his purposes. But he tells it repeatedly; having heard about the arrival in Hobart Town of a new immigrant ship, he rushes to the dock and selects the best-looking woman he can find. Barely an hour later a friend spies him in the street with his bride-to-be and steals her away from him.

So Johnny returns to the ship and finds its captain.

'Hullo,' says the captain, 'what do you want now?'

'Another wife,' I says.

'Why, confound you, how many wives do you want? You took the best looking girl on the ship a few minutes ago.'

'Yes, but my mate took her away from me and now I want the homelyess-looking girl you have got and I will marry her.'

Her name is Eliza Cobb, described by one historian as 'unattractive, ungainly with a pock marked face and a caste eye'. Truth is, she has not just stepped from an immigrant ship looking for a new chance in a new world. The boat is just another female convict ship, like the one William Lushington Goodwin so memorably steered to the new country.

Cobb had been sentenced to seven years for kidnapping a four-month-old baby while serving as a maid at a home in Kensington, possibly not long after giving birth to a baby of her own which had died. She and Johnny will remain childless while the Batmans will bring eight children into the world, seven daughters and a son.

Maybe that's one of the reasons little Johnny cares so much about legacies, about making sure history is written in his hand. There is no-one else to do it for him so if he has to twist the facts a little this way and that, so be it.

Like that plot by the Aboriginals to murder every white in the settlement – and how you, William, wanted to see it happen. Johnny Fawkner can twist and turn. But you should see him spin.

25

YOUR NAME BLACKENED;
MASSACRE AVERTED;
A MISERABLE DEATH

Didn't take long, did it? A few months after rejoining these white men and what have you come to realise? They are as aroused and engaged by the same petty arguments and disputes as the tribes you lived with for more than 30 years. Their vindictiveness, their need for revenge, their desire to assert superiority over a rival, it's all the same. Nothing has changed. You're still caught between warring factions and the only difference is that the white men are not interested in working within the land. They are here to change it, forever.

A day barely passes without another boat arriving from Van Diemen's Land to disgorge its stinking load, a white plague destined to inflict as much damage to Aboriginal land and culture as bullets and disease.

Forget *Teredo navalis*, that indestructible bivalve worm that loves nothing more than dining out on the hulls of wooden ships. Sheep by the thousands, soon to soar into the millions, are being shipped bleating across Bass Strait to fill these new pasture lands. Within just a few years their hooves will turn much of the earth into a hardened mass, causing water runoff and turning plains into dust bowls. Their teeth will gnaw away at much of the native plant life; the yam daisy and many nutritious berries will virtually disappear. The numbers of native animals, including the kangaroo, will begin to decline. The land will ache.

It all happens so quickly, tidal forces so strong that once unleashed they can never be stopped. There is land to be claimed, homes to be built, boundaries to be drawn, Aboriginals to be won over and, if not, chased away or hunted down. Two centuries later one noted historian will regard what takes place around Port Phillip Bay as one of the 'fastest land occupations in the history of empires'. At the same time the annihilation of the Aboriginal people and their culture will also be one of the swiftest ever experienced. No-one knows how many Aboriginals live in Victoria when Batman's treaty is struck. Best estimates range between 30,000 and 60,000. Within the space of two generations there will be little more than an estimated 800 left.

It's as if you already know how this is all going to end because once it starts there is no pulling back. You will always be seen by many of the whites as sympathetic to the Indigenous people. And by the Aboriginals who showed you so much respect for three decades? As the land grab quickens and their numbers begin to rapidly decline they will grow ever more suspicious that you are nothing more than a simple instrument of the men hell bent on taking their hunting grounds.

Look at that little Johnny Fawkner and the Batmans, eyeing one another off across a few pathetic parcels of land, always probing and testing one another. There's a clash in February 1836. Henry Batman, drunk as usual on rum and the power handed to him by his ailing brother, tells Fawkner he can continue building a house but the Port Phillip Association owns all the land and will seize his place at some stage.

Fawkner writes back: 'I cannot account for the manner in which you act towards me. I do not deserve to be treated as you continue to use me. Only two days ago you shot one of my dogs close by your men's fire. The day before yesterday you would have shot another dog of mine . . . only your piece misfired . . .

'I beg leave to tell you that if I had thought proper to act towards your brother as you seem inclined to act towards me I could have injured him severely, for most of your men are ready to leave you.'

A few days later Henry writes back to Fawkner: 'Sir, you say my piece miss fire at your bitch, it is a bloody lie, and so is the whole of your letter.'

On it goes, this clash of egos, the Batmans resentful over Fawkner's presence on the Yarra River, Fawkner bitter because he is . . . little Johnny Fawkner. Why, when he casts an eye across the fields and sees Henry and his wife lurching about in the middle of the day, stone drunk as usual, it is easy for Fawkner to take the moral high ground. Truth is, the depravity of the Batmans means even a man like Johnny can sense the hand of God on his shoulder. Back in October, just a few days after settling here, Fawkner had written in his diary: 'Cloudy day. I performed divine service this day by reading the prayers usually read in the established church, to our own people and Wm. Buckley.'

It takes Fawkner a little time to set about demonising you, to start bending and twisting those facts.

But here is how it begins.

Just weeks after arriving in Port Phillip, little Johnny will make a diary note that 'the blacks we learnt intended to murder us for our goods'.

It will be three decades before he elaborates on this threat. Like Batman, Fawkner realises it is better to forge relationships with the Kulin people than to go to war with them. One of them is a young man, Derrimut, a leader or *arweet* of the Yalukit Willam, a horde who have roamed the area around Port Phillip for tens of thousands of years and can still tell stories of the times when the bay was a vast plain. The Yalukit Willam is one of six main language clans among the Bunurong people and white fellas fascinate Derrimut. He has accompanied Fawkner and his men on fishing and hunting expeditions. But the gulf between languages remains a problem and a reluctant Fawkner will come to rely on you to bridge the gap.

According to Fawkner – later in life when he is busily using every opportunity to cast himself as the original and only founder of Melbourne – Derrimut warns of an imminent attack on the settlement by tribes from the north of Port Phillip and repeats the warning a few weeks later, giving Fawkner and his men enough time to arm themselves and prepare for any attack. Fawkner, Henry Batman and a handful of others fire several rounds of buckshot to scare off the northern tribesmen. Then they round up the remaining Aboriginals lingering around the camp and haul them across to the other side of the river in their bark canoes, burning them before returning to the settlement.

Say what you like about John Fawkner, but don't say he does not have a flair for the dramatic. 'Derramuck came this day and told us that the natives intended to rush down upon us and plunder our goods and murder us. We cleaned our pieces and prepared for them . . . I and two others chased the blacks away some distance.

'I do not believe that one of us would have escaped. But fortunately for us the Melbourne party of Aborigines was favourable to us. They felt thankful for the things we gave them.' Fawkner had ordered one of his men, William Watkins, to learn the locals' languages and to forge as close a relationship as possible with the Aboriginal tribes around the Yarra.

'He taught them words of our language and very readily learnt theirs and two of these sons of the soil, named Baitbanger and [Derrimut], formed a friendship with him and the latter told Watkins of the plan to murder the whole party, in order to possess themselves of our goods etc etc . . .

'Watkins could not make out the words used by [Derrimut], who appeared much excited. I therefore called Buckley to explain what information the boy Watkins could not make out. Buckley, having been 32 years with these blacks understood their language fully, and he at once declared that the Aborigines had agreed to murder all the white people by getting two or more of their fighting men alongside each of our people, and upon a given signal each of us were to be cut down by blows on the head with their stone tomahawks . . .

'The half savage Buckley declared that if he had his will he would spear [Derrimut] for giving the information.'

There it is. Did you even see that allegation coming? It's a severe one – according to Fawkner you view Derrimut as a traitor to the Aboriginal people. You – William Buckley – would prefer to see all the whites massacred and this settlement put to the torch.

It is a charge hard to believe. Just a few months earlier you prevented a similar massacre taking place on the shores of Indented Head. Since then you have done nothing but try to keep the peace. When you finally met John Batman here in Port Phillip you organised several hundred Aboriginals to greet 'King John' and Batman had been so impressed he could not 'refrain from expressing my thankfulness to that good providence which threw Buckley in our way, for certainly he has been the medium of successfully establishing between us and the natives an understanding which, without his assistance, could never have been effected to the extent it has been . . .'

You have sat with tribal leaders and explained the motives of Batman's people 'and the consequences which might arise from any aggression on their part', as well as promising them swift justice if white men ill treat any Aboriginals. That message will always be remembered. Listening and watching on will be an 11-year-old boy, William Barak, who will become the last *ngurungaeta* of the Wurundjeri-willam clan.

Decades later Barak will recall how 'Buckley told the blacks to look at Batman's face, he looks very white. Any man that you see out in the bush not to touch him. When you see an empty hut not to touch the bread in it. Make a camp outside and wait till the man come home and finds everything safe in the house. They are good people. If you kill one white man white fellow will shoot you down like kangaroo . . .'

Besides, you are the only man who fully understands what Derrimut is saying. Would it not be easier for the threat to be lost in translation? There is no doubt you are beginning to doubt the wisdom of your return to white culture; you're going to grow increasingly surly with officialdom over the coming 18 months as all the talk about respecting the natives and their land comes to nothing. But slaughter on the scale Fawkner is claiming? You have been friendly with Derrimut. You know his people; during your travels with the Wadawurrung you will have passed through Bunurong lands and traded with them.

The simplest explanation is that Fawkner is at it again, inflating his own importance, tickling the truth a little further than necessary, showing the world how it is he, not Batman, who is able to reach out and bridge the two cultures.

The man's inconsistencies are as common as the enemies he creates and pursues. On the final day of 1835 a newspaper in Hobart Town, *The True Colonist*, publishes a letter from Fawkner, whose supply of ink seems endless. Johnny has taken a set against John Helder Wedge, who has informed Fawkner that he is trespassing on land owned by the Port Phillip Association. Fawkner has just read an account of Wedge's tour of the land near Indented Head a few months earlier and how Wedge claimed he had discovered three rivers and a lake.

'Please to contradict Mr Wedge's assertion . . . Buckley discovered them to Mr Wedge. He, Mr Wedge, also says that he established a manufacture of baskets. This is utterly false: the basket trade, Buckley says, was carried on before he joined the Blacks thirty-two years back . . . almost the whole of his letter is false or delusive, but it is like his language while here: he first asserted he was only employed by the Company [the Port Phillip Association] to survey land, but had no interest in it: the next day he declared he was a partner.'

It's not unusual for Fawkner to build up a head of steam when on the attack and this is no different. He pours on the bile, noting that the local Aboriginals did not like Wedge.

And then this: 'He never mentions the great exertions of Mr Henry Batman, who has done wonders here with the blacks . . . Mr Batman has kept them in good order, and with the able assistance of Mr William Buckley, I don't doubt but the settlement will eventually become of importance – fine feed both for sheep and cattle . . .

no perjured villains swearing people's lives away, to please a Botany Bay Magnifico . . .'

So let's get this straight. Fawkner is full of praise for you and the Batmans? But wasn't he supposed to have been horrified just a few weeks earlier to learn you were threatening to spear Derrimut? The man is a mess of contradictions. But he is at least consistent on one point. He signs his letter: 'John P. Fawkner. Pascoeville, Fawkner's River, Port Phillip'.

His river. His town. His idea.

—

His blackfella, too. So fond does Fawkner become of Derrimut that he will take him to Hobart Town the following year along with another influential Bunurong man, Baitbanger, for a show-and-tell session with Lieutenant-Governor George Arthur, who will present Derrimut with a drummer's uniform. It is easy to picture the scene; little Johnny Fawkner triumphantly returning to the island that for so long had looked the other way whenever he tried to better himself, rubbing shoulders – finally – with the elite of Van Diemen's Land, showing off his latest acquisition.

It is a grand occasion. The resident English artist Benjamin Duterrau is summoned to paint a portrait of Derrimut. After a year living and working alongside Fawkner – the pair have even traded names, a significant act of bonding among many of the Kulin – Derrimut usually wears European clothing supplied by little Johnny. But this would be jarring to the colonial eye. So Derrimut is stripped down, a kangaroo skin draped around his hips, the scarring on his muscular upper torso exposed. Beyond the cliché, though, it is Derrimut's face that captures the observer. Framed by a mass of curly black hair and a thin beard, and with his left eye slightly larger than the right, he has an almost mischievous look on his face, as though he is laughing at all the attention he is receiving.

But amid all this bonhomie emerges a darker sign of things to come.

One of those present for Derrimut's visit is the English botanist Daniel Bunce, who years later will travel with Ludwig Leichhardt during his second attempt to cross Australia. Bunce, who will go on to marry one of Batman's daughters, will record in his journal the arrival in Hobart of 'some distinguished visitors from Port Phillip, which had just been discovered by Mr John Batman, in the persons of two of its princes, or chiefs: Derrimut, King of the Werriby District; and Betbenjee, of the adjoining district, two brothers . . .

'Of the two native chiefs, a singular instance of the effects of strong drinks may be related. On their arrival they both got extremely intoxicated and they both felt the sickening effects the following morning. Poor Derrimut was induced to taste "a hair of the dog that bit him" and recommenced his debauch, and still continues a drunkard to this day.'

Well, John Fawkner is right about one thing. That cold day when he stares into the grave, wondering how many more in the fledgling settlement grog and its evils will send back to the soil? Derrimut has had a taste of it and, like so many of his people, will never escape its hold. Fully in its grip he will earn a reputation as a dangerous drunk, violent at times and difficult to control. The grog will add to his growing disillusionment with white people. They will no longer fascinate but disgust him. He will stand up to them, arguing his people should be left to live peacefully on their tribal lands. But despite his efforts the remnants of his tribe will be forced to settle on a mission station north-east of Melbourne by the early 1860s.

But before then the new parliament of Victoria will hold an inquiry into the condition of the state's remaining Aboriginal people. One of those to appear before it in 1858 is the politician William Hull, a man who, like Fawkner, has earned much of his living by selling grog.

Hull relates a recent encounter with an embittered and fatalistic Derrimut and his evidence will become one of the saddest and most poignant tales about dispossession in Australian history.

'The last time I saw him was nearly opposite the Bank of Victoria,' says Hull. 'He stopped me and said "you give me shilling, Mr Hull."

'"No," I said. "I will not give you a shilling. I will go and give you some bread."

'He held his hand out to me and said "Me plenty sulky you long time ago, you plenty sulky me; no sulky now, Derrimut soon die" and then he pointed with a plaintive manner, which they can effect, to the Bank of Victoria.

'He said "You see, Mr Hull, Bank of Victoria, all this mine, all along here Derrimut's once; no matter now, me soon tumble down."

'I said "Have you no children?" And he flew into a passion immediately.

'"Why me have lubra [woman]? Why me have picanninny? You have all this place, no good have children, no good have lubra, me tumble down and die very soon now."'

Derrimut dies in 1864 in the Benevolent Asylum, a broken and embittered man in his early 50s. His body is interred in the Melbourne cemetery and Fawkner chips in for a tombstone to commemorate the man he claims helped save the early settlement. But there is nothing remotely Aboriginal about his funeral. Derrimut's coffin will be lowered into the deep ground, down there among the waiting worms, accompanied by the usual solemn Christian rites.

In death, as in life, still trapped between two worlds.

TEARS AT FAMILY REUNION; RAPE; A NASTY RUMOUR SPREADS

The lengths some people will go just to lay eyes on the wild white man of Port Phillip . . .

The unpredictable waters of Bass Strait have become a tempest. Howling gales have whipped the sea into a swirling froth. Waves crash against the side of the boat. This is no place for a hardened sailor, let alone a lawyer with a cherubic face, tousled blond hair and doe eyes. Joe Gellibrand should be back home in his sitting room in Hobart, reading poetry and listening to his wife play the piano. But no, the man has insisted on voyaging to Port Phillip and he will get there no matter what is hurled in his way.

Joseph Tice Gellibrand may have the soft hands of a lawyer who works indoors but he is not a man to back down from a fight. He is a controversial figure in Van Diemen's Land. Sacked as Attorney-General by George Arthur, he has been described as a 'vulgar' attorney by the island's Chief Justice. He has much at stake in the future of Port Phillip. Back in the 1820s he and his friend John Batman had applied unsuccessfully for a land grant to run sheep and cattle in the region. Now the opportunity has come to reverse that refusal. Besides, Gellibrand is the author of Batman's 'treaty' with the Kulin.

The man wants to see what his words have bought him, and how this whole scheme has managed to conjure up the almost mythic figure of William Buckley.

But first, Gellibrand and William Robertson, another member of the Port Phillip Association, must survive this horrendous late-January crossing of Bass Strait. It's a ship of horrors. More than 100 sheep perish by 'injuries and suffocation'. The storm also wreaks havoc with hay supplies and they are soon forced to feed the surviving sheep flour and water. Forced to land at Western Port, the party decides to make the 90-kilometre trek to the new settlement overland. Gellibrand may be a good lawyer but a bushman he is not. 'In passing through one of the valleys I found the gleams of heat extremely oppressive and which brought on violent palpitations and a termination of blood to the head,' he observes in his diary.

He is forced to lie under a tree to recover and then turns to the most reliable medicine of the era – calomel tablets. Made from mercury chloride, calomel is often used as a purgative and its popularity will not wane until the end of the 19th century when its toxic effects are finally discovered. But all that is a long way in the future for Gellibrand. 'I lay down for about two hours and finding the heat very oppressive I took three grains of calomel and in half an hour afterwards took another pill.'

Six days later the tired party finally reaches the Yarra – saved only by a series of Aboriginal water wells – and discover a fledgling settlement of about a dozen turf huts. The next morning, still recovering from the hot trek and anxious about hundreds of sheep that have gone missing because hired shepherds have not watched them closely enough, Gellibrand holds his first meeting with the Association's prize asset – its wild white man.

He finds you to be 'of nervous and irritable disposition and that a little thing will annoy him much'. These are traits you often show when meeting people for the first time. It has been six months since you walked out of the bush and when you are not feeling like an exhibit in a sideshow, then you are refereeing disputes and trying to keep the peace between two colliding cultures. But unlike many of his colleagues Gellibrand peers a little deeper, putting down your 'irritable disposition' to the 'peculiar situation in which he has been placed for so many years'.

Out of all the characters and people you will meet, Gellibrand will come the closest to understanding your moods and motives.

'I am quite satisfied that he can only be acted upon by kindness and conciliation, and that by those means he will be an instrument in the hands of providence in working a great moral change upon the Aborigines. He is not at all desirous of occupying any land or having sheep but is highly pleased at the idea of being appointed superintendent of the natives with a fixed stipend so that, to use his own expression, "he may know what he has to depend upon" and be enabled to make a few presents to his native friends.'

Gellibrand wants to journey to Wadawurrung country and asks you if you would like to accompany him. 'He seemed very much pleased at the idea but stated he did not think he could walk so far. I then proposed he should ride, which seemed to gratify him very much and in consequence I engaged a large cart horse of Mr Fawkner's for that purpose.'

A few days later the Gellibrand party reaches Indented Head and he learns 'to my extreme mortification' that the local Aboriginal people have fled the small base after being threatened with guns for stealing a sack of potatoes. 'They had pulled up the roots and taken the potatoes and then planted the roots in the earth again thinking they should not be discovered . . .'

The next morning – 5 February – they set out to find the Wadawurrung. To ensure they are not frightened by a group of armed men on horseback, Gellibrand directs you to advance while the rest follow a safe distance behind.

'Buckley made towards a native well and after he rode about eight miles we heard a *coo-ee* and when we arrived at the spot I witnessed one of the most pleasing and affecting sights.

'There were three men, five women and about twelve children. Buckley dismounted and they were all clinging round him and tears of joy and delight running down their cheeks. It was truly an affecting sight and proved the affection which these people entertained for Buckley. I felt much affected at the sight myself and considered it a convincing proof of the happy results which will follow our exertions if properly directed.

'Amongst the number were a little old man and an old woman, one of his wives. Buckley told me this was his old friend and with whom he had lived and associated thirty years. I was surprised to find this old man had not a blanket and I enquired the cause and was much concerned to learn that no blanket had been given him because he did not leave that part of the country and proceed to Dutigalla [a Kulin word for 'tribe' and one of the early colonial names for Melbourne] . . .'

Gellibrand has few blankets of his own but insists on handing one to you to give to the old man. Apart from the joy he expresses at your family reunion, Gellibrand has also noticed something else about you.

'[As] soon as Buckley crossed the saltwater river and obtained a view of his own country, his countenance was much changed and when we reached Geelong he took the lead and kept us upon the trot. He seemed quite delighted and proud of his horse.'

How could you not be happy? Gellibrand's son, Tom, shoots a large musk duck for your dinner. The next morning you get to lead these men through your homelands, back among familiar territory. You lead them up river to the place now officially known as Buckley's Falls, show them a hollow tree that often provided you shelter at night, explain to them the art of catching eels. And while you admire Gellibrand, another member of the party begins to earn even more of your respect.

William Robertson, a tall Scottish grazier who provided much of the funding for Batman's first expedition to Port Phillip, is only a few years younger than yourself and his strength and endurance impresses you. Robertson and Gellibrand do not have horses and have been walking for the past six days while you take the lead on Fawkner's large draught horse. Gellibrand is still a tad worse for wear after that crossing of Bass Strait. He can probably feel more 'violent palpitations and a termination of blood to the head' about to occur and, according to one report many years later, Robertson carries Gellibrand's knapsack for him.

This is where another of those stories about William Buckley begins. The rumour will spread that Robertson's display of chivalry so captivates you that you give the man thousands of acres of land. Right here, on this spot among the Barrabool Hills just to the west of what will become Geelong. Legend will have it that you will tell Robertson the clans of the Wadawurrung gave you this large tract of land and that this is now his land. It is a story hard to believe but it will spread for years. Perhaps it explains why Robertson will be so generous when you and John Morgan sit down to write *The Life and Adventures*. Other graziers, jealous about Robertson's growing empire, will reportedly ask his permission to enter this land before taking their herds or flocks through it.

Exhausted or not, Gellibrand is pleased with what he has seen; enormous plains ideal for grazing sheep, gentle rolling hills and enough water on the 40,000-acre allotment Wedge has measured for him to sustain a decent business. 'I consider the representations of Mr Batman fully borne out and from the account given by Buckley I have every reason to believe there are millions of acres of equal quality extending to the westward.'

He is just as impressed with the Indigenous people: 'a fine race of men, many of them handsome in their persons and all well made. They are strong and athletic, very intelligent and quick in their perceptions. They have fine foreheads, aquiline noses, thin lips and all of them very fine teeth. I did not observe a single man with a decayed tooth . . . I feel not the slightest doubt but they may be all brought to habits of industry and civilisation . . .'

But by the time the party returns to the settlement on the Yarra, Gellibrand the explorer with blistered feet quickly becomes

Gellibrand the attorney, a man quick to get up on those sore feet. About 150 Aboriginals have gathered at the settlement 'and I learnt with much concern that an act of aggression had been committed upon one of the women which required my immediate attention'.

Gellibrand finds a young Aboriginal woman lying on the ground, covered with a kangaroo rug and suffering from a 'violent contusion' on the back of her head 'which I understood had been inflicted upon her by her husband'. He learns the woman had been making her way to the settlement to visit her mother when a shepherd on one of the adjoining allotments had seized her, tied her hands behind her back and taken her back to his hut. He had kept her there all night 'and either that night or the next morning abused her person'.

After finally reaching the settlement she has told her friends about the incident 'and they immediately apprised Buckley of it to obtain redress.

'The natives are particularly jealous respecting their women,' writes Gellibrand in his diary, 'and they consider any intercourse of this kind as a contamination, and in every case punish the women, frequently even to death.' Gellibrand addresses the 100-strong assembly with you translating, telling them he is determined to punish the white man responsible for the initial assault and 'protect the natives to the utmost of our power'. But Gellibrand the lawyer must also point out that white man's law does not yet extend to this new settlement and the guilty party would have to be sent 'to their own country to be punished'. He is a man with unusual views for his time. Years earlier, when George Arthur had declared martial law and escalated the Black War, it had been Gellibrand who stood up at a public meeting in Hobart and expressed concern that Arthur's move was officially condoning the murder of Aboriginals.

Two men are hauled down from the shepherd's hut and held before the young woman, who has been lifted from the ground.

Your turn to be the attorney, William. You ask her if either of the two men before her is guilty of the assault. She says no – but they were in the hut when another shepherd had brought her in, tied up. Gellibrand orders an immediate search for a third man before stepping forward to address the two shepherds.

'I then explained to the two men the wickedness of their conduct and how justly they would be punished if the natives had inflicted an injury upon them and gave orders that as soon as fresh shepherds could be obtained they should be removed from the settlement under the terms of their indentures. I directed the other man to be immediately sent for and if the woman identified him as the aggressor that he should be removed from the settlement by the first ship . . . and publicly taken away as a prisoner.'

Gellibrand turns to Buckley to explain 'to the whole tribe the course which I had directed to be pursued and I could perceive by the expression of their countenances that they were highly satisfied. I then endeavoured to make the poor woman understand how much I commiserated with her situation and I tied around her neck a red silk handkerchief (with which she appeared much gratified).'

Gellibrand is soon on a boat back to Van Diemen's Land, along with Batman and his wife and children, who will finally return to settle permanently in April. The lawyer returns a few weeks later with more of his sheep – this time finding the Bass Strait journey more to his liking – to discover the young woman reconciled with her husband and living at the settlement because it is 'a place of security'. He learns that the offending shepherd has already been removed to Van Diemen's Land and 'Buckley informed me that the measures which had been adopted respecting this transaction had given great satisfaction to the natives generally'.

A job well done. But Gellibrand can't help but wonder at the limitations of the law in Port Phillip. The shepherd was back in Van Diemen's Land and likely to go unpunished. 'It was in fact all the punishment which we had the power, but not all that we had the will to inflict.' If Gellibrand feels handicapped by the lack of law and order, he remains optimistic about the future of what will become Melbourne. In early 1836 anything seems possible – the settlement, he writes, could 'render this in a few years one of the most important colonies under the British crown'.

And in William Buckley he believes they have a man to help make it happen.

—

Funny how men can look at the same thing and come away with such different conclusions. When Gellibrand looks at you, he sees a large tool to be used, a key that can help unlock millions of acres of grazing lands without staining it red by going to war with the natives.

But other men see you so differently. George Russell is one of them. Scottish born, he arrives in Port Phillip as yet another prospective grazier. He first sees you on the banks of the Yarra as his boat pulls in. He is not in the best of moods. The schooner *Hetty*, which carried Russell and 800 of his sheep across Bass Strait, began taking on water in the bay after its inexperienced skipper beached it the day before. The sheep were landed and Russell has now made his way to the settlement in a small boat. He has already heard plenty about the wild white man and will be one of many to repeat a suspicion that is probably started by Fawkner – that you murdered and ate your fellow convicts after escaping from Sullivan Bay.

'Buckley . . . and a few blackfellows were keeping up a conversation with others on the opposite side, talking at the pitch of their voices in the native language . . . he was a tall, ungainly-looking man, about six feet four inches in height. His looks altogether were not in his favour. He had a shaggy head of black hair, a low forehead, shaggy overhanging eyebrows which nearly concealed his small eyes, a short snub nose, and his face very much marked by small pox.'

Russell says this many years later. Fair to say he is unimpressed. In fact, he concludes that you are 'such a man as one would suppose fit to commit a burglary or a murder . . . he was a very ignorant, uneducated man. The government expected that he might be useful in reconciling the native population to the settlers; but he was indolent and never did much in that way.'

Now why would George Russell say that? He has very little to do with you, apart from one quick exchange where, walking past Batman's house, he sees you putting together its brick chimney: 'He seemed to be very well pleased with his work and asked me if I did not think it was pretty good work for a man who had lived thirty years with the blacks.'

But there's always a reason – a motive that is never far from the surface. Russell knows you lived with the Wadawurrung for all those years and he is going to take a dim view of those people once he settles just outside Geelong. 'The natives as a class were very deceitful, and very little reliance could be placed in them,' he will say in his memoirs. Russell is one of those men who see the Aboriginals as little more than a nuisance, people with no real relationship to land that really belongs to grazing animals. His organisation – the Clyde Company, a rival of the Port Phillip Association – does not even bother with meaningless treaties like the one offered by Batman. In fact Russell will join several groups in the years to come, hunting down clans who have stolen sheep or property belonging to the Company.

That rumour that does the rounds about how Buckley gave land to William Robertson? George Russell, a rival of Robertson, is the man who spreads it. And that, William Buckley, is how this world works.

27

THE WORD OF GOD

It is not often that a man has his prayers answered, much less feels God's guiding hand on his shoulder. But Henry Reed is blessed like that. He is only 25 and everything he touches seems to turn to gold. He is already building an impressive property and business portfolio and he knows all the right people. In Launceston he has become friends with John Batman, so close he stands as witness to the man's marriage to Eliza in St John's church. But not even Batman, that crafty and resilient bushman, can help Henry Reed right now. Someone – some *thing* – far more powerful is required.

It is the Year of Our Lord, 1831. Reed is on board the *Bombay* on a quick journey home to England when one of those truly biblical storms comes out of nowhere, whipping the sea into a maelstrom. Wind and rain lash the deck. The ship is tossed from the peak of one wave to the next. Reed is certain his time has come, that the next crashing sound he hears will be the *Bombay* exploding into splinters and taking all her passengers down into the black cold depths of the Atlantic.

And then all is quiet. Reed is not being washed away – it's his fears and doubts that are draining from his body. Calmness has taken hold of him. It can be only one thing – *the hand of God!* – and suddenly Henry Reed understands why, as he counted his money at the end of each day back in Launceston, there had been 'an aching heart in the midst of prosperity, and with all the world could do for me my soul was not satisfied'.

The storm, exhausted by all that fury, disappears as quickly as it arrived and Reed looks to the sky and gives thanks: 'I saw all the mercies and deliverances of God; and when I saw them how astonished I was at the ingratitude of the wretch who had been watched over by that loving God and not even thanked him!

'. . . I was conscious that I had hold of God and that God had hold of me.'

Reed returns to Launceston and while he will lose none of his business skills, his life will now be devoted to spreading the Lord's words. And so in late 1835 he decides to head to Port Phillip to see how his friend Batman's little settlement is faring (he has loaned Batman 3000 pounds for the venture) and, most importantly, spread the word of God among the heathen natives.

He finds this sorry excuse for a colony – just three shabby sod huts – sorely lacking in enlightenment. Each morning he preaches and sings and celebrates the work of the one true Being who had so graciously saved his life four years earlier.

'The congregation had in it William Buckley, the escaped convict who had been living in a state of wilderness and barbarism with the natives for over thirty years, the brother of Mr John Batman, and three natives from Sydney who but imperfectly understood the English language. I had prayers in the hut with these five men every day, read the scriptures, expounding to them the Word of Life, and telling them of the love of God for poor sinners . . .'

After that Reed heads out with the natives. 'The Yarra Yarra tribe "corroboried" to me, and alone I accompanied them up the river and lived with them. Having gained all the information I required I returned to Launceston, the Lord having mercifully preserved me whilst living with them in the wilderness.'

Reed's visit is just the first of what will become a worn trail of preachers and moralisers making their way to Port Phillip. You meet them all, don't you, all of them spellbound by your 30-year journey among the 'savages'. A spirited revival of evangelicalism began in London at the start of the 1830s and now its doctrine of salvation is being spread to the outer reaches of the Empire. These men of God have many questions for you but one keeps recurring. What did you do to lift these heathens out of their savage ways? Did you not teach them there is only one true God? You always have the same answer, mumbling about your own personal safety. Truth is, you were baptised in that bulging little church back in Siddington and like everyone else you no doubt believed in God. But . . . well, hard to imagine anyone, let alone a man who dispenses words the way Johnny Fawkner bestows compliments, standing in front of a Wadawurrung clan explaining the mysterious ways in which God moves.

The Reverend Joseph Rennard Orton is the next of the Lord's helpers who makes his way to you. He is a Wesleyan missionary who epitomises the Empire's new anti-slavery stance and its determination to Christianise the world. In the 1820s he had been posted to Jamaica where he quickly grew appalled at the treatment of the plantation slaves. He had watched helplessly, his indignation rising, as slaves were whipped for petty offences and forced to work 18–20 hour days. Many had been left so disabled that, according to Orton, they were left with 'bodies almost eaten up by disease – so sorely affected with scorbutic humours that in some instances their limbs were literally rotting from their bodies'.

Slavery was anathema to the civilised man; not only was it physically repulsive but it 'corrupted the morals, induced idleness, theft, debauchery and duplicity; all of which strongly character-ised the negro slave, particularly petty theft . . . it being difficult to convince a slave that there was any moral evil in taking his master's provisions'.

Orton and another missionary were charged 'with seducing the negroes into dangerous notions of the rights of men' and thrown into a fetid prison cell for 10 days. He barely slept, kept awake at night by 'barbarities beyond description'. The experience left him shaken and physically he would never be the same again. Appointed to run the church's outpost in Van Diemen's Land and to also take responsibility for Port Phillip, he makes the journey across Bass Strait – and you are one of the first he meets. Orton does not fall prey to the pre-conceptions held by so many others. He senses something different, something deeper in this Wild White Man he has heard so much about.

'He is a man of thought and shrewdness,' Orton will say in a report to the Wesleyan Missionary Society in August 1836, 'a proof of which he has exhibited in the policy he has adopted with the natives – particularly in carefully avoiding to mix in any of their party feuds, by which means he has kept on terms of friendship with all . . .'

Yet Orton is perplexed. He finds you very willing to listen to religious instruction 'and sometimes flattered myself that he was under the influence of good impressions'.

There you go again. Gruff old William, always giving these civilised white men what they want. Well, up to a point.

'He informed me that during the whole period of his heathenish sojourning he never forgot to acknowledge one Supreme Being, upon whom he daily depended . . . and yet, strange to say, I cannot learn that he used the least effort to instruct the natives but descended and conformed to all their barbarous habits without endeavouring to raise them in any degree.'

It's not as though Orton does not try to discover if the Aboriginals believe in a God. He uses the 'minutest observation' and 'strictest inquiry' but cannot detect a sliver of evidence to support any belief in a Supreme Being. But he does discover that 'since Europeans have settled among them they seem to have imbibed the ludicrous notion that the white people are their ancestors returned to them – and that after they die they will 'jump up white man'.

Orton is a man who knows what it is to sacrifice oneself for the good of the Lord. He can only explain your unwillingness to try and convert the Wadawurrung down to one thing – 'his incompetency to convey instruction (for he is totally uneducated), his inertness of disposition and the policy he deemed prudent to adopt. His admissions are that it would have been useless and might have endangered his personal safety.'

He grills you, of course, on the subject of cannibalism and 'though evidently unwilling to disclose such deeds of darkness, yet in several conversations which I had with him he most distinctly asserted the awful fact'.

Orton is the first minister to conduct a formal church service in the new colony. More than 100 Aboriginals attend and Orton begins to read from the book of John with more than a little apprehension 'lest our devotions would be interrupted by their noise and restlessness, for they are usually exceedingly loquacious and in their social intercourse maintain a constant jabber and confusion'. But it goes off without a hitch, the Aboriginals sitting quietly and at one stage are 'struck with silent admiration' when a hymn is sung.

Orton is reminded of his time in Jamaica 'but with this appalling drawback – that these poor creatures were totally ignorant of and not able to receive the proper truth which I was endeavouring to explain. The mingled feelings of pitiful commiseration and compassionate desire which were wrought in my breast are not to be described.'

It is not hard to picture you there, a quiet smile forming beneath that beard of yours as Orton does his best to convey God's word to the Aboriginal people. How many times have you seen this since that day you walked out of the bush? How many well-meaning white people have you come across who simply don't even know where to start when it comes to trying to fathom the rich and complex culture it took you more than 30 years to appreciate?

—

Henry Reed. Joseph Orton. Next to take his turn is another missionary, George Langhorne, sent by NSW Governor Sir Richard Bourke to establish a government-sponsored mission to protect the Aboriginals. Langhorne has a lengthy meeting with you and does his best to record what you tell him about your experiences while living among the Wadawurrung. But it is a difficult exercise, one that Langhorne labels 'extremely irksome' because he finds your command of English still limited. Is that why he calls you 'James' instead of William?

It's easy to assume that you have decided to be difficult and are growing tired of these men. It is about 18 months since you met Batman's party at Indented Head and almost everyone who has had something to do with you has said how quickly you regained the English language. But there is no disguising your disenchantment with the way things have turned out; the mischief-making of Johnny Fawkner, the illness that is now consuming Batman, the ongoing loss of your people's lands and the sheer rudeness and arrogance of so many of these white pastoralists.

Langhorne finds a man who 'appeared to me always discontented and dissatisfied and I believe it would have been a great relief to him had the settlement been abandoned and [he] left alone with his sable friends'.

Certainly, the story you tell him is similar to the one John Morgan will publish with you in 1852. There are some inconsistencies – you say you used a boat as part of your escape from Sullivan Bay (and of course you fib to him about ever living with an Aboriginal woman). But most discrepancies can be put down to language difficulties, your disgruntled mood and the unreliability of Langhorne's memory and notes.

For 30 years you always had a place to escape to when the fighting and talk became all too much. You could head straight to the coast, down to the Karaaf with your little hut with its endless supply of fish and solitude.

But here in Port Phillip there is nowhere to go, no way to escape from people like . . . John Hepburn.

Hepburn is typical of those white men descending on the country of the Kulin nation. He is a former seaman whose business running a steamer between Sydney and the Hunter has gone belly-up. He has joined a party of would-be pastoralists who set out on an arduous overland expedition from New South Wales to Port Phillip. It takes Hepburn a while before his sea legs leave him; eight miles into the journey he had tumbled off his horse to the amusement of his fellow travellers, a mishap that set the tone for the rest of the trip.

It takes the party more than six weeks before they reach the settlement and, tired and saddle-sore, they are far from impressed. The Promised Land has no accommodation for weary travellers and is nothing but a motley collection of huts – 'slabs stuck in the ground, forming a roof and covered with earth'.

So who is the first man he sees? He could have stumbled into Fawkner's hut and spent hours being regaled with stories about how little Johnny has founded this . . . err . . . thriving metropolis. But no, the first person he meets is William Buckley.

Hoping to extract information about available grazing land in the district, Hepburn asks you where his group might go to snatch themselves some of this precious ground that is now the talk of the entire country.

It isn't hard to picture his face as you quickly roll out a succession of monosyllabic answers. That simpleton routine works just like a charm.

'I found him what he had been represented,' Hepburn will say about you years later, 'a very stupid fellow not possessed of any knowledge of the country.'

Say what you like about William Buckley, Mr Hepburn, but is it possible to say something nice?

'Before taking leave of Buckley I may be allowed to observe that all writers on this to-be-a-great empire have lost sight of this man, who laid the foundation stone (if it may be considered so) of this interesting colony. Buckley built chimneys of bricks imported from Van Diemen's Land, for Mr Batman. This I consider constituted the foundation of the capital of Victoria, which seems to have been entirely lost sight of, but never less is true.'

MURDER MOST FOUL; BLOODTHIRSTY REVENGE; VICIOUS CALUMNY

Promises, promises. These white men have made a lot of them in the past few months. They keep saying they don't want a war with the black man and will do their best to protect them. Batman, Gellibrand, Wedge and the others – all insistent that white man's justice will apply equally. Well, here's a chance for them to live up to those words, an opportunity for you, William, to take their measure.

You heard a rumour a couple of weeks ago that bark strippers in Western Port, almost 50 miles south-west of Port Phillip, had been up to their usual mischief and had attacked a group of Aboriginals. You alerted Wedge and sent word for the wounded to be brought to the Yarra. Here they are now, limping into the settlement. The parents of one teenage girl have carried their daughter on their backs the entire way. John Wedge is shocked – given his past he may well be overacting a tad – and picks up his quill to send a letter to the authorities in Hobart Town.

'It appears the natives were fired upon soon after sunrise whilst lying in their huts and one young girl about 13 years of age, was wounded in both her thighs, the ball passing through one into the other, grazing the bone in its passage . . . her parents were obliged to carry her on their backs . . . and it is apprehended that she will not recover the use of her legs.

'To rescue this poor girl the mother took her in her arms and in carrying her away was fired at and wounded in the arm and shoulder with buckshot. Notwithstanding this inhuman attack the natives persisted in removing the girl and two more of them, a girl and a boy, also received wounds.'

Outrages like this are nothing new. Isn't this one of the reasons why you avoided places like Western Port and the land around Portland? The year before Batman made his way into Port Phillip, a group of Portland-based whalers went to war with the Kilcarer gundidj clan of the Gunditjmara people. It will take years before the details emerge and how a dispute over a beached whale turned into a gruesome massacre. The Gunditjmara will say only two men of the Kilcarer gundidj survived. Several white historians will estimate the death toll at anywhere between 60 and 200 in what will become known as the Convincing Ground massacre. According to George Augustus Robinson, who becomes the Chief Protector of Aboriginals in the Port Phillip District at the start of the 1840s, 'the circumstances are that a whale had come on shore and the natives who fed on the carcass claimed it was their own. The whalers said they would "convince them" and had recourse to firearms . . .'

Wedge fears that more incidents could see conflict escalate: 'Unless some measures be adopted to protect the natives a spirit of hostility will be created against the whites, which in all probability will lead to a state of warfare between them and the Aborigines, which will only terminate when the black man will cease to exist.'

New South Wales Governor Richard Bourke issues a proclamation warning that anyone 'guilty of any outrages' against the Aboriginals will be brought to trial in the Supreme Court. He dispatches the police magistrate of Campbelltown, George Stewart, to Port Phillip to investigate and while Stewart does not venture down to Western Port, he reports back to Sydney that the whalers responsible for the attack have already left.

Stewart does not venture down to Western Port. What sort of investigator is this man? All this talk about justice and the man does not even visit the scene of the crime? Could you picture the same happening if we reverse the situation and it is whites who are attacked? Well, you won't have to wait for very long.

—

Charles Franks is a man of 'strict integrity' and 'gentlemanly deportment' who has joined this flood of sheep farmers descending on Port Phillip. It is early July 1836 when Franks and his shepherd are found dead near Mt Cottrell, 20 miles west of Melbourne, the rear of their heads struck so violently with a tomahawk their skulls have been pushed into the earth.

Franks is the first free settler to die at the hand of Aborigines. News of his murder spreads quickly. A real gentleman, a figure who commanded enormous respect throughout the northern half of Van Diemen's Land, dead at the hands of ruthless savages? A meeting is hastily convened at the settlement and a party of men, including several of John Batman's Sydney Aborigines, mount their horses and head out to find the perpetrators and exact revenge.

In Launceston, William Lushington Goodwin cannot contain his outrage. On 30 July the *Cornwall Chronicle* unleashes a tirade strident even by its standards. 'We learn that a party of settlers assisted by the Sydney natives . . . started in quest of the murderers, whom they were fortunate to fall in with at no great distance from where the bloody deeds were perpetrated.

'Many of them were clothed in the articles of dress they had plundered from their victims. A quantity of provisions and other stores were, likewise, in their possession, which left no doubt as to their identity. The avenging party fell upon the guilty about daylight in the morning, having watched them the previous night and, putting into effect a preconceived plan of attack, succeeded in ANNIHILATING THEM.'

Is this not the sort of ruthless, strong-arm tactic of which Goodwin fully approves? He writes that the offending tribe are a particularly treacherous people, despised by the rest of Port Phillip's Aboriginals and can now be presumed to have been 'swept from the face of the earth'.

'In the death of Mr Franks the colony has to deplore the loss of one of its brightest ornaments . . . his docile and compassionate disposition insured to him the respect and esteem of every one who enjoyed his acquaintance. The "ANNIHILATION" of the whole body of Port Phillip natives, in our opinion, would afford an insufficient revenge for the murder of such a man.'

Swept aside are any suspicions that Franks was antagonistic toward the Kulin people; that he hated sharing food with them and despised the way other settlers in the area put up with their thieving and begging. Another settler, Robert Von Stieglitz, will remember how Franks shared some lead with him to help devise a few little 'blue pills' (bullets) to keep the nuisances away.

Trifling details, are they not? The important thing to men like Goodwin is the swift action and retribution carried out to avenge the two men's deaths. In the same issue as the *Cornwall Chronicle*'s breathless report on the murder of Franks, Goodwin also publishes a letter to the editor. It is worth examining this letter closely because it exposes a campaign that has already begun to undermine you.

The letter coincides, not surprisingly, with the return to Launceston of John Pascoe Fawkner, who is on his way to Hobart Town for that show-and-tell session with his Aboriginal friend Derrimut. The letter is unsigned but it reeks of little Johnny. All those nice words he had to say about you at the start of this year are now history. It only took a few weeks for him to start sowing seeds of distrust. In February he recorded a dispute about possum skins, writing that he believed Henry Batman had been using you to stop the Aboriginals from trading with Fawkner and his men. 'I find him [Buckley] forbidding the natives to sell us any skins or birds,' Fawkner had written. 'He wants them all himself.'

This letter in the *Chronicle* announces that the author has 'just arrived from Port Phillip' and throws a quick punch at the Port Phillip Association: 'Mr Franks had only a few days previous to the dreadful occurrence removed his sheep to the river Ax, being desirous not to encroach on the land claimed by what is called the "Company" who, by the bye, have no more claims to the land than you and I.'

Jab.

Who else but Fawkner could manage to find a way to link the unfortunate murder of a man to the massive amount of land holdings enjoyed by John Batman and his associates?

'Mr Franks received one blow on the right temple with the back part of a tomahawk, the side back part of the skull presented two large cuts which must have caused instant death . . . The head of his shepherd was so dreadfully shattered that his brains had to be buried on the spot. Their tent was plundered of all provisions, blankets and firearms and their bodies conveyed to the settlement where coffins were prepared for them.'

Gasp.

But what follows is just as sinister.

'I must take upon myself here to observe the disgraceful conduct of the monster Buckley: when the bodies of Mr Franks and his man were brought to the settlement he objected to them being placed in his hut; he did not attend the funeral and was observed, as it passed, laughing at the truly melancholic procession.'

William Buckley is at the heart of it all!

'He did not assist the parties who immediately had gone out in search of the murderers and it is generally believed by his best friends, namely the "Company", that he is at the bottom of all the mischief that has taken place in the new colony and, unless he is speedily removed, I very much dread the results, he having already threatened to join the natives. It is to be lamented that the progress of colonisation in so fine a country, one so well adapted for sheep and cattle grazing, should be checked in its growth by the conduct of one man who is more savage than the Aborigines with whom he has lived and associated for thirty years.'

What do you have to say for yourself? In your book with John Morgan you will only note that 'an affray had taken place between the natives and some of the settlers, in which two of the latter were killed. I know nothing of the circumstances, as the affair occurred more than twenty miles from the settlement . . .'

It's entirely possible you laughed – or at least smirked – when the coffins of Franks and his servant passed by your hut. There are others who will say they heard you chuckling, standing there next to John Batman's smithy as the cortege passed you by. These people fear you, fear what you are capable of unleashing. An erroneous newspaper report is about to appear in Van Diemen's Land saying you have already taken to the bush and are busy organising a resistance movement. This report will be quickly quashed but it does tell us about the concerns in Port Phillip about your allegiances. One of the old settlers will quote Gellibrand as saying you told him you would prefer to go back to the Wadawurrung: 'He said it was the white people's fault. This latter part I heard Mr Gellibrand say myself – they thought he might go back to them; then, what mischief he could do.'

Did you laugh as Franks' body passed by, or were you being sarcastic as you contemplated all the hollow promises and talk about swift justice? It is now a year since you walked into Batman's camp at Indented Head and all those early hopes you had are disappearing. Fawkner's poison is clearly beginning to affect others. First impressions are always important and for any visitor or prospective settler arriving in Port Phillip, they are often gained by the first person who meets them off the boat. And who is often the first man waiting with open arms to welcome them? Indefatigable, tireless little Johnny, that's who.

—

Henry Hawson must have stepped from his boat on the Yarra and had Fawkner's arms lovingly wrapped around him – that is, unless little

Johnny was checking the man's waistcoat pockets for loose change. Hawson is yet another of these pioneering types who wants to see the land for himself. He has come all the way from Newfoundland, a large island off the Canadian east coast, and has heard the new colonies of New Holland offer a magnificent return on investment. But he quickly decides Port Phillip is not for him; the land is lush and a man could probably make a fortune with sheep and cattle. But there is great uncertainty over whether NSW Governor Richard Bourke will send police or even a military force to give it some decent law and order. And besides, the way the land is being seized from its traditional owners leaves him feeling almost . . . queasy.

Hawson will write a lengthy letter to a former colleague in Newfoundland as his ship sails out of Port Phillip Bay. The consequence of no law enforcement, he writes, is that 'some of the stock keepers have committed offences against the blacks, who have retaliated by killing . . . settlers – a prelude, I fear, to constant war between the parties, until the blacks shall be exterminated, or driven far into the interior, a most horrible alternative.'

A hastily installed form of government might convince the natives that any outrages committed against them were actions by unauthorised individuals, suggests Hawson. Only then would they gain confidence that they could find some form of protection.

But alas, writes Hawson, there is the problem of this man Buckley. Hawson tells his colleague that Buckley was granted a free pardon on the basis that he would use his influence among the natives 'to preserve a good understanding between them and the whites – this he agreed to; but the supreme authority refused to sanction the compact and he has consequently stirred them up to avenge the wrongs which he supposes himself to have sustained.

'He is now their leader and possesses uncontrolled authority over the tribe; it is said that he has several wives of the native women and a great number of children by them.'

There it is again – more misinformation and outright lies. William Buckley angry and bitter over not receiving his pardon? You have it.

You have seen it. Why, earlier this year the King made it official and God knows the number of men you have boasted to about finally being a free man.

Hawson's letter is a sombre one and he raises issues few potential settlers at Port Phillip are even contemplating. 'I fear that these occurrences will prevent my settling in this delightful country,' he writes. 'Can it be reconciled to the principles of the Christian religion, of common sense, or of any system of morals – that foreigners can take possession of the land of others . . . by murdering and exterminating the natives . . . I should feel like an accessory to murder and a receiver of stolen goods.'

It is highly possible you will never learn of Hawson's views – or even hear about that anonymous letter in Goodwin's *Cornwall Chronicle*. But you do know that there are forces moving against you. Still, even if half of what they say about you is true, why would the British government offer you a job?

29

DEATH, BUT NO JUSTICE

William Buckley, employee of His Majesty's Government. Seven simple words – but who would ever have imagined them forming a sentence?

Interpreter William Buckley. Reporting to the Chief Police Magistrate. Must be a little hard to keep a straight face and stifle the laughter building inside you. But that balding man sitting opposite you is serious. Captain William Lonsdale has been sent to Port Phillip as commandant and police magistrate, effectively taking charge of this lawless land. He is under orders from the British government to hire you and if you don't believe that, this is what the NSW Governor Richard Bourke has told him:

'It will be one of your most important duties to protect the Aboriginal natives of the District from any manner of wrong, and to endeavour to conciliate them by kind treatment and presents. You will continue to employ, as the medium of communication with them, the European named "Buckley" who has so long resided amongst them, allowing him the same salary as he now receives from Mr Batman and his associates.'

Turns out you and Lonsdale have much in common. He was born in the Netherlands in October 1799 – in the very week those French and Dutch forces were overwhelming you and the rest of the Duke of York's coalition army. Then, while you were off in the bush with the

Wadawurrung, he was serving with the 4th (King's Own) – your old regiment. No wonder you will always remember this day and how Lonsdale 'enquired very particularly into my history and sufferings'.

The man certainly wants you by his side. Bourke has made that clear. The Governor is under orders from London to start taking control of Port Phillip before the Fawkners and Batmans of the world turn it into a fiefdom of their own. Bourke has instructed Lonsdale that when it comes to the Aboriginals he must treat them kindly and 'maintain friendly relations with them and improve by all practical means their moral and social conditions'. Of course, they will need to understand that no matter a person's colour, everyone must obey the laws of England. But before all that, your salary needs to be arranged.

Lonsdale says your pay will be 50 pounds a year – exactly what you are currently given by Batman, as per orders. But that's not quite satisfactory, is it? You've been watching men like Batman and Fawkner over the past year and you have noticed that no-one ever accepts a first offer.

Well, thank you very much, Mr Lonsdale. It would be an honour. But surely after the work I have already performed in this settlement I should be entitled to an increase in salary? Say, 60 pounds, with rations?

Lonsdale agrees and, along with the salary increase, gives you a new horse. Much of this role will now involve travelling to outlying stations and regions around Port Phillip, trying to keep the peace and reporting back to Lonsdale on the frequent territorial disputes between settlers and Aboriginals. But the role will also require helping to find a site for new barracks and a storehouse. Doesn't take long for you to get to work. Many of the local Aboriginals have been wary of going anywhere near the 30 red-coated marines who arrived on the warship *Rattlesnake* with Lonsdale. But Interpreter William Buckley soon has them hauling loads of building materials to various sites around the settlement, rewarding them each 'with boiled meat and biscuit; and this sort of employ they followed with great cheerfulness'.

Your life is settling down. In a few weeks a census of sorts will be carried out in the settlement so Lonsdale can understand the numbers. Among those surveyed is a 'Buckley, William. Arrived: 1803. No. of horses: 2. Residence: Wattle and shingle. Under cultivation: 1 acre, garden.'

—

These, however, are not times for peace and tranquillity. Barely a week after your meeting with Lonsdale comes word that one of the most prominent Wadawurrung men, Woolmudgin – head of the Wadawaurrung balug clan who took you in all those years ago – has been tied to a tree, shot at close range and his body dumped in the Barwon River near Geelong. Despite everything you have seen this news must come as a shock. You knew Woolmudgin and his people for many years. The man is an *arweet* whose reputation extends far beyond Wadawurrung land. He was one of the first Aboriginal leaders to meet with Batman's group of men at the depot in Indented Head.

Lonsdale dispatches you and two constables to investigate and apprehend John Whitehead, a convict shepherd alleged to have murdered Woolmudgin. Whitehead works for a local station manager with ties to the Port Phillip Association, Frederick Taylor, and what a cruel piece of work Taylor turns out to be. He is already earning a reputation as a notorious hater of blacks. It was Taylor who had seized Woolmudgin and tied him to the tree, claiming the man had threatened a local worker with a tomahawk. Taylor will say he left the roped-up Woolmudgin under the supervision of Whitehead while he went off to notify the authorities about the Aboriginal man's capture. But Taylor is being disingenuous. Why would a shepherd open fire on a tied-up man unless his boss had given him the order? Everyone will suspect Taylor urged Whitehead to shoot Woolmudgin. Lonsdale will write that he 'entertained a strong suspicion that he had given strong encouragement to the prisoner [Whitehead] to commit the murder'.

Can you taste that sourness again? Can you swallow a little more of white man's justice?

Whitehead is sent to Sydney for trial but is acquitted because of a lack of evidence – and witnesses. Where is Taylor, the key witness?

Why, he jumped on the first boat that would take him to Van Diemen's Land.

But he'll be back. Three years later Taylor will lead an assault on the Tarnbeere gundidj clan of the Djargurd Wurrung people at Mt Emu Creek, near modern-day Camperdown. It will become known as the Murdering Gully massacre, a brutal and indiscriminate slaughter of more than 35 men, women and children. Armed and on horseback, Taylor and a posse of shepherds approach a gully containing an Aboriginal camp near the dormant volcano of Mt Noorat. Within minutes dozens are dead, their bodies ripped apart by musket fire. While a handful of survivors make it to a local church mission to report the crime, Taylor and others dispose of the bodies by burning some and dumping others in local water holes. As word spreads of the massacre and authorities begin to investigate, Taylor employs his usual modus operandi after committing an outrage – he jumps on an American whaling ship and makes his way to India.

The man is untouchable, even if every damn thing he touches is left blood-stained and in pain. He will return to Victoria within a few years, this time leading a band of pastoralists into the Gippsland region where massacres of the Gunai people will take place. Teams of imported coolie labourers will desert Taylor because he treats them so harshly.

This is the point, William, where we are supposed to bring a smile to your face and tell you how Taylor, having spent time in India, discovers there is truly such a thing as karma. That what goes around, comes around, that eventually the strongest warriors from a local clan creep into his home one night, take him into the bush and dispatch him upstairs to be judged by his own God.

But you know it doesn't happen like that. You've already seen how white man's justice works in this new frontier. Frederick Taylor will reach a respectable age for the era, dying at home in his mansion, a wealthy 62-year-old who spends years laundering his reputation to the point where the local papers say he passed away 'an old and respected colonist'.

That, really, is white man's justice. The well-intentioned Governor in New South Wales, that well-intentioned boss of yours, William Lonsdale, and all those well-disposed preachers . . . ultimately all of their words don't mean that much. Nice intentions. But the only real intention at work here is to make a profit.

—

Well, here's something else that won't surprise you. The Year of Our Lord, 1837, begins in the new settlement with little Johnny Fawkner getting into another fight. On New Year's Eve he gets into a stoush with one of Lonsdale's marines, private James Duckworth, over a pig Duckworth has caught and taken to a nearby tent.

When the charge is heard in court on 3 January, Duckworth says he was on his knees 'endeavouring to secure the pig' when Fawkner appeared and 'shoved me down having previously seized me by the collar of my jacket. I told him I would kick his backside away if he did not go about his business. He said he had as much business there as I had as the ground was his and he would have the tent pulled down. I then put my threat into effect and kicked him, as besides having collared me and shoved me down he made me lose the pig I had in my charge . . . he then ran about a dozen yards, picked up a stone and hit me on the head with it which cut me in two places.'

Fawkner is fined four pounds and costs are also awarded against him. Later in the year a charge of assaulting one of his servants, allegedly drunk at the time, will be dismissed. And then he gets into a fight with John Moss – a rival publican – the pair grappling in the dirt because Fawkner objects to Moss guiding a horse carting a load of earth through one of his allotments.

It's a never-ending list, Fawkner the offender and Fawkner the offended against. A year later he will be fined 10 shillings for assaulting John Batman's storeman, William Willoughby, in a dispute over money.

The power and influence of the Port Phillip Association is already beginning to fray; all the hopes and dreams of those first 12 months have already been dashed by a decree from London and Sydney that they are nothing more than squatters on Crown land; eventually the British government will pay the Association 7000 pounds as 'compensation' for their attempts to form the first real settlement in the area.

By then the mythic qualities of John Batman – Bonwick's 'man of nerve . . . powerful frame and daring courage . . .' – will have also faded. The strength in his legs is vanishing and his nose is being eaten away by that syphilis raging through his body. At the funeral of Charles Franks six months earlier, Fawkner had watched his rival struggle to walk up the small hill to the cemetery.

Batman will soon begin to hide his disfigurement by draping a handkerchief over his face. The illness will weaken him to the point where the once 'virile and adept' bushman will be reduced to a pathetic sight, relying on his Sydney Aboriginals to drag him about in a make-shift perambulator whenever he has to make a public appearance.

But Batman is not just hurting physically. Remember that curse we mentioned hanging over the Batman name? How William Todd will die in a macabre way in hospital trying to swallow his shirt? Batman's wife Eliza, perhaps finding her husband's deteriorating condition distasteful, has begun an affair with that storeman William Willoughby. And then she will suddenly leave on her own for England, returning in late 1839 to discover Batman has died and left just five pounds for her in his will.

Nothing seems to end well. The year before his brother's death, Henry Batman will be sacked as a police constable for taking a bribe. Yes, only in Port Phillip could a man like good ol' rum-swilling Henry become a police officer.

And then, in 1845, Batman's only son, John Charles, will drown in the Yarra River while fishing. Eliza, who by now has married William Willoughby, writes to one of her daughters to inform her of the loss and includes a locket of her son's hair 'which I cut off myself before he was put in his coffin . . .

'Every effort was made to get the body, but to no purpose till next morning when several of the blacks dived in different parts of the river and were successful in finding him. Oh, my dear child, had you but seen him you would never have forgotten his countenance: no person would have thought he was dead, he looked as if he were in a quiet sleep with a heavenly smile on his sweet face . . .'

The funeral brings the settlement – now the town of Melbourne – to a sombre halt. Even Batman's fiercest rivals cannot help but be moved by the occasion and the loss. More than 150 flower-carrying children follow John junior's hearse toward the cemetery before his coffin is lowered into place, just above the casket containing his father.

Not even Eliza, a woman so accustomed to being on the run, can escape the curse. Unlike her son she will not leave this world in such an unblemished way. Seven years after the drowning of John junior, the body of a female 'of rather abandoned character' will be found in an old home in Geelong, beaten almost beyond recognition. The victim, 'Sarah Willoughby', will eventually be identified as 'Eliza Callaghan'. By then the name Batman will have faded from view and little Johnny Fawkner will have proven himself to be the most stubborn bastard of them all.

30

ENOUGH IS ENOUGH

A Sunday morning in early March 1837 and it is time for the good reverend to tend to his flock. What a flock it is, the greatest gathering of important people the settlement has seen. NSW Governor Richard Bourke is here, along with the rest of the senior crew of HMS *Rattlesnake*, which has just arrived from Sydney. Also pressed into this small weatherboard building is William Lonsdale and a group of soldiers. Someone has ordered a gang of convicts to fill the spaces and make sure it is standing room only. And of course, who can miss the towering figure of William Buckley?

Governor Bourke is about to make another adept career move, officially naming the settlement Melbourne, after Lord Melbourne, the current British Prime Minister, William Lamb. It is time for the Empire to officially seize this land from the likes of Batman and Fawkner.

Bourke's face has a large and vicious scar along his jawline. Another veteran of that ill-fated campaign against the French in Holland in 1799, Bourke was shot through the jaw, and while the skin and muscle eventually healed, it still gives him pain and affects his speech.

The Reverend George Langhorne looks out at the crowd and prepares to speak. Bourke has sent him to Melbourne to establish a government mission for the Aboriginals. The Governor has a favourite theory he wants proven. Take all your lower-class whites – you know, the convicts and servants and the rest of the great unwashed – and get them together with the Aboriginals. Before long you will have a new race and all those problems both creeds constantly create . . . why, they will disappear, replaced by a new breed of more civilised men.

Langhorne isn't too sure about this idea. But Bourke is the Governor, after all, and the man who has sent him to help protect the Indigenous people. There is already a dispute going on about where this mission should be located. Some want it close to Melbourne. Langhorne presses for it to be established down at Western Port, perhaps on French Island.

'Such nonsense, young man,' Bourke will tell him. 'You will have your throat cut.'

Langhorne opens his Bible and looks up. Pressed against the windows of this makeshift church are more than a hundred black faces, staring in at this strange gathering of white fellas. Just a day or so earlier, *Interpreter William Buckley* had made sure Bourke's arrival in Melbourne was accorded the appropriate pomp. All those natives, lined up in neat, orderly rows with no idea the man they were greeting had issued a decree 18 months earlier that effectively wiped away any notions they were the traditional owners of the land. It was Bourke who had introduced the concept of *terra nullius* – in large part to stymie the plans of the Port Phillip Association. But his proclamation in October 1835 – that Australia belonged to no-one until the British Crown seized it – would resonate for almost two centuries.

One of those travelling with Bourke, Captain Phillip Parker King, will write that a 'small tribe of natives, headed by Buckley, were drawn up on the road side, who stared with all their eyes at the "Gubernoz". Compared to Buckley they appeared to be of diminutive size, but are fine looking men, and by no means so short, for Buckley measured 6ft 6in. He acts now as interpreter for the commandant and is a very useful person in that capacity.'

So how appropriate is it that Langhorne should look out at what he will later recall as his 'motley congregation' and turn to

Luke, 15:3–7. It's the parable of the sheep, one of the most memorable passages in the good book. What other lesson could Langhorne choose? The sheep is the only reason why everyone is crammed into this makeshift church.

Langhorne begins his reading and tells them how Jesus had turned to his followers and asked them: 'Which of you men, if you had one hundred sheep, and lost one of them, wouldn't leave the 99 in the wilderness, and go after the one that was lost, until he found it?'

Langhorne stares at his flock. He has their attention. 'When he has found it, he carries it on his shoulders, rejoicing. When he comes home, he calls together his friends, his family and his neighbors, saying to them, "Rejoice with me, for I have found my sheep which was lost!" I tell you that even so there will be more joy in heaven over one sinner who repents, than over 99 righteous people who need no repentance.'

Every time Langhorne glances at his audience he sees you looking miserable and downcast. 'Often as I glanced at his desponding countenance, contrasted with the excitement and glee manifested in the faces of his former sable companions at the windows, I would have given something to have read his thoughts and theirs.'

Sermon over, the crowd shuffles from the church. You follow Langhorne out of the door and pull him aside. You want to discuss that passage from the Book of Luke.

'I could not help thinking,' you say to Langhorne, 'I was so like that lost sheep in the wilderness.'

—

You're not the only one. As you unburden yourself to the reverend there are growing fears for the safety of one of the most important men to have helped found this settlement.

Joseph Gellibrand had landed in Geelong in late February with his friend, the solicitor George Hesse, and the two had set out to inspect a new sheep station before heading to Werribee and on to Port Phillip a week later for Governor Bourke's arrival. According to their stockman, William Akers, they have missed a crucial river junction and continued riding west into largely uncharted territory. Gellibrand, the notoriously hopeless bushman with no sense of direction, had insisted they continue west but Akers, now fearing for his safety, had refused to go any further and left the pair to find their own way to Melbourne.

Bourke will delay his departure for Sydney for a couple of days, hoping to meet Gellibrand. In the meantime, having overseen the drawing up of street plans for new Melbourne, Bourke heads out for a tour of the country and, of course, he takes Interpreter William Buckley as part of his expeditionary force. In Geelong the party will travel down the Barwon River and visit Buckley's Cave and Buckley's Falls.

Already the legend is growing. There is plenty of time for talk as Bourke's party covers hundreds of miles. At one stage, with the party camped near Werribee, you tell the Governor your story; how you eked out a pathetic existence for those first few weeks on the run eating shellfish until you were welcomed by one of the clans who treated you with food and kindness.

Phillip Parker King, travelling with the Governor, writes: 'By degrees he [Buckley] became quite satisfied with their mode of life, clothed in an opossum skin and relishing all their "delicacies" such as grubs and raw flesh. He lived in every way as one of them. Food was always supplied to him and he took no part in procuring it. He meddled not in their quarrels or joined against the enemies of his tribe. In fact, he appears to have eaten, drunk and slept for the space of 30 years, quite happy and contented, and without much desire to alter his lot.'

By the end of March, Bourke is preparing to leave for Sydney and there is now talk that Gellibrand and Hesse must have been killed or captured by 'hostile tribes'. Two separate search parties have returned with nothing but rumours. So naturally they turn to you. Well, you're hardly going to decline. You like Gellibrand – 'his humane considerations for me will never be forgotten' – and you head out into those endless plains you know so well, taking a small group of trusted Aboriginals with you.

But you return a week later, seething with anger. You had met Gellibrand's son, Tom, who had a posse of prospective settlers from Van Diemen's Land with him as part of a search party. They had joined you, following the spoor of Gellibrand and Hesse's horses until it faded on a plain that had been recently burned. Further west you saw a native camp and 'having reason to think it was not a tribe likely to receive the white men in a friendly manner', you asked the rest of the party to remain behind.

At first the Aboriginals ran off. They had never seen a horse before, or a large white man on it wearing white man's clothing. But just as you began winning their confidence, Tom Gellibrand and his party of white men rode up, frightening the tribe.

Well, that was just about enough. Combined with the Bourke expedition you had just spent close to a month in the saddle, riding hard and putting up with the jibbering nonsense of white men who think they knew better. Back in Melbourne you go straight to Lonsdale, who in turn sends a missive to Bourke in Sydney: 'He [Buckley] met with some tribes that are not in the habit of visiting the stations. From one of them he learnt that two white men on horseback were seen passing onward to the west when the grass about there was burning . . . he says he could find no clue to discover that any murder had taken place . . .

'Now Buckley appears very much annoyed with some of the people who went out also. He says they paid more attention to see what the country was like, than to pay attention to the search.'

It never ceases to surprise you, does it . . . that potential pasture-land could be more important than the lives of two of your fellow men.

It's not the end of the matter, though. Far from it. Two men from Van Diemen's Land – Anglican preacher Joseph Naylor and his associate Charles Parsons – arrive in Port Phillip representing the families of the missing men and demanding assistance for a new search.

Go out again with idiots who know nothing about the land? You tell all this to Lonsdale and he agrees you should instead go out on your own.

But your horse needs to rest; its back is sore from carrying a giant halfway across the state. After a couple of days you are ready to resume the search for Gellibrand when an Aboriginal man rushes into your hut shouting that your horse is bleeding. John Batman is with you and both of you run outside to find the horse has been hamstrung – 'all the hind sinews of his legs having been cut through by some white, or other savage'.

If you didn't sense it before, then now you know there are forces at work that want you gone. In the meantime, Naylor and Parsons, disillusioned and angry, have departed for Geelong. They form their own search party and are joined by a war party of Wadawurrung men. Within days they have captured a man from the Colac area, Tanapia, a member of the Kolakgnat clan of the Gulidjan people and said to be an enemy of the Wadawurrung. Claiming to have extracted a confession, Naylor will report that the Wadawurrung then kill a young Aboriginal woman before turning their spears on Tanapia.

It smacks of a revenge killing and even by the standards of the time few people fully believe Naylor. You hear about it when you reach a sheep station in the area after having sailed from Melbourne to Geelong to get another horse. As far as you are concerned the search is now over. 'It was an inexcusable murder,' you will say in *Life and Adventures*, 'for there was not the least reason to believe that the poor people who had been so mercilessly sacrificed had anything to do with the death of Mr Gellibrand or Mr Hesse, neither was it known at that time whether they were dead or alive.

'This affair gave me great pain because, from my long association with the natives, I thought such destruction of life anything but creditable to my countrymen; but on the contrary, that they were atrocious acts of oppression.'

That old feeling – the need to escape, to get away – begins to return. The problem is, William, you are no longer a young man. And where will you go?

In September an opportunity to get out of town presents itself: a prisoner needs to be transported to Van Diemen's Land and Lonsdale allows you to take him to Launceston. After delivering the prisoner to the local jail you catch up with an old shipmate from the *Calcutta*. Doesn't take long for news to spread quickly that the Wild White Man is in town.

'Buckley, the Anglo-Aboriginal of Port Phillip, is on a visit to this island,' reports the *Launceston Advertiser* on 14 September. 'He is a strapping upright fellow, about six feet and a half high, and apparently none the worse for his thirty year sojourn among the savages of New Holland. We understand that he has taken to warm blankets, clothing and good diet, very kindly again.'

You have also taken kindly to this island. Convicts have been trying to escape from here for decades. It might just be the place for a former one to call home.

31

'A YET DEEPER SHADE
OF WRETCHEDNESS'

Convicts? Foster 'Flogger' Fyans knows how to deal with the bastards. It's a great mystery to him – not to mention a source of growing annoyance – why so many people are now pushing for a greater leniency toward the criminal class. It's . . . well . . . *unfathomable*. Governor Bourke is one of them – not long ago he tried to limit the number of lashes a convict could receive to 50 strokes of the cat-o'-nine-tails.

Fifty lashes? A man was only warming up by that stage. Fyans couldn't tell you how many convicts he'd had strapped to the triangle and flogged until the yard was carpeted in skin and blood. Punishment – harsh but just – was the only way to keep prisoners in check. He had tried to explain this once to a pair of touring Quaker missionaries. They had asked him about the process of whipping a man and Flogger, leaning back in his chair, no doubt a gleam in his eye, got straight to the point.

'The first lash . . . the skin rises not unlike a white frost . . . the second lash often reminds me of a snowstorm . . . the third lash . . . the back is lacerated dreadfully.'

The two missionaries groaned, glanced at one another and uttered a couple of prayers.

But Fyans wasn't finished. 'The painful feelings then subside . . . for the blood flows freely.' He then offered to have a convict flogged – God knew there was a never-ending line of them to choose from – so that these men might better judge the process and its effects.

'No . . . we thank thee,' said the missionaries, eager to find the door.

This Fyans . . . not exactly the sort of man you are likely to warm to, is he? But meet him you must. He's on the ship with you returning to Melbourne from Launceston having just been appointed the police magistrate for Geelong. As it happens both of you have served with the 4th (King's Own). But any similarities end there. You're tired and have never had any time for trumped-up little men. And Fyans will hardly have time for you, either, given your convict background. Apart from his sadism, Flogger is also a snob of the worst kind; just the sort the British Army specialises in producing.

Fyans is an Irishman who survived a cholera pandemic during his time in India and eventually moved to Sydney, where he was appointed second-in-charge of the notorious penal colony on Norfolk Island. Even by the standards of the time Norfolk was renowned for its cruelty. Convicts sent there – usually the most hardened and difficult to discipline – would often prefer suicide or hanging to serving out their time.

It was a special kind of hell, a place where nightmares played out in full daylight. A prisoner might receive 100 lashes for singing a song, 200 for defying a soldier's orders and up to eight months in solitary confinement for refusing to work. The blood-soaked grounds of the whipping yard were dried black. It was here, amid an orgy of unrestrained violence and payback, that Fyans earned his nickname.

In 1834 several hundred convicts staged a coordinated uprising. Like most rebellions of the time it was ill-conceived and within hours had been put down as Fyans – his commander restricted to bed with a timely migraine – relished the opportunity of once more wielding a sabre and gun in pitched battle.

Hunting down escapers through gardens and a field of sugar cane, Fyans' men of the 4th were as bloodthirsty as their boss. 'The men were very keen after these ruffians,' Flogger will recall years later. You can almost hear him sighing with nostalgia. 'It was really game and sport to these soldiers . . . "Come on out, my honey" – with a prick of the bayonet through both thighs or a little above.'

. . . Or a little above.

Now wouldn't that be a just punishment for rebels who could not be regarded – let alone treated – as men? Just a little stab to the nether regions. When one of the rebel ringleaders was found at the foot of a hill dying slowly from bayonet wounds, Fyans defied a doctor's request and had the man dragged back to captivity in chains – on his back and across a stony field.

The recriminations went on for months. Fyans ordered new irons for the convicts, the insides roughly chiselled to gouge ankle flesh with every movement. He paid the floggers tobacco to choose a random prisoner and tighten the ropes binding their arms until blood ran from their fingertips. And there were lashings, thousands of them, so many that the penal colony's whips began falling apart and a frustrated Flogger began questioning the quality of the men wielding them.

Having distinguished himself on Norfolk Island, Fyans was promoted to commander of the Moreton Bay settlement and had famously overseen the rescue of Eliza Fraser, one of the survivors of a ship that had been wrecked by coral on its way to Singapore. Heavily pregnant, Fraser had given birth to a baby that died just days after the wreck and had been taken in – against her will, she would claim – by an Aboriginal group for several months on what would become Fraser Island. The story of Eliza Fraser would echo for more than a century to come, burnished by myth and so many distortions until the truth of what really happened was completely obscured.

But wasn't that the problem with so much history? A man was better off worrying about his own place in it. The rescue of Fraser had taken place the year before and the only thing that mattered now was that Flogger Fyans was on his way for another adventure.

—

A couple of photographs remain of Fyans. In one, wearing a top hat that hides his bald head, his face is austere and highlighted by a long sharp nose. Later in life the lens will capture him again and that face will have filled out, leaving the nose less pronounced. But his eyes will remain the same, hard and all knowing, the look of a man who has rarely been racked with self-doubt or uncertainty.

Fyans will forge a decent reputation for himself in Geelong and throughout the western district of Victoria, acclaimed for helping the settlement gain access to fresh water. They will name streets and suburbs after him. A man of action he certainly is. But getting along with William Buckley is something beyond his abilities.

'I stared when I saw the monster of a man,' Fyans will record in memoirs that many historians will regard as self-serving and unreliable.

It is late September 1837. Lonsdale wants Fyans in the Geelong area as soon as possible and who else does he order to accompany him but the one man who knows the Wadawurrung and their land better than anyone else. According to Fyans, who wants to set out immediately on the 50-mile walk, William Buckley is 'rather sulky, wanting to put it off for a week'.

Two days later, according to Fyans, the pair of you begin the trek.

'Now for the road, Mr Buckley . . . have you no blanket?'

'Nothing.' Good old sullen William Buckley. Never been good at hiding those feelings, have you?

Fyans hands over a piece of pork and a large slice of damper.

'"What?" He said looking down on me. "Carry damper and pork? I don't care for such things. I can feed myself. You may do as you like."'

Fyans tells you carrying the food supplies will have to be shared. 'The long fellow took the charge but soon tired of it. Relieving him of this small parcel, only a few pounds of weight, before we reached the native track to Geelong . . . I found that I was to be the carrier. With great difficulty he kept up until we arrived at the Werribee River, where Mr Simpson had a sheep station. Buckley engaged himself during the night. In the morning he, if possible, was more discourteous and with difficulty I could get him on his legs.'

The next 12 miles pass in silence. Fyans is clearly intimidated but growing increasingly frustrated. By the time you reach the You Yangs, a series of rugged 300-metre-high granite ridges that stud the Anakie plain a dozen miles from Geelong, it is time to stop for water at a small creek.

Fyans offers you some pork, damper and a cup. 'Seating himself in sulkiness on the bank, thrusting his legs into the stream to the knees, thus he remained for about a quarter of an hour, when again I asked him to eat something.

'Without a reply, pulling from his belt a tomahawk, he proceeded to an old tree, cutting and hacking it in particular places, extracting large grubs, eating them with much relish. He continued at his repast for nearly a quarter of an hour.

'"Well, Buckley, are you ready?"

'"For what?"

'"For Geelong."'

According to Fyans' account, you say, 'It is too far for me to pull away there.'

Fyans insists, 'Why, Buckley, you must come on with me.'

But you refuse and Fyans continues on toward Geelong, 'on a dreary path in a strange and wild country unknown to me, and then seldom frequented by Europeans'.

You eventually join Fyans in Geelong a day or two later, helping Flogger look for a site for a permanent settlement with a fresh water supply. And then you organise a muster of the local Wadawurrung. By Fyans' count there are '275 of all classes – men, women and children'. As you interpret for the new police chief, flour, blankets and clothing are handed out. But Fyans, nervously eyeing off the large mob, decides the two dozen tomahawks sent down from Sydney to be distributed to the local Aboriginals should instead be thrown into the river.

'The natives saw this preparation, and I kept some distance from them with my double barrelled gun, accompanied by Mr Patrick

McKeever, district constable, also alarmed; it had the effect of making the natives retire, the interpreter Buckley telling them to do so. I was exceedingly happy at the result, not having the slightest trust in Buckley; and I may now add, my conviction is that the natives assembled wishing an opportunity to murder every person in the place . . .'

You can no longer put up with this. A day later you receive permission to return to Melbourne. The Reverend Langhorne has lost his battle to set up an Aboriginal mission far to the east and away from the town, and must settle for a site just south of the Yarra River. He has plans to use you as an interpreter to the Boonwurrung and Woiwurrung people but it soon becomes clear that won't work. According to Langhorne, '. . . unfortunately I was placed on the Yarra with a tribe who identified Buckley as one with a tribe with whom they were constantly at war'.

You're trapped now, caught between worlds. Only one option left.

'I could not calculate on one hour's personal safety from either one party or the other,' you will recall years later. 'Under such circumstances, for if our lives had been lost or cattle stolen in any locality where I happened to be stationed, prejudice or vindictive feelings might have been brought into play and I should have been sacrificed.'

Someone – probably Batman or Wedge – drafts your resignation letter to Captain Lonsdale. Dated 9 October 1837, it states: 'I do myself the honour respectfully to request that you will be pleased to accept my resignation as interpreter to the Aborigines and special constable for this district from this date, as it is my intention immediately to proceed to Europe . . .'

Europe? Well, that plan does not last long, and directions were never your strong point. You're going south – south to Van Diemen's Land.

But first you need to secure your future. A man in his mid-50s needs to think about such things. A petition is sent to Governor Bourke in Sydney 'praying that he may receive the indulgence of a grant of land . . . in order that your petitioner may not in his old age be reduced to distress'. It adds that your advancing years and absence from the white world for 32 years mean you are 'unable to gain his livelihood and further he has, by joining his countrymen, so far displeased . . . the natives of Port Phillip that he could not with safety, comfort or satisfaction . . . again join them'.

Bourke has a soft spot for you and writes to Lord Glenelg in London recommending an annual pension of 100 pounds. Lord Glenelg is Charles Grant, a long-time politician and the son of a former chairman of directors of the British East India Company. He is known as a ditherer and it will not be until June the following year that he writes to Bourke's replacement in Sydney, George Gipps, saying: 'I do not see any sufficient reason to justify the grant of a pension as suggested by Sir Richard Bourke. Buckley has already obtained presents and a salary of 75 pounds a year for his services which he has rendered, but especially when taken in connection with his former history they do not appear to me sufficient to warrant any further remuneration from the public.'

Your *former history*. There really is no escaping it. On 28 December 1837, you board the cargo ship *Yarra Yarra*, bound for Hobart Town. Behind you, the country in which you have spent the majority of your life continues to change. The boats keep disgorging their loads of sheep and cattle, the white men keep squabbling over land and money and the people who took you in, who protected you for 32 years, are being trampled by the white stampede.

You have no idea that six months earlier a requiem for their souls was laid out in the pages of a British parliamentary report. After months of inquiries and testimony, the House of Commons' Select Committee on Aborigines made a bleak and often poignant finding about the fate of the nation's dispossessed.

'The inhabitants of New Holland, in their original condition, have been described by travellers as the most degraded of the human race,' the report said. 'But it is to be feared that intercourse with Europeans has cast over their original debasement a yet deeper shade of wretchedness.

'These people, unoffending as they were towards us . . . suffered in an aggravated degree from the planting amongst them of penal settlements . . . it does not appear that the territorial rights of the natives were considered, and very little care has since been taken to protect them from the violence or the contamination of the dregs of our countrymen.

'The effects have consequently been dreadful beyond example, both in the diminution of their numbers and their demoralisation.'

It's doubtful that Foster Fyans ever peruses a copy of the committee's report either. It is not the sort of bedside reading for a man of action and firm views who now finds himself in a world that grows softer by the year.

Later in life he will write to Charles La Trobe, the first Lieutenant-Governor of what will become the official state of Victoria. A gold rush is about to engulf the land that Batman and Fawkner and so many others long believed would prove to be the richest in the nation. But Flogger Fyans has a more important subject to discuss; the thorny and difficult question of apprehending and putting on trial Aboriginals who may have committed theft or other outrages in far-flung regions of the country.

'It's a difficult thing to apprehend natives, with great risk of life on both sides,' writes Fyans. 'On the Grange, and many parts of the country, it would be impossible to take them; and in my opinion, the only plan to bring them to a fit and proper state is to insist on the gentlemen in the country to protect their property, and to deal with such useless savages on the spot.'

PART IV

WILLIAM RETREATS FROM BOTH WORLDS

WILLIAM BUCKLEY, AKA 'GIANT HACHO'

Now this just might be the thing to keep all those prostitutes and drunks in their seats for once. The Wild White Man from Port Phillip, live on stage! Who knows, with a little luck everyone might get through the night without another brawl erupting and spilling on to the dirty streets of Wapping.

Just who had the ridiculous idea of putting a theatre down here among the brothels, slaughterhouses and slums of this sewage-ridden suburb of Hobart?

Not that the town couldn't do with a dose of real culture. Might actually lift spirits a little and add some polish to this raw and rowdy frontier. But down here? Talk about a rose among thorns. The Theatre Royal is a majestic Georgian building, an edifice of sophistication and grandeur, its stone blocks stained with convict sweat. And what did they do? They put a tavern beneath the auditorium called The Shades – a seedy joint overflowing with rum-swilling sailors and hookers. It has its own entrance to the theatre pit and for the gentry in the boxes above it's often hard working out just what spectacle to concentrate on – the music and the theatrical plays, or the cockfights and the drunken melees.

There's little relief once you get outside, not unless you happen to be a connoisseur of stinking tanneries and butcheries and all those cheap tenements and flophouses of flood-prone Wapping.

Mean streets, these, just the sort of squalid lanes and alleys where you might bump into that legendary receiver of stolen goods, Ikey Solomon. One of the most famous convicts of all time, Solomon is now a free man on the condition he stays away from Hobart. But how can the old fence resist wandering by to catch up with old friends and soak in a little more of his growing fame? Charles Dickens' latest novel, *Oliver Twist*, is being serialised in the British papers right now and its main character, Fagin, is said to be based on Solomon, the 'Prince of Thieves' who trained hordes of London orphans to pick pockets.

But even Solomon's stature pales next to the celebrity status of Mr William Buckley. You have only been in Hobart for a week and you haven't been able to step outside without someone wanting to shake those large hands and make those ears bleed with hundreds of questions about Port Phillip and your life among the Wadawurrung.

In fact, that is how this whole damn theatre business began in the first place.

There you were, loping down the street, revelling in the knowledge that little Johnny Fawkner wasn't around the corner plotting his next move against you, when a man came out of nowhere and asked if you would like to go to the theatre with him. Well, of course you did. Hard to remember the last time you actually went anywhere for pure enjoyment, let alone *the theatre*. You had a regular seat at some fine performances under the stars for 32 years and if the Theatre Royal could put on a show half as good as the corroborees you have seen, it would be time well spent.

Turned out to be a pleasant evening. You liked what you saw and at the end of the show one of the performers wandered over and asked if you would like to return – but this time to the stage. That sounded like an offer too good to refuse. What a kind and generous proposal. Say what you like about William Buckley, but don't say he never grabs an opportunity when it presents itself. It's just that . . . you can be naïve, can't you? It's why some folk will suggest you can come across as being a little . . . *simple*. You think they are going to put a seat on the stage for you where you can watch the entire performance without your hulking frame blocking the view of those behind you.

Not really a man of this world, are you? You may have just spent two years among some of the most deceitful and duplicitous men God ever put on this earth, but it's been almost 40 years since you rubbed elbows with the sort of urgers and lags that inhabit Wapping. So put this down as another of life's lessons where, once again, you will leave people feeling as though you have let them down.

—

You can't blame John Moses for trying. The man needs bums on seats. This Wednesday night – 17 January 1838 – is his big night. A benefit for John Moses and the new Theatre Royal has never seen the likes of it. Making its debut: the play *One O'Clock – or The Knight & the Wood Demon*, a gothic romance from the pen of the English writer Michael Lewis.

A day before the performance the local papers are filled with late breaking news. 'The grand spectacle which had such an unparalleled run in London, the Wood Demon (in which will be introduced, in the character of Giant Hacho, Mr William Buckley, just arrived from Port Phillip), to be followed by a pantomime, with all its amusing fooleries . . .'

The Giant Hacho himself! Never heard of him? Here's an extract from 'The Penny Playbook' from the show's run in London: '. . . in an almost impregnable castle on the sea coast dwelt a terrific giant named Hacho, who delighted in securing all the beauteous damsels who came in his way, and confining them in his castle, till they yielded to his infamous desires, after which, he mostly put them to a horrible death . . .'

Staging the play in Hobart is a coup for Moses, who arrived in town in 1820, courtesy of His Majesty's convict fleet. He's a theatrical type. He has a ruddy face and hazel eyes that poured tears of regret when he appeared before a judge in Westminster for stealing a watch. 'I beg for mercy,' he cried out during his trial. But that performance hardly helped. Seven years' transportation to the colonies. He served his time and since then has worked hard to fight his way back to respectability – well, as best a man can do in these colonial times when being Jewish puts you just a couple of rungs above the Indigenous population on the ladder of respectability.

The local papers don't mind publishing sarcastic stories about members of what they call 'the money-lending tribe'. But the *Colonial Times* does have some sympathy for Moses. The day before his benefit it writes that through 'the exertions of Mr Moses, the theatre has been for months past kept in highly respectable and peaceable order, it being his duty to superintend the management of the tickets taken, and the audience generally. His situation, in a colony like this, must be anything but agreeable; but he invariably does his duty and has therefore claims upon the public. The pantomime is spoken of as certain to please. Since writing the above, we find Mr Buckley, the Port Phillip giant, is to perform in the first piece.'

So let's get this straight. A week ago you were *Interpreter William Buckley*. Now you're *William Buckley, Actor*? This is surely your greatest – and quickest – transformation. It was only six days ago that you disembarked from the *Yarra Yarra* and strode in to the colony with a cool sea breeze at your back, the ship's skipper, John Lancey, by your side. Lancey may have been the captain of the boat that carried Johnny Fawkner's team of first settlers to Port Phillip but he never let the man's bile affect his view of you. He took you to a local bank to cash a cheque and by the time you arrived at the Duchess of Kent for a little light refreshment, word had already spread through town that the Wild White Man had arrived and was looking to settle down. So many people wanting to catch a glimpse of you, to confirm with their own eyes that you actually do exist and have not been a figment of the imagination of men like William Lushington Goodwin.

You have woken this morning at the home of William Cutts, the licensee of the Black Swan hotel, a man who has been kind enough to give you somewhere to stay for a few weeks until you find your bearings. The news is already spreading about your coming appearance.

Well, that won't be happening, will it?

You quickly let it be known you will not be up on stage 'exhibited as the huge Anglo-Australian giant'. Damn thing sounds like a freak show and haven't you just spent two years trying to escape from one? The news is relayed 'very much to the mortification' of Moses, who now has to find another lumbering figure to play the role of the Giant Hacho. But Moses is a professional and of course he will find a way to get on with the show.

But if William Buckley is a man who cannot escape his past, so too is John Moses. A few months after the premiere of *The Wood Demon*, Moses discovers one of his actresses has stolen two valuable stage dresses. The matter goes to court and after a lengthy debate Moses decides to withdraw the charges when it becomes clear he can't win the case.

The *Colonial Times* no longer has any sympathy for Mr Moses. Once again it is time to poke fun at his Jewishness and dwell in some good old-fashioned racism of the era. It quotes Moses telling the court that the dresses were valuable and had been worn by a duchess at Queen Victoria's recent coronation: 'Dey ver vort eight coinees and ver vorn by a Tuchess at the Queen's crownashun.'

Just in case the reader is in any doubt about the man's heritage, the *Times* ends its report by saying he would like his stolen property to be returned. 'Vell, vell, I am shatisfied,' he is quoted. 'Let me have my trasses.'

33

ASSISTANT STOREMAN BUCKLEY

Now listen. You may be the talk of the town but there is also another large and ageing veteran making news in Hobart. The *Bussorah Merchant*, a 530-ton teak vessel that has seen better days, is sitting in quarantine in North West Bay, a four-hour walk south of those squalid Wapping streets. For the past few weeks its passengers have been recovering from a five-month nightmare that saw the bodies of more than 60 children sent into the deep.

The *Bussorah Merchant* left Cork in Ireland in August with almost 300 free emigrants hoping to escape their homeland's poverty and civil unrest. They must have thought they were in safe hands with Morgan Price, a doctor who had been at sea for more than 25 years tending to the health of passengers on Navy and merchant vessels. Here was a man who knew only too well how cruel those months on board could be; how disease could spread so quickly that, before you knew it, bodies were being thrown overboard morning, noon and night. It was not just illness, either, that could move through all that oak as stealthy and deadly as . . . well, that stubborn bastard of the seas, *Teredo navalis*. Cram hundreds of people into a ship that has already been at sea for 20 years, a vessel that has already made three long trips to New Holland, and the smallest of slights could be magnified, reactions blown out of all proportion. A decade earlier, as the *Bussorah Merchant* sailed from London to Madras, a soldier had shot dead the ship's serving surgeon.

So Price was taking no chances on this voyage. Those on board who could read would have seen the General Regulations notice he nailed up for everyone to see. It was a fine list from a man doing his best to keep them safe; bedding in the dingy recesses where the poorest passengers spent their nights would have to be brought on deck and scrubbed with holystone twice a week; there would be 'no smoaking' between decks and every male emigrant 'must be shaved every Wednesday and Saturday and every individual to be mustered every Thursday and Sunday when they are required to have on clean linen'.

But Price had known these rules could only do so much. The rest would have to be left in God's hands.

'You are required strictly to attend to the sacred commandments, in order to attain a knowledge of those truths,' Price instructed the passengers. 'I earnestly recommend you to the frequent reading of the Scriptures, and to seek opportunities in your spirits before God, when you are at your work, as He knoweth every secret thought.'

Well, Price did not have to fear his passengers' loyalty to the Lord. It did not take long for these poor Irish passengers to huddle together and pray for mercy and forgiveness as the *Bussorah Merchant* ploughed its way through the heaving seas toward Hobart Town. Smallpox and measles soon began to spread and within weeks the first of many tiny bodies shrouded in calico were buried at sea.

It would become a voyage that later historians would cite as an example of 'ignorance of good hygiene . . . four women and sixty four out of one hundred and thirty three children died, mostly of measles and smallpox'. It is difficult to imagine what those months at sea must have been like for those on board; waiting to see whose child would be next, every cough and itch closely – and fearfully – examined.

The passenger list, a grim register of tragedy and misfortune, reads as though the ship was carrying an entire village of workers. There were labourers and shepherds, carpenters and sawyers, plasterers and cabinetmakers.

A wheelwright and his wife from Cloyne, John and Ellen Cosgrove, buried three of their six boys at sea. A 29-year-old sawyer and his wife from the small town of Fermoy, Edward and Ellen Fennessy, watched their daughter Peggy die from smallpox, her body ravaged by sores and blisters. Soon after they lost their other children – Mary Anne, John and Edward – to measles.

James Byrne, a labourer from Balriggen, and his wife, Mary, surrendered two of their three measles-affected children to the deep. So too did William and Ellen Clancy of Aghada.

The Lord, it turned out, had not knoweth all. He had failed Morgan Price and that meant the surgeon had failed his passengers. And now the *Bussorah Merchant* has been forced to spend more than five valuable weeks anchored in North West Bay, its owners no doubt counting every lost day without cargo. Within the next few days its quarantine will be over and its surviving passengers will finally step on land for the first time in five months.

So, William. You may ask what all this has to do with you. Well, among those fortunate emigrants who have survived this hellish journey from Ireland is a woman who will soon become your wife.

—

In the fast, sing-song cadence of the Cork accent, words tumble into one another quickly like a trail of falling dominoes. It's a musical dialect with a throaty Irish 'r'; what the experts will one day call a *velarised alveolar approximant*. Its speed, combined with a patter of unrounded vowels, can be confusing to those not from the southwest of Ireland. A goat becomes a *gawwwt*. The word 'top' comes out as *tahp*. To those passengers who first laid eyes on her, the *Bussorah Merchant* must have seemed a *tahp bawwwt*, the vessel that would take them from poverty to the Promised Land.

So it's understandable that the poor soul charged with putting together the ship's manifest had some difficulties. Daniel Eagers, a 34-year-old stonecutter keen for a new life in a new land, suddenly became Daniel Higgins. Naturally, his 24-year-old illiterate wife, Julia, was also given this new surname along with their two-year-old daughter, Mary Ann.

This little island they have come to is hardly the land of opportunity. Two years ago the Lieutenant-Governor George Arthur protested to London about the large numbers of labourers being sent his way because they were taking work his tens of thousands of convicts could be carrying out. Now his replacement, Sir John Franklin, a man less interested in the outpost as a penal settlement and more concerned with having Van Diemen's Land declared a free, self-governing colony, has suspended assisted immigration. The Eagers family might well be one of the last to make it here under a system that guaranteed skilled married men a 20-pound advance.

That 20 quid will have to last them for some time. Jobs for skilled labourers are scarce, particularly stone-cutting, seen more as fine, backbreaking work for convicts. It may also explain why Daniel Eagers will shortly leave Hobart for Sydney to join an overland cattle drive heading to Port Phillip.

But first, the Eagers need somewhere to live. They will make their way through the grimy streets to Hobart Town's Immigrants' Home. And who will they meet at this fine establishment?

None other than . . . *Assistant Storeman William Buckley*.

—

While you get an opportunity to rest that weary body, the days also pass in a blur of new faces. But it is the old ones you enjoy meeting most and no-one will do more to get you back on your feet than Joseph Johnson.

Joe was one of your shipmates on the *Calcutta* and has done very well for himself. He had been 26 years old when he was sentenced to death for horse-stealing in Crown End and, like you, had that term commuted to life before being sent to the hulks in Langstone. Perhaps it was the separation from all those bad influences back home.

Or maybe Joe always had a kernel of entrepreneurship in him and David Collins' decision to come to Van Diemen's Land finally gave it that chance to flourish. He certainly moved quickly. After receiving a conditional pardon in 1809 he was given a grant of 140 acres and has now turned that into more than 5000 acres. He has a large house in Green Ponds, properties across Hobart and has become so wealthy and successful he has paid for relatives – two nephews and their families – to join him from England and share in his riches.

All these accomplishments have given him a sheen of respectability along with rare access to the powerful; in fact, you could say Joseph Johnson has become one of them. But despite all these achievements he has never forgotten where he came from. He greets you like the long-lost friend you are. You're both old men now with so many stories to share. He insists you must stay with him in that grand house he calls *Tissington*, named after his native village in Derbyshire. Where to begin? You have spent more than 30 years living on the land; Johnson has spent the same time profiting from it.

But after three weeks of this – 'being tired of an indolent life' – you beg him to organise an introduction to Sir John Franklin so you might capitalise on your new celebrity and find a way to make a living. Joe Johnson is a man for whom all doors open in Hobart and within days you arrive at Government House for breakfast with Sir John and his wife, Lady Franklin.

The Lieutenant-Governor is another of those men the 19th century specialises in producing, a Navy man who somehow always manages to turn up when history is being made. He was at the Battle of Copenhagen with Horatio Nelson. He was a midshipman on board the HMS *Investigator* when it made the first circumnavigation of Australia under the command of Matthew Flinders. And he was on board the HMS *Bellerophon* at the Battle of Trafalgar when Nelson, on board the *Victory*, was shot through the spine by a sniper.

But it is not just the sea that calls out to Franklin. Twenty years earlier he led an expedition charting the rugged north-east coastline of Canada. Over the next two years more than half of his force perished from starvation, survivors like Franklin forced to chew on their leather boots and eat the moss clinging to the cold rocks. Whispers of cannibalism would linger for years. Now there's something for you. Want to boast about all those shellfish you were forced to suck down all those years ago, those days and weeks when you thought you would collapse from being so famished? This man knows what it is like to go hungry. There are colleagues of his who still call him 'The Man Who Ate His Boots'.

Perhaps that is why Sir John looks so well fed these days, his balding head softened by a chubby face and a fleshy chin that droops dangerously close to his collar and silk tie. Take a good look at him because chances are you won't be seeing much more of the man after this meeting. In just a few years he will head back to the Arctic to lead an expedition to chart the remainder of the famed Northwest Passage, that legendary route Europeans have spent centuries exploring as a potential path to Asia. It will also be the last Lady Franklin sees of her 59-year-old husband, whose disappearance will earn him a special place in 19th-century history.

As commander of the expedition Sir John will take 130 men, two ships – the *Erebus* and the *Terror* – and three years' worth of supplies into the frigid, iceberg-laden seas around Lancaster Sound. The expedition is never heard from again, its fate uncertain until Inuit Eskimo discover the *Terror* floating in an ice-bound cove, the *Erebus* long broken into pieces by the vice-like pack ice. Dozens of search parties will be sent out over the next 40 years and Sir John will become mythologised in song and legend. But it will take another 150 years until the fate of Franklin and his men is revealed. Human bones found on one of the islands in the Northwest Passage will contain traces of tuberculosis and possible lead contamination from tinned food that turned bad. Other bones – broken and previously boiled – will indicate attempts at extracting marrow. Most of the men, it seemed, either froze or starved to death as they ran out of companions to dine on.

So if Sir John is enjoying his breakfast, no-one should complain. He asks you if there is anything he can do to make your life a little easier. Having seen what Joe Johnson has accomplished, you tell him a small allotment of land would be nice.

But that won't be happening. 'His excellency said he could not grant land,' you say in *Life and Adventures*, 'but that he would see what could be done in the way of finding me employment.'

Assistant Storeman at the Immigrants' Home. Perhaps not the greatest of occupations. But then, what exactly can you do these days? You're too old to haul bricks. And these colonists have no need for an Aboriginal interpreter because they effectively wiped them off the face of the earth years earlier. You've made it clear that acting is not your passion. So let's make do with what you have been given.

Besides, you get to meet the Eagers family. Julia is a tiny woman, clearly devoted to her precious daughter, particularly after that voyage of the *Bussorah Merchant*. She might be a little hard to understand when she talks in that tumbling, lilting Cork accent. But all you have to do is listen closely. You are, after all, a man from Cheshire who mastered Wadawurrung.

34

'A CERTAIN MORAL AND INTELLECTUAL COMPOSURE'

This raucous place they call Hobart Town. What do you see as you stride down streets of cobblestones and sawdust and horse dung on your way to your storeman's job at the Immigrants' Home? There are convicts with calloused hands hauling stone slabs, carpenters furiously sawing and hammering, blacksmiths swinging their mallets like Thor himself, pounding hot metal against their anvils until it bends to their will. The chill of autumn might be in the air but the entire town is perspiring, toiling in rivers of sweat and industry.

Hard workers, most of them, diligently obeying the directive from Colossians 3:23: 'Whatever you do work heartily, as for the Lord and not for men.' But not a single one can hold a candle to those few brave souls tasked with the hardest occupation in this town.

The clergymen.

Spare a thought for those who must spread God's word. 'He is placed as it were in the very gorge of sin, in the midst of the general receptacle for the worst characters in the world . . . of necessity compelled to take the "Bull by the horns", to grapple at the very gates of hell if he would rescue a soul from the headlong ruin to which he is hurrying.'

These are the words of Charles Medyett Goodridge. He knows a thing or two about standing before those gates of hell and staring into its flaming abyss. Goodridge lives in Hobart for many years, working as a ferryman on the Derwent, earning his keep transporting livestock across the river; a man never far from a salt breeze and a swaying deck. In the early 1830s he publishes a book with a deceptively dull title – *Statistical View of Van Diemen's Land*. But its pages are far more than a turgid catalogue of lists and numbers. They come to life as Goodridge guides us on a virtual tour of the good, the bad . . . and the very bad, of which there is plenty.

It is why the man insists that a Hobart preacher has the toughest job in town: 'This truth will be painfully impressed upon the mind of any one who views the streets of Hobart Town during the time of divine service. Idle men and women may be seen loitering here and there . . . some standing impatiently around the doors of the public houses, waiting until the hours of public worship are over when the houses may be opened and they may go in to continue their carousing.'

A pastor's duty, he says, is the most important a man can undertake, 'but in these penal colonies it is extreme. He has to struggle with the enemy at close combat, face to face and foot to foot, and to brace himself up to the utmost point of exertion . . . his zeal and industry will readily show themselves by the character and success of his works in the pulpit.'

Good fire and brimstone stuff, this, straight from the hand and heart of a man singed by those very flames of hell.

Charles Goodridge is another Robinson Crusoe, a shipwreck survivor who lived off penguin eggs and the raw brains of sea elephants for two years. Really? Just how many of these characters can one century produce? Back in the early 1820s he had been a merchant sailor on the *Princess of Wales*, a cutter sent to the rugged limits of the Southern Ocean with enough salt in its hold to preserve the skins of 10,000 seals. The men would be dumped on rocky outcrops in the middle of the cold sea for weeks at a time, their small rowboats turned upside down to shelter them against the icy winds, the skin torn from their hands as they crawled across jagged boulders, hunting prey in such numbers that within decades the industry would be on its knees.

As with any decent Robinson Crusoe experience, a huge storm came out of nowhere and its monster swell seized the *Princess of Wales*, dashing her against rocks and leaving her crew stranded. This small band of sealers spent the next two years eking out a miserly existence, the blubber of walruses their only fuel, their raw brains a rare source of protein and their skins the only protection against the extreme weather. But what put steel in these men's hearts and hope in their minds? The only reading matter they managed to salvage from the wreck was a single copy of the Bible and it was in the pages of the good book, read by the flickering glow of a blubber-fuelled fire, that Goodridge was reminded each night that God had not forgotten him, that if he continued to believe in Him those gates to hell would remain locked.

Salvation eventually arrived in the form of a passing ship making its way to Hobart Town. But no sooner had he set foot in Van Diemen's Land than Goodridge was struck by the sheer meanness of the town and its 'want of charity'. A bid to raise funds for the crew attracted just a few pounds. Money, it seemed, was good for one purpose. 'The vice of drunkenness was extremely prevalent, more particularly among the convicts, but I am sorry to add it greatly pervaded all classes.'

While Goodridge would go on to praise many aspects of life in Hobart before making his way back home to England, he never forgot 'the most humiliating scenes of drunkenness, disgusting indeed to the spectator'. And that, in large part, is why he insists the preacher of Hobart has the toughest job in town.

'The great work of reformation must begin with him. If one mode of exhortation does not succeed he must try another, and his mind must be continually on the rack to discover the best means of accomplishing some part at least of the great work before him.'

—

Well, if those Hobart preachers have their work in front of them, just what sort of fate awaits the Reverend William Waterfield? He arrives in Hobart in March 1838 and in just a few weeks will make his way to Port Phillip to become Melbourne's first appointed congregational minister. Waterfield is a devout and private man who shuns parties and public displays of any sort of exuberance. Melbourne will sorely test his patience. Over the next five years he will see people out and about on the streets on Sundays, engaging in all sorts of riotous behaviour . . . like walking . . . and laughing in public on a day reserved for contemplating the Lord's work. Waterfield will peer through his window and refuse to join these outrageous scenes because his 'mind was too harassed'. He will be mortified to discover a couple sharing his home who, on Christmas Day, suddenly begin singing before getting up to . . . well . . . it's almost too obscene to put down in words . . . but they . . . well, they stand up and start . . . *dancing*.

But before his departure for the Gomorrah that is Port Phillip there is one man he insists he must meet. Yes, another of God's workers wants to talk with you and gain some insight into those heathen natives he will be forced to contend with once he crosses Bass Strait.

On 28 April the Reverend William Waterfield writes in his journal that he is introduced to you after dinner and the usual questioning begins immediately. 'I . . . asked him many questions and found that the natives had no idea of a Supreme Being or a God of any kind, that all the future state that they believed in was that when they died they would be turned into white people and visit again their own land.

'Buckley was a man about 6ft 6in. He informed me that the native fruits were very few and were something like the black and white currant. He thought the people were quite harmless. They avowed no chief but were on equality with each other.'

So far, so good. But then Waterfield throws a question your way that has to do with another of those myths that have built up around you, that you were part of a group of British soldiers who staged a mutiny in Gibraltar in 1802. It's a story that has circulated for years.

Yes, there was a mutiny in Gibraltar. And, yes, six soldiers involved in that mutiny were put on board the *Calcutta* at the last minute as it sailed for Port Phillip. But no, you were not one of them. When that mutiny was being staged you were making your way to the hulks at Langstone.

'He would not acknowledge to having been at Gibraltar,' writes Waterfield, as though he does not quite believe you. 'He denied it altogether. He was originally a bricklayer but did not attempt to teach it to the natives. I was pleased with the interview.' He's not a man for extensive details, our Reverend Waterfield.

But there are others who do manage to extract far more information. All types have been beating a path to your door since your arrival in Hobart. One of the first was Dr John Lhotsky, who sat down with you just a few days after that ridiculous attempt to get you on stage at the Theatre Royal.

An eccentric Polish explorer and naturalist, Lhotsky is a divisive figure in Van Diemen's Land. He is debt-ridden and hounded by several local newspapers that claim his request for public donations to develop his private collection of rocks and specimens into a museum is nothing but a scam. He will soon leave for London but the scorn he has earned from Hobart's polite society will follow him. 'Here he assumed the rank of Gentleman,' reads a typically scathing assessment of the man in *The Tasmanian*, '. . . and the pomposity of a great Philosopher, mineralogist, geologist and every other *ist* imaginable . . .'

We'll never know how Lhotsky manages to sit you down. Perhaps, as that historian and noted pedicurist to the rich and famous James Bonwick might say, he employs 'the steamy vapour of the punch-bowl'. But it's an exclusive interview that not even *The Tasmanian* can decline; no matter how much it loathes the good doctor.

Lhotsky, in fact, should have considered adding another *ist* to his many titles – that of journalist – for he has a natural talent wide-spread in this era for taking the truth and . . . stretching it a little.

'Buckley must have been a splendid young man, being nearly seven feet high,' writes a clearly impressed Lhotsky, unfortunately shattering any claims he may have to being a man of science and a master of measurement. 'Even at the present moment there is something original, but quite sedate about him. His features have been rather darkened by thirty-two years exposure to the sun of Australia, and there is certainly something stern and "savage" in them, however thoroughly softened by a certain moral and intelligent composure, if I shall call it so.'

Did you hear that? *A certain moral and intelligent composure.*

'Upon being asked whether the blacks were in the habit of killing their sickly or deformed offspring, he paused a good time very significantly, and replied that they do no such thing; but, on the contrary, that they treat their children with the greatest care and tenderness.

'Buckley being so deeply and justly attached to a race of strangers, amongst whom he had lived for so many years, I mentioned that they doubtlessly treated him well after they became better acquainted with each other; but the answer which I received, and I believe a tear glistened at the same time in his eye, was that they had treated him from the very first like one of their own.'

Lhotsky is . . . almost spellbound. 'It was very satisfactory, and at the same time touching to me, to find a civilized European feeling so deeply (as I saw he did) the kindness which he had received from (what we call) savages.'

So impressed is Lhotsky that he goes on to give us a hint as to why some of his critics have come to regard him as a tad pompous: 'I was forcibly reminded of an old adage of mine, viz., that "it is easy to despise mankind, but difficult to comprehend it!"'

Well, the man doesn't mind quoting himself. But his interview with you is the best piece of press you've received in a long time. If we didn't know any better we'd be tempted to think all that hob-nobbing around Hobart – rubbing those immense shoulders with the powerful, pressing those huge hands into the palms of the rich and influential – is having an effect, stripping away your layers of naivety and replacing them with a *certain moral and intelligent composure* . . .

What a pity you still have to work for a living.

35

GATEKEEPER, AUTHOR, PORTRAIT SUBJECT

Your curriculum vitae please, William. Time to update it again. Mind if we have a look? Can't quite make out that date of birth but it seems as though you are now in your late 50s? It says here you've had quite a few jobs over the years, too. You were a bricklayer? A soldier? There's quite a lengthy gap after that. Took a lengthy stint of long service, did we? Then a role as an interpreter, followed by — well, let's ignore that 24-hour career as an actor — the job of assistant storekeeper.

Time to add another to the list. *Gatekeeper William Buckley.*

The Immigrants' Home is being closed after three months because all those surviving passengers from the *Bussorah Merchant* have been resettled. Daniel Eagers, that stonecutter from Cork, is apparently heading off to Sydney soon to join an overland expedition to Port Phillip, leaving his wife and small daughter behind in Hobart. The rest of those Irish pilgrims have found other lodgings so your services are no longer required. Instead, the government has found a new position for you. Would you mind popping down to Liverpool Street? There's a large house opposite the colonial hospital that shouldn't be too hard to find. It's filled with women and children and someone needs to keep an eye on the door. Quickly.

It is late May 1838, and the government is under pressure to improve the squalid conditions inside its workhouse for female convicts, the Cascades Female Factory. What a disaster it has turned out to be; a remodelled distillery sitting in a swamp at the foot of Mt Wellington, down where the sun never shines and the only thing that grows is mildew. Not even the man who put the Theatre Royal in the middle of Wapping could have come up with this. There are hundreds of women prisoners crammed into small, unventilated rooms. Settlers have been complaining that many of the inmates sent to them to act as servants arrive on their doorsteps in a filthy state, nits crawling through their unkempt hair. Many of the women are disease-ridden, others suffering severe mental illnesses that go untreated. The only health problem that is not an issue is obesity – dinner is a quarter pound of bread and a pint of soup. What a nutritious broth it is, too. The regulations stipulate the preferred recipe to be 25 pounds of meat to every 150 quarts of soup, boosted with vegetables or barley. But vegetables are often unavailable so the chef whips up what the French would call a *bouillon*, which the inmates know only as lukewarm water with tiny, floating pieces of unidentifiable meat.

For pregnant and nursing mothers, conditions are even harder. In 1834, 10 children died within six weeks. When a coroner's inquiry subsequently visited the site it found more than 60 mothers had been living in a dormitory only 40 feet long and 11 feet wide. In the past eight years one in every four children have died within the Factory's walls.

Even the press – no great fans of convicts male or female – has been hounding the government over this 'miserable place . . . the most unfitting place in the whole colony for the prison of women, children and infants'. So the Convict Department has assigned a house in Liverpool Street to act as the new nursery. Your role as gatekeeper will be to keep an eye on the comings and goings of these female convicts who, according to the papers, make 'their exits and entrances just when and how they please . . . these women are openly disgraceful – drunkenness and cohabitation being continually practiced and all from the miserable penuriousness of the government'.

So would you mind heading down there right now?

—

It must be over the next year that news filters back to Hobart that Daniel Eagers has been killed. The only source we will have for this is your *Life and Adventures*, where you will say Daniel went to Sydney 'thinking to better himself . . . but whilst on a journey he afterwards undertook overland to Port Phillip, he was killed by natives near the Murray River; thus leaving his family unprovided for'.

When the news of his death is confirmed you propose to the widowed Julia and she accepts. It is – and let's choose our words carefully here – an *unusual* union. These are certainly times when desperation brings couples together; convict women often marry free men (see John Batman and John Pascoe Fawkner) while older, newly widowed men are known to take their female servants for brides. Your friend Joseph Johnson will do just that in a few years' time when his wife, Elizabeth, passes away, marrying his housekeeper who will, in a rather unfortunate memory lapse on her part, turn out to have a husband back in England who eventually travels to Australia to reclaim her. So necessity often conquers love as the driving force behind many unions.

But as the Reverend Thomas Ewing stands before the pair of you inside St John's Anglican Church on Monday, 27 January 1840, even he must find the differences between you a touch remarkable.

William Buckley is at least 58 years old and despite the care you will have taken to comb your hair and trim your beard, there is no disguising that receding hairline.

Julia Eagers is 26.

You're a giant.

She is . . . diminutive.

You have been described – unfairly – as a mindless lump of matter.

She is, clearly, the smartest person in the church.

Julia knows Hobart is no place for a widow and her young daughter. She only has to glance at all those soulless buildings around the corner from the church that form the Orphans Asylum to know what often happens to young children whose parents can no longer provide for them. There are hundreds of them living in harsh and miserable conditions; underfed, often bashed and at the mercy of scarlet fever and measles epidemics that break out every few years.

The Reverend Ewing – one of those men Charles Goodridge wants us to believe has the hardest job in town – also happens to be headmaster of the orphans' school. Ewing is one of those 19th-century preachers who delight in the complexity that God has given nature; his days off are often spent prancing through fields with a butterfly net, examining algae and collecting specimens. The famous British ornithologist John Gould will name a species of bird after the man – Ewing's Acanthiza.

Within a year Ewing's name will be associated with something far more sinister when allegations surface that he has sexually molested one of the orphan girls. While an investigation will clear the married preacher of any criminality, he will eventually lose his position as headmaster because of his 'impudence'.

But that is a year away. In front of him right now stand Mr and Mrs Buckley. The church, newly consecrated, is all convict stone and sturdy beams hauled down from the slopes of Mt Wellington. Do they ring the large bell donated by the King to announce your marriage? And by the way . . . have you told Julia that she is not your first wife?

Not long after your wedding, a letter announcing you have just been married will arrive in Port Phillip. Its contents will be read to some of the Wadawurrung people who formed your family for 32 years, among them Purranmurnin Tallarwurnin, the woman who says she was your wife. They cried when you left for Van Diemen's Land. With this news that you have settled down with an Irish woman, they will cry again, too. Now they know Murrangurk will never return.

—

Good thing you married Julia. Soon after the wedding you contract typhus, a bacterial infection they often call jail fever. You thought you were coming down with the flu for a few days until a week later when you noticed the beginnings of a rash. It didn't take long for it to spread and for the fevers to kick in. Hobart has had a few typhus epidemics and body lice usually spread them. That convict nursery where you work. It must be nit headquarters. Typhus can lead to delusions and ultimately death – it has killed hundreds of millions of sufferers in the past couple of centuries. But thankfully 'the kind attentions I received from my wife and her daughter . . . at length restored me to health, but not to such health as I had previously enjoyed; my privations and exposure in the bush, with increased years, having no doubt materially damaged my naturally strong constitution'.

Those are your words – or at least the words John Morgan writes on your behalf. It's about this time that you must meet the man. Your absence from work because of illness, coupled with your already low salary, means things have grown quite tight. Someone – perhaps Morgan – petitions the government in 1841 on your behalf in which you 'humbly solicit your Honour . . . to allow rations to be issued to his wife and child on account of the smallness of his pay as well as for numerous duties which petitioner has to perform'.

There's the usual trail of memos and notes sent to various bureaucratic departments. There is even talk that your measly half a crown a day be increased by sixpence. But when the petition finally lands on the desk of Sir John Franklin any hope of improving your lot comes to a quick end. The Lieutenant-Governor who was all over you at breakfast three years earlier has no sympathy for your plight. The Man Who Ate His Own Boots effectively tells you to chew on yours. 'The Lt Gov . . . has directed me to inform you that he cannot approve of the petitioner prayer being granted, neither does His Excellency think it necessary to increase the petitioners pay.'

But in this paper trail there is one telling sentence that sums up how this town works. One of the bureaucrats writes: 'I certainly think

Buckley's pay is small being only half a crown a day with his rations, but I cannot [vouch for] his wife to be placed on rations as she forms no part of the Establishment.'

The Establishment.

Now he could be meaning that Julia is not a government employee and therefore not entitled to a weekly food subsidy. But it's hard not to detect a whiff of snobbery in those words. It's just the sort of condescending elitism that riles John Morgan, the man who will now have to help you find a way to boost your income.

—

These years in the 1840s are hard ones; scrapping by on that meagre salary in a series of rented homes, trying to provide for Julia and her growing daughter. By the end of 1842, when your work with the convict nursery is moved to Dynnyrne House in South Hobart, Morgan appears to have finished writing *Life and Adventures* because a small advertisement appears in the *Colonial Times* in early December with the headline 'New Work'.

It's an ad that is surely written by Morgan, a lover of the complex inverted sentence: 'Preparing for the Press, and will be published in this colony by the undersigned, if a sufficient number of copies are ordered previous to the 1st of March, 1843, the life and extraordinary adventures of the Anglo-Port Phillipian Chief WILLIAM BUCKLEY, thirty two years a wanderer amongst the Aboriginal Natives of Australia Felix. The work will be embellished with twelve plates, descriptive of the costumes, habits and manners of the Aborigines. One volume, octavo, boards: price 21s.'

But Morgan's dreams of wealth and fame as the new Daniel Defoe, along with your hopes of securing some much-needed cash, will have to be put on hold. Not enough readers with inquiring minds, it seems, make their way to the printer's office at 39 Elizabeth Street to register their interest. Over the coming decade similar advertisements will appear in the press. Yet the manuscript will continue to languish on Morgan's desk.

It's not that your name and fame has been forgotten. People still point you out when they see you. Many will never forget the sight of the ageing giant strolling the streets with his tiny wife, one end of a looped handkerchief around your arm, the other around her hand. Just so the both of you can go out arm-in-arm like everyone else. In 1848 the papers will carry a story that originates in *The Geelong Advertiser* – a paper owned by little Johnny Fawkner – so full of exaggerations about your years in Port Phillip that a letter from you appears in the Hobart press saying 'every word of it is totally at variance with the truth . . . I further beg to state that I never gave any person an account of my adventures . . . except the person who wrote the manuscript and which I have now by me.'

But the manuscript continues to gather dust on Morgan's desk. It will not be until late 1851, just as the gold rush in Victoria begins to transform Melbourne into a pulsating vibrant city, that Morgan finally stands up at a meeting of the Mercantile Assistant's Association and gives a reading from several of its pages. The book is finally published in March 1852, and William Robertson, one of the old members of the Port Phillip Association and now part of the landed gentry of Victoria, acts as trustee. Morgan is mindful of the accusations thrown at Defoe after the publication of *Robinson Crusoe* – that he had used Alexander Selkirk's experiences and profited enormously from them without a penny going to the man who provided its inspiration.

By all accounts it is a success; extracts are published across the country and overseas. The *Colonial Times* says 'the life of Buckley would be an instructive addition to many a family library, and its perusal furnish no small pleasure during the long winter evenings . . . the Aboriginal character, in its lowest depths, is truthfully depicted and the painful illustrations with which this little work abounds must excite pity in every Christian bosom for the fast declining tribes of the sister colony'.

The money from the book sales must be invaluable. Your job as gatekeeper ended in 1850 and you have been getting by on a paltry annual pension of 12 pounds. Morgan concludes *Life and Adventures* with a plea for the Victorian government to grant you some form of financial reward for all you have done. 'Let us then hope that some additional provision will be made for him, so that he may never have cause to regret (on account of poverty) his return to civilisation, or the services rendered to those of his countrymen who found him in his solitude and restored him to what he hoped would provide happiness for the few remaining years of his extraordinary existence. In all the surrounding prosperity, arising out of the increase of flocks and herds and gold, surely Buckley may be permitted, in a very small degree, to participate?'

Accompanying the book is a sketch of you by the artist Ludwig Becker, a German artist and naturalist who has only just arrived in Van Diemen's Land and is paying his way around the island by painting miniature portraits of notable people. Becker is a gentle and sensitive man with an unruly red beard who will die in 10 years from scurvy and dysentery as part of the disastrous attempt by Burke and Wills to cross Australia from Melbourne to the Gulf of Carpentaria. The artist's perceptive nature becomes apparent when, years later, he develops his sketch into a life-sized oil portrait. It will be the only colour representation of William Buckley that will endure down the centuries and Becker manages to give you a rare sense of nobility.

It's the type of portrait normally found in one of those aristocratic English manors, hanging high on the wall of a private library or sitting room, an impression of a man of wealth and stature, not one spending his final years in penury. It is one of two misleading aspects of the painting. No-one ever said you were a handsome fellow. Becker has done you a favour, removing that unsightly mole high on your left cheek, softening your features to leave a dignified, if slightly austere, lasting image.

But there is no mistaking the hanging brow and the pair of haunting eyes. They stare impassively back at the observer, the look of an ageing man who has seen far more than he can ever tell.

36

'THE ORIGINAL DISCOVERER OF PORT PHILLIP'

That quill must feel strange in your hand. You have mastered two languages in your life but you have never known how to put them down in words. Perhaps these last few years might not have been so hard if you had known how to read and write. But it's all too late now for that. So take that quill, place it between your fingers and press gently on the paper before you.

It is Tuesday, 6 September 1853. Julia's daughter, Mary Ann, has just married William Jackson, a 30-year-old labourer, in the same church where you tied the knot 13 years earlier. The reverend needs you and Julia to leave your mark as witnesses on the wedding certificate.

Perhaps you are hesitant. Nervous. You certainly haven't done this very often because it looks as if you press the quill on the page just a little too long; the ink runs, turning the only mark we will ever find from your hand into something closer to a blob. Julia doesn't fare much better, dragging her finger back over her cross to leave a faint smudge.

Not that it really matters. Today is all about the future, not the missed opportunities of the past. Hard to imagine that the young girl whose mother you married all those years ago is now a grown woman. Despite all the hardship of recent years, Mary Ann can read and write and in just a few years she and her husband will move to Sydney where they will bring 11 children into the world.

You are now a man in his 70s and the last 12 months should have been a little easier after the publication of the book. Seems all that pleading on your behalf by Morgan, all those petitions requesting an acknowledgement of services rendered, finally paid off. At the start of this year the Victorian Legislative Council voted to give you a 40-pound gratuity. In fact, the original motion put to the elected representatives was that 'Forty pounds be voted to William Buckley as the original discoverer of Port Phillip . . .'

The original discoverer of Port Phillip.

Well, didn't that set off little Johnny Fawkner. That title, combined with your name in the same sentence . . . in an instant that furnace of bile inside the man was ablaze, a molten river of hatred just waiting to spill over. Fawkner is a member of the Legislative Council, of course. Why wouldn't *the original discoverer of Port Phillip* occupy a position of power and influence? He fronts up to every sitting of the Council, a velvet smoking cap pulled over those wispy white hairs, an appropriate black cape swung over his shoulders, never missing an opportunity to remind everyone that they would not even be here if it were not for him.

What's that phrase of his? 'The country is (*cough, cough*) something indebted to me.' Little Johnny's asthma is never good in the summer with all those swirling hot winds and pollen flying through the air and when the Council moved to give you that 40 quid in early January, Fawkner must have been wheezing like a broken piano accordion.

The motion was eventually shortened and the 'original discoverer' line omitted. But that wasn't enough to appease Fawkner. He had stood there in the Council and loudly opposed any payment to you because you had 'injured' the colony. Then he brazenly claimed that when Charles Franks had been murdered back in 1836, 'it was proposed to form a party to follow and apprehend the murderers.

Before this could be done, Buckley rode off and informed the blacks so that they escaped.'

It's the sort of slur you have let stand in the past, perhaps only hearing about second-hand. But not this time. No doubt Morgan authors the response that later appears in the Melbourne newspapers where you 'publicly solemnly deny having done so, although under all the circumstances of my long residence among them and the kindness I had received at their hands for thirty two years, perhaps it would have been a pardonable act of mercy . . .'

You demand Fawkner apologise and set the record straight because his claims 'have occasioned me more sorrow and uneasiness than I can describe . . . so far from my having at any time acted treacherously towards the first settlers, I solemnly declare I did all I could to benefit and protect them from injury. All persons but yourself readily acknowledge this.'

Of course, there is no apology from Fawkner. Johnny never says sorry. He will bide his time like a patient sniper for two more years.

In 1855 the Council will vote to give you a more substantial recognition – an 88-pound annuity. Mr Fawkner, the Honourable Member for Talbot, will then take to his feet again to oppose the motion, saying you were a – *cough, cough* – thief in your younger days, that you had done everything within your means to turn the Port Phillip Aboriginals against the – *wheeze, wheeze* – white settlers and that you had even *eaten* your fellow escapers – those 'lags' who ran off with you into the bush just days after Christmas in 1803.

William Buckley . . . cannibal.

The members of the Victorian Legislative Council are used to Fawkner's barbs and exaggerations. Hugh Childers, the Collector of Customs and a man who will go on to become a key member of the British cabinet, begs the council not to bow to little Johnny's wishes because William Buckley is now a very old man who is 'totally unable to provide for himself in his old days'. And then Edward Grimes, the Attorney-General, takes to his feet sensing an opportunity to gain a laugh at Fawkner's expense. He questions Fawkner's claim that you had rendered no services whatsoever to the Port Phillip colony and refers to recent legislation preventing ex-convicts from Van Diemen's Land visiting the thriving Victorian goldfields.

'By the honourable member's own account Buckley had eaten three old lags,' says Grimes. 'Now, if every free man in this community had rendered such services, there would have been no necessity for the Convict's Prevention Act; nor would the colony have been inundated with old lags from Van Diemen's Land.'

According to press reports, the Council's chamber is filled with roars of laughter and the vote to give you 88 pounds goes through easily.

But preventing you from receiving a government pension is not the only wish of little Johnny Fawkner that is denied.

Remember that day all those years ago when he stood in that new cemetery in Port Phillip, peering into the depths of a newly dug grave? There was something Fawkner wanted known. He wrote about it in his journal that night. He didn't want to be buried down there in the dark moist earth where all those squirming worms were just waiting to eat his mortal remains.

Fawkner instead wanted his body placed on a burning pyre, the way they used to send those Viking warriors to Valhalla, a display of stubbornness and grandiosity that would forever sum up the man.

When he dies in his home in 1869, at the age of 76, all those decades of fighting and scheming and doing whatever it took in order to make history remember him will have paid off. Except for one thing.

Acclaimed as the grand old man of the state of Victoria, more than 15,000 people will throng the streets to watch the funeral procession. Some will no doubt be there in their black top hats and waistcoats just to make sure the coffin lid has been tightly sealed and little Johnny has no way of staging a final act of defiance. More than 150 carriages will form the funeral cortege. Bells will sound and several minutes of silence will be held.

But at the end of it all there will be no burning pyre for John Pascoe Fawkner. They will lower him into the ground to join the worms like everyone else.

—

Stubborn bastards. Where would we be without them? Four days before Christmas in 1855 a single-seat chaise cart makes its way down the steep incline of Constitution Hill, Hobart Town. Where have you been, William? Mary Ann and her husband, yet to leave for Sydney, live in Antill Ponds, about 40 miles north of Hobart, so perhaps you are on your way home from visiting them. These gigs make it easy for an old man with tired legs. But they are not the most stable of contraptions and when your horse suddenly stumbles, the wooden wheels slide and you are hurled violently out of the cart and on to the ground.

According to some reports you are unconscious for several minutes as passers-by come to your aid. When you regain consciousness you are in pain and cannot move your arms and legs and so they carry you to the nearby Swan Inn and call for a doctor. It does not take long for news of the accident to spread. The man whose name 'has become almost a proverb from his lengthened and intimate association with Australasia met, we regret to say, with an accident on Friday . . .' reports one of the newspapers. 'Fears are entertained that at his advanced age the accident will terminate fatally.'

A safe assumption to make about any person in their mid-70s who has been thrown to the ground and paralysed. But they don't know what a hard man you are. You're going to fight this all the way. By 8 January the doctors decide there is little they can do to ease your pain, so you are taken to St Mary's Hospital in Davey Street, an institution for the 'labouring classes' who despise the nearby colonial hospital that treats convicts.

It must be a painful journey, every tortuous bump in the road adding to the agony. You're going to remain in St Mary's for 11 days until, at the request of yourself and Julia, who is beginning to go blind and can no longer care for you on her own, you are taken to the home of a friend and local baker, William Bridger, where around-the-clock care can be provided. It also won't cost you anything, will it? The daily fee at St Mary's is six shillings and by the time you are discharged the amount owing is more than three pounds – a quarter of the annual pension the Van Diemen's Land government gives you.

All your life you have managed to find a way out of a difficult situation. But there is not going to be any grand escape this time.

On 30 January 1856 you take your final breath.

—

They bury you the following Saturday at St George's burial ground in Battery Point. John Morgan is there and Joseph Hone, a former London barrister who has become a friend in recent years, also joins the procession to the grave. But there are none of the surviving members of the Port Phillip Association, that group of wealthy men who used you to keep the peace with the Aboriginals as they set about taking their lands. John Wedge, the author of your successful request for a pardon and now a prominent member of the Tasmanian Legislative Council, fails to show because 'other imperative engagements prevented him'.

So it is left to the Reverend Henry Fry to commit your body to the Lord as it is lowered into an unmarked grave. Perhaps there are plans to erect a suitable headstone later when the distraught Julia and Mary Ann and her husband manage to come into some money.

But that will never happen. Just a couple of months after the funeral a motion to posthumously pay the 88-pound gratuity to William Buckley is withdrawn by the Legislative Council of Victoria. There is no explanation given, but even the most charitable will not have a difficult time suspecting whose hand might be behind this final snub.

It is a move that incenses John Morgan. The old newspaper editor, who has never used one word when he could use 20, takes out a lengthy advertisement in the local Hobart papers railing against the decision. 'The Government of Victoria has refused all assistance to the widow of the late William Buckley, in aid of the payment by her of the expenses of hospital, lodgings, medical and other attendance and of the funeral,' says Morgan. 'These expenses and liabilities amount to nearly fifty pounds which, it was hoped, the Victorian Government would have paid and also that its legislature would have voted an annuity for the widow, sufficient to afford her food and shelter; she being . . . nearly blind, and therefore incapable of labour.'

Morgan announces that he has secured the mayors of Hobart Town and Launceston to preside as Treasurers over a fund that will hopefully raise enough money to pay off the debts and 'whatever balance may remain shall be applied (by weekly stipend) for the support of the widow, so long as it may last'.

Nothing further exists on the record as to the success of Morgan's fund-raising campaign. But a century and a half later the faded admissions book for St Mary's Hospital will show the amount owing of three pounds and six shillings was never paid.

Your death, her failing eyesight and all those debts are too much for Julia. Six months after the funeral, a small, sad paragraph appears buried deep in the columns of the *Hobart Courier*.

'The widow of the late well-known Mr Buckley is an inmate of H. M. General Hospital, laboring under temporary aberration of mind.'

It's hard to think of that tiny woman with the lilting Irish accent slowly going mad, locked away amid all that squalor, her vision fading, alone with her grief, her future bleak without you.

But surely, in her more lucid moments, Julia can still remember the days when she, like so many others, walked with a giant by her side.

OTHER LIVES

Julia Buckley never fully recovered from her 'temporary aberration of mind' or her fading eyesight. She moved to Sydney in the years after William's death to be with her daughter Mary Ann and son-in-law. She died in the Hyde Park Asylum on 18 August 1863. She was 49.

Mary Ann Jackson also died at the age of 49 on 17 May 1883. According to a death notice in the *Sydney News*, she passed away from 'cerebral apoplexy' – what doctors now call a stroke. She was buried in the Balmain cemetery and was survived by her husband and 10 children. Her two eldest daughters were married in the months after her death.

John Morgan lived for another 10 years after the death of his friend William Buckley, passing away in April 1866 at the age of 74. He was married and had one daughter. According to the *Tasmanian Morning Herald*: 'In late days Mr Morgan had fallen into considerable pecuniary distress in consequence of his having been unable to obtain settlement of certain claims for a remission order for land.' One of his biographers, Peter Bolger, would write: 'He died in 1866 as he had lived – lonely, annoyed and frightened.'

John Batman was 38 when he died, effectively broke after borrowing heavily to buy land. He was buried in the old Melbourne cemetery but was later exhumed and placed in the Fawkner cemetery, named after his nemesis. His home on Batman's Hill was taken over by the government shortly after his death and used as administration offices. By 2018 a social movement to erase his name from public places and monuments culminated in the federal seat of Batman being renamed Cooper in honour of an Indigenous rights activist. Several 'Batman' parks around Melbourne were also in the process of being renamed. Bronze sculptures of Batman and John Fawkner were also removed from the streets of Melbourne by the city council and placed in storage. Despite its flaws, his formal agreement with the Kulin people in 1835 remains the only treaty ever offered to Australia's original inhabitants.

John Pascoe Fawkner remains widely commemorated around Melbourne, including the two suburbs Fawkner and Pascoe Vale. Several parks and a private hospital also honour his name. He hand-wrote the first nine editions of Melbourne's first newspaper, the *Port Phillip Patriot*, and, after weathering financial problems in the 1840s, emerged as one of the city's most influential and controversial figures. He never lost his hatred for the Port Phillip Association and made rancorous speeches in the Legislative Council against squatters. While regarded as a liberal who pushed for greater rights for married women and a relaxation of divorce laws for deserted wives, he unsuccessfully opposed moves to introduce universal manhood suffrage – the concept of 'one man, one vote'. A year after his death in 1869, Fawkner's 70-year-old wife Eliza married 44-year-old John Walsh. She died at the age of 79 and was buried with her husband.

James Bonwick published more than 60 books and papers, ranging from school textbooks and his biography of John Batman to screeds on Irish druids and the wool trade. He was appointed archivist for the New South Wales government and also transcribed a great deal of original source material for the Queensland government. He dabbled in mysticism and never lost his passion for the temperance movement. He died at the age of 89 in 1906 in Sussex, survived by five children.

David Collins' wife, Maria, petitioned the Colonial Office several times requesting financial aid after the death of her financially ruined husband in Hobart in 1810. She was granted an annual allowance of 120 pounds in 1813 in 'consideration of her husband's services . . .' She died in 1830.

King George III suffered a major relapse of his mental illness in 1810 after the death of his much loved daughter, the 27-year-old Princess Amelia. The following year, as George descended into permanent insanity, almost blind and racked with severe rheumatism, the Parliament passed the Regency Act, allowing the Prince of Wales to act on his behalf until George's death at the age of 81 in 1820. George III fathered 15 children – two died in childhood. His reign continues to divide historians. Some have labelled him a tyrant, others viewing him as a more benevolent leader who steered England through the greatest social and political upheavals in millennia.

Sir George Arthur was recalled against his wishes from Van Diemen's Land in 1836 and went on to become Lieutenant-Governor of Upper Canada and, in 1842, Governor of Bombay. The architect of Tasmania's Black War died a wealthy man, in part due to his heavy investments in land during his tenure in Van Diemen's Land. These investments were described by some critics of the time as a 'matter of notoriety'.

John Helder Wedge left Port Phillip in 1838 for England. When he returned to Van Diemen's Land five years later following the death of his father, he married Maria Medland Wills. Wedge was 50 at the time and Maria died in childbirth a year later. He became a member of the Tasmanian Legislative Council and went on to serve in the short-lived ministry of the second Premier of Tasmania, Thomas Gregson. Wedge died in 1872 at his home on the Forth River in the island's north-west. He was 79.

Alexander Selkirk returned to pirating after his rescue by Captain Woodes Rogers. He famously led a crew in pursuit of several wealthy Spanish women who had fled up a river in Ecuador, seizing gold and jewels hidden inside their clothing. He completed an around-the-world voyage as sailing master of the *Duke* in 1711. Selkirk later joined the Royal Navy and, while serving on an anti-piracy mission off the coast of Africa in 1721, died of yellow fever and was buried at sea. He was 45.

Foster Fyans was an influential figure in the founding of Geelong, a derivation of the Wadawurrung word *Djillong* ('land' or 'cliffs'). In 1840 he was named Commissioner of Crown Lands for the Portland area pastoral district. Prone to hosting balls with turban-wearing servants, Fyans' eccentricities also included hiding jewels and diamonds in homemade furniture. He married Elizabeth Cane in 1843. She died 15 years later at the age of 42. Fyans died in 1870. He was about 80 years old.

Robert Knopwood served as a magistrate and clergyman in early Hobart until 1828. He never lost his liking for strong drink and entertaining. His work habits were criticised as 'dissipation' by NSW Governor Lachlan Macquarie. He retired on an annual pension of 100 pounds and also received a series of land grants, but his later years were beset with financial problems and bitterness toward Lieutenant-Governor Arthur. Knopwood was at one stage accused by the bushranger Michael Howe of being connected to his gang. The reverend also adopted a young girl, Elizabeth Mack, shortly after the death of her mother. She lived with him for many years and Knopwood was shattered by her death in childbirth. He died in 1838 at the age of 75. His diaries remain one of the few first-hand records of the difficult early years in Hobart.

James Hingston Tuckey was captured by the French along with the rest of the crew of the *Calcutta* in 1805. During his nine-year imprisonment he married Margaret Stuart, the daughter of an East India Company ship commander. He also wrote a monumental and highly acclaimed work on maritime geography, a 2500-page tome published in four volumes. The captain of the *Calcutta*, Daniel Woodriff, praised Tuckey in an inquiry into the capture of the ship, saying 'his courage, cool intrepidity and superior abilities as a seaman and officer . . . render him most worthy of the attention of the Admiralty'. Tuckey died in October 1816, off the coast of the Democratic Republic of the Congo. His diaries about his journey into the Congo were published posthumously. His wife and four surviving children were granted pensions by the Prince Regent on behalf of the incapacitated King George III.

William Marmon, Buckley's regimental colleague who sailed with him on the *Calcutta* and formed part of the escape party in late December 1803, made it back to the settlement at Sullivan's Bay suffering from scurvy, just in time to join the *Ocean* as it sailed for Van Diemen's Land. He became a free man in 1818 and advertised his intention to leave for England in 1821.

Captain William Lonsdale acted as Chief Magistrate of Port Phillip until 1840 when he became the colony's sub-treasurer. By the early 1850s he was Victoria's first colonial secretary and treasurer until he left for England in 1854. He died in London in 1864.

Joseph Johnson married his housekeeper, Jane Baird, 11 months after the death of his first wife, unaware that 'Baird' was already married to an Englishman, William Hadden. When Jane left him following the arrival in Hobart of her original husband, Johnson advertised that he was not responsible for any debts she may have incurred. She later made successful claims for much of his property.

Reverend George Langhorne oversaw the establishment of Port Phillip's first Aboriginal mission, believing he had been asked to encourage the 'intermixture by marriage of the Aborigines among the lower order of our countrymen as the only likely means of raising the former from their present degraded and benighted state'. The project was an abject failure marked by food shortages, police brutality, political tension and the inability to understand Aboriginal culture and customs. It was closed in 1839 as pressure by white settlers for more land increased. Langhorne became a pastoralist and died in 1897.

William Lushington Goodwin's constant attacks on the Establishment of Van Diemen's Land cost him hundreds of pounds in defamation payments. He sold the *Cornwall Chronicle* after being declared bankrupt in 1842 but continued to act as proprietor. He then underwent a significant rehabilitation, becoming an alderman on the Launceston City Council and being appointed to several senior government positions. He died in 1862 at the age of 64 in George Town, Tasmania. Goodwin's wife, Sophie, continued to manage the *Chronicle* until it was merged with the *Launceston Times* in 1869.

WADAWURRUNG CLAN NAMES AND LOCATIONS

Clan name	Approximate location
Barere barere balug	Colac and Mt Bute stations
Beerekwart balug	Mt Emu
Bengalat balug	Indented Head
Berrejin balug	Unknown
Boro gundidj	Yarrowee River
Burrumbeet gundidj	Lakes Burrumbeet and Learmonth
Carringum balug	Carngham
Carininje balug	Emu Hill station, Lintons Creek
Corac balug	Commeralghip station, and Kuruc-a-ruc Creek
Corrin corrinjer balug	Carranballac
Gerarlture balug	West of Lake Modewarre
Keyeet balug	Mt Buninyong
Marpeang balug	Blackwood, Myrniong, and Bacchus Marsh
Mear balug	Unknown
Moijerre balug	Mt Emu Creek

Clan name	Approximate location
Moner balug	Trawalla station, Mt Emu Creek
Monmart	Unknown
Neerer balug	Between Geelong and the You Yangs (Hovells Creek?)
Pakeheneek balu	Mt Widderin
Peerickelmoon balug	Near Mt Misery
Tooloora balug	Mt Warrenheip, Lal-lal Creek, west branch of Moorabool River
Woodealloke gundidj	Wardy Yalloak River, south of Kuruc-a-ruc Creek
Wada wurrung balug	Barrabool Hills
Wongerrer balug	Head of Wardy Yalloak River
Worinyaloke balug	West side of Little River
Yaawangi	You Yang Hills

Source: Clark (1990)

THE FIRST PEOPLE

In the 1830s up to 60,000 Aboriginals were believed to live across the land that later became the state of Victoria. Less than a century later an estimated 500 remained. While they were subjected to the same pressures of frontier violence, introduced diseases and dislocation experienced by Indigenous people elsewhere in Australia, the occupation of their lands in Victoria took place at an unprecedented pace. The pastoral and grazing invasion decimated traditional food sources, from kangaroos and other fauna to the yam daisy, forcing more to turn to towns where the ready availability of sugar, rum and tobacco compounded other emerging health problems. Alcoholism, dysentery, typhus fever and syphilis shattered families and traditional clan structures and among the hardest hit were the tribes who originally lived around the Melbourne area – the Woiwurrung and the Boonwurrung. Four years after a group of clan leaders from these tribes signed the so-called Batman treaty, little more than 200 remained.

In that same year, 1839, George Augustus Robinson was appointed Port Phillip's Chief Protector of Aborigines following a recommendation from a British government inquiry. Robinson, a believer in conciliation, had been responsible for the relocation of most of the remaining Tasmanian Aboriginals to Flinders Island, particularly the Big River and Oyster Bay people. By 1835 there were fewer than

150 Tasmanian Aboriginals left from an estimated population of more than 5000 before white settlement. Robinson's time in Victoria was unimpressive as Aboriginal people were lured or herded into remote missions, often in unfamiliar land or in territory previously occupied by rival tribes. Several other initiatives supported by London, including the introduction of a Native Police Force, also ended in failure.

The ratio of deaths attributable to violence for Aboriginals and whites in this era was 12:1 and the Wadawurrung were among several tribes that suffered significantly at the hands of unauthorised hunting parties. By the end of the 1860s the majority of Wadawurrung had been moved to reserves and missions away from traditional lands.

A census in 1871 reported only 65 Aboriginals remaining in Wadawurrung country.

ACKNOWLEDGEMENTS

It took more than 150 hard-working crew members six months to ensure HMS *Calcutta* safely sailed from England to Port Phillip in 1803. There were times when it felt like I had far more people helping me trace the extraordinary journey of William Buckley. There is not space to mention everyone who made a contribution. But it would be remiss not to highlight the assistance I received from the State Library of Victoria, the State Library of NSW and the National Library of Australia, particularly its impressive digital resource Trove. In Melbourne, Des Cowley of the SLV's Collection Development and Description section provided sound advice and steered me in several key directions. His colleague, Greg Gerrand, allowed me to sit down one afternoon and, with gloved hands, very gently turn the pages of William Todd's calf leather diary, an extraordinary document that records the moment Buckley returned to white society.

Professors Tim Flannery and Richard Broome were also invaluable guides in the early research. Flannery's introduction to the 2002 edition of *The Life and Adventures of William Buckley* remains one of the most insightful explorations of Buckley and his experiences. Tim's passionate advice took me in several new directions. Professor Broome, one of the most authoritative voices on Australian Aboriginal history, gave me much to think about.

Professor Alan Cooper, the Director of the Australian Centre for Ancient DNA, is one of a team of researchers who have revolutionised our understanding of ancient Aboriginal history through pioneering DNA sampling work. He read a draft of a critical section of the book and patiently highlighted areas that needed improving.

Many thanks also go to Dr Stefan Petrow of the University of Tasmania, who steered me in the direction of Jacqueline Fox, the author of a highly praised biography of the former Chief Justice of Van Diemen's Land, John Pedder. Jacqueline found previously undiscovered material relating to Buckley in the archives and was a tremendous resource on the island's colonial times, as well as being a valuable sounding board. Thanks also to the staff of the Rare Book Collection at the University of Tasmania and the Tasmanian Archives.

In England there was only one man to turn to when it came to uncovering faded historical documents in Cheshire – the 'History Detective', Tony Bostock. A retired policeman who has lost none of his prosecutorial skills, Tony seemed to instantly uncover information and papers that would have taken me months. In the village of Marton, Roger Lomas, a landscape architect and the managing director of urban design company e*SCAPE, helped me understand the countryside around Buckley's birthplace. Books, papers, theses and other key resources are mentioned in the bibliography. But it would be remiss not to highlight the importance of Marjorie Tipping's seminal work, *Convicts Unbound – the Story of the Calcutta Convicts and Their Settlement in Australia*, along with that astonishing body of work, the foundation series of *Historical Records of Victoria*.

Jill Baker – as she often did during our time in newspapers – rescued me when I was drowning in doubt, patiently going through an early draft of the book while trying to write one of her own.

Alison Urquhart at Penguin Random House Australia is one of the publishing industry's greatest enthusiasts and she saw the possibilities of this book long before I did. Her passion for this project made it happen and, ultimately, led me to the watchful eyes and careful hands of two brilliant editors – Michael Epis and Patrick Mangan.

Their suggestions on the book's structure as well as their ability to save me from many errors – factual and grammatical – were invaluable. Any remaining faults must rest with me.

But when it came to writing *Buckley's Chance*, I always had the sense that two other people were looking over my shoulder, critiquing every sentence. One of them, of course, was William Buckley. The other was Les Carlyon, the master storyteller himself, a man I had been fortunate to call a friend and mentor for more than 30 years. He fell ill and passed away as this book began to form. A day didn't pass when I did not wonder what he would think of this passage or that chapter. Like everyone else whose life he touched and influenced, I will continue to sorely miss his voice and advice and regret that I never thanked him enough for his wisdom and encouragement.

ENDNOTES

PROLOGUE
1. **There is a full moon in hell ...** based on the moon's phase for the evenings of 26–27 December 1803. www.moonpage.com.
2. **No punishment can be fitting enough ...** Details of the escape are drawn from the diary of Robert Knopwood, daily notices by David Collins at the Sullivan Bay settlement, *Convicts Unbound* by Marjorie Tipping and John Morgan's *The Life and Adventures of William Buckley*.
3. **He has come up with a solution for this ...** The looped handkerchief Buckley used while walking with his wife in Hobart is reported by various sources, including *The Narrative of George Russell of Golf Hill* (edited by P. L. Brown).

PART 1
CHAPTER 1
4. **It is dark and damp ...** Descriptions of life on the prison hulks are drawn from several sources including *The Scots Magazine*, July 1770; www.royal-arsenal-history.com/woolwich-prison-hulks.html; Hughes, Robert, *The Fatal Shore*; Campbell, Charles F., *The Intolerable Hulks: British Shipboard Confinement, 1776–1857*.
5. **Imprisoned on the *Portland* ...** George Lee letter to Sir Henry St John Mildmay, 24 January 1803, Bentham papers, British Library.
6. **So best leave the most colourful description ...** Vaux, James Hardy. *A New and Comprehensive Vocabulary of the Flash Language*.
7. **'These guards the most commonly of the lowest class ...'** Vaux, James Hardy. *Memoirs of James Hardy Vaux*.

CHAPTER 2

8. **She's an old ship, this one . . .** Tipping, Marjorie. *Convicts Unbound*; Colledge, J. J., *Ships of the Royal Navy: The Complete Record of All Fighting Ships of the Royal Navy from the Fifteenth Century to the Present.*

9. **More than 500 of you – 300 convicts . . .** Tipping.

10. **She was built in John Perry's yard . . .** Currey, John. *Sullivan Bay: How Convicts Came to Port Phillip and Van Diemen's Land.*

11. **Two men are losing their heads . . .** The trial of Edward Marcus Despard has been the subject of many books, including a shorthand account of the trial by the brothers Joseph Gurney and William Gurney in *The Trial of Edward Marcus Despard for High Treason*, 1803, available online. Description of his execution from Jay, Mike. *The Unfortunate Colonel Despard.*

12. **The effects of this new Industrial Age can be seen . . .** Jackson, Lee. *Dirty Old London – the Victorian Fight against Filth.*

13. **War has long been its greatest industry . . .** Haythornthwaite, Philip. *Redcoats – the British Soldiers of the Napoleonic Wars.*

14. **And ruling over this divided kingdom . . .** Many historians and doctors now believe King George III suffered from porphyria, a disorder that affects the nervous system. Researchers who discovered traces of arsenic in samples of the king's hair reported their findings in the medical journal *The Lancet* on 23 July 2005.

15. **Many were sold to private contractors . . .** Hughes, Robert. *The Fatal Shore.*

16. **There are more than 160 offences . . .** Tipping.

17. **The smell will reach its climax . . .** Halliday, Stephen. *The Great Stink of London.*

CHAPTER 3

18. **In late 700 AD . . .** One of the best descriptions of the Marton Oak has been written by Julian Hight, author of *World Tree Story: History and Legends of the World's Ancient Trees* (2012).

19. **But Offa is a man . . .** Encyclopaedia Britannica.

20. **And suddenly you find yourself indentured to Robert Wyatt . . .** Morgan, *The Life and Adventures.*

21. **Apprenticeships in the late 18th century . . .** The London Lives project, Digital Humanities Institute, University of Sheffield. www.londonlives.org/index.jsp.

CHAPTER 4

22. **The scum of the earth . . .** Haythornthwaite.

23. **Hard pounding this, gentlemen . . .** as quoted by Sir Walter Scott, *Paul's Letters to his Kinfolk* (1815).

24. **They will celebrate Old Nosey in ballads . . .** Some of them include *Nosey the King of Waterloo and his row dow dow iddy iddy pipe clay nose* and *Poor old King Nosey is getting old*. Source: Muir, Rory. *Wellington: Waterloo and the Fortunes of Peace*, 1814–1852.

25. **The Secretary of War will stand up . . .** Haythornthwaite.

26. **One regiment employs the 42-inch dwarf . . .** Description of John Heyes from *The Gentleman's Magazine*, Volume 83, Part 1; Volume 113 (January to June 1813).

27. **There is little they won't try in the quest . . .** Haythornthwaite.

28. **One soldier who joins the ranks . . .** ibid.

29. **Little wonder John Gaspard Le Merchant . . .** *The United Service Magazine and Naval and Military Journal*, 1843, Part II.

30. **Alcohol has become a peculiar British disease . . .** Howard, Martin, MD. 'Red Jackets and Red Noses: Alcohol and the British Napoleonic Soldier'. *Journal of the Royal Society of Medicine*, Vol. 93, January 2000.

CHAPTER 5

31. **'A swarm of bees, here on the battlefield? . . .'** Haythornthwaite.

32. **The little Frenchman's sore arse . . .** Mason, Phil. *Napoleon's Haemorrhoids: and Other Small Events That Changed the World*. Skyhorse. 2008.

33. **More bloodshed before another embarrassing retreat . . .** The campaign in the Netherlands also became well known for one of the more bizarre incidents during the Napoleonic Wars. A soldier with the 31st, John Cames, buried a colleague, Robert Hullock, who had been shot through the jaw. But Hullock was not dead, just in shock. He eventually came to his senses and clawed his way out of the ground. Years later, as the pair served on another battlefield, Hullock spent a few spare hours digging a 10-foot grave. Asked what he was doing, Hullock said: 'Building a grave for Cames . . . it will puzzle him to creep out as I did.' Letter by Asaph Shaw, Lt., 31st regiment. *The United Service Journal and Naval and Military Magazine*, Part III, 1831, pp.380–1.

34. **Restoring Prince William to power . . .** Descriptions of the 1799 campaign drawn from various sources including *The Campaign in Holland*, 1799 by Terry Astley (Subaltern), Henry Bunbury's *A Narrative of the Campaign in North Holland*, 1799 and *Anglo-Russian Invasion of Holland* (Wikipedia).

35.   **Some of them had placed leather pads in their shoes . . .** Haythornthwaite; Galofré-Vilà, Gregori, Dr. *Heights across the Last 2000 Years in England.* University of Oxford. 2017.

36.   **'We can shew a peasantry of heroes . . .'** *The Works of Samuel Johnson*, Volumes 1–2. 1837, p.403.

37.   **'The faces of the bravest often change colour . . .'** Hughes, Ben. *Conquer or Die!: Wellington's Veterans and the Liberation of the New World.* Osprey Publishing. 2010.

CHAPTER 6

38.   **Good looking man this Collins . . .** Descriptions of David Collins from Currey, John. *David Collins, a Colonial Life.* The Miegunyah Press, 2000.

39.   **The wife of a convict, fair to the eye . . .** Ibid; Tipping.

40.   **'I have always thought that nature designed me . . .'** Letter to his father, 12 September 1791. Collins papers. Vol. 1.

41.   **'I have just had two letters from my father . . .'** 8 June 1775. Ibid.

42.   **The Queen had been married off to her first cousin . . .** Ward, Adolphus William. *Dictionary of National Biography*, 1885–1890. Vol. 9.

43.   **It had been a 16-year-old David Collins . . .** Currey.

44.   **'. . . a collection of old, worn out, useless men . . .'** Collins letter to Lord Hobart, 4 March 1804. *Historical Records of Australia*, Series III, Vol. 1.

45.   **'I think and hope that my evil genius . . .'** Collins letter to his mother, 23 December 1802.

46.   **Collins has his looks and standing . . .** Shortly before the departure of the *Calcutta*, Collins filled out his final will leaving his sparse assets and funds to his wife, Maria. His appointment as Lieutenant Governor of the Port Phillip venture followed years of behind the scenes manoeuvring. Patronage was instrumental to promotion within the British government at this time and Collins had been corresponding for years with the Home Secretary, Lord Sydney, who constantly hinted that Collins was on the cusp of receiving an important role. But nothing ever materialised and when Lord Sydney died unexpectedly, Collins turned, among others, to Sir Joseph Banks. In a letter to Banks he wrote: 'I have at all times considered your protection, had not the unexpected death of my patron, Lord Sydney, at a moment when his influence was about to be extended in my favour, compelled me to throw myself on you, Sir, for the patronage I have so untimely lost in his Lordship.' Banks, who was known to have the ear of King George III, replied, '. . . I have my doubts of being able to effectually serve you when a man of Lord Sydney's interest has so long solicited your cause in vain.' Letter to Banks, 8 July 1800. State Library of NSW. Series 72.017. Banks reply to Collins, 8 July.

47. **Have you seen that small boy . . .** Tipping; Anderson, Hugh. *Out of the Shadow: the Career of John Pascoe Fawkner*; Billot, C. P. *The Life and Times of John Pascoe Fawkner*; Fawkner, John Pascoe. *Melbourne's Missing Chronicle: Being the Journal of Preparation for Departure to and Proceeding to Port Phillip.*

48. **Desperate to stay out of the prison rooms below . . .** Tipping.

49. **'A woman whom I did not know . . .'** Langhorne, George. *Reminiscenses of James [sic] Buckley . . .*

50. **Compared to Captain Mazot's troubles . . .** Accounts of the trial of William Buckley and William Marmon taken from the *Sussex Weekly Advertiser*, issues 2 August 1802 and 9 August 1802, and Tipping, Marjorie.

51. **Hanging is not the swift form of execution . . .** Public hangings did not stop in Britain until 1868. At the time of Buckley's trial, there were few standard procedures in place for executions. Variously sized ropes and knots were employed by executioners and full and partial decapitations were not unusual. A standardised method of estimating the drop required – based on the weight of the victim's body – was not introduced until late in the second half of the 19th century.

CHAPTER 7

52. **'. . . asking for additional, often-used letters . . .'** Currey.

53. **'Nancy must mind her spelling . . .'** Collins letter to Henrietta, 11 November 1776. Collins Papers. Vol. 1.

54. **'Duncan Campbell had been up to his usual tricks . . .'** Hughes, Robert. *The Fatal Shore*. Campbell had been a merchant seaman and ship owner who earned five pounds for each convict he took to America and on the return leg imported large amounts of tobacco. His niece was married to Captain William Bligh, who at one stage worked for Campbell. After the War of Independence Campbell managed England's prison hulks for 25 years. Campbell, Charles. *The Intolerable Hulks: British Shipboard Confinement, 1776–1857.*

55. **The sheep had only been slaughtered the night before . . .** Hughes.

56. **. . . the ship's skipper, Daniel Woodriff . . .** This was Woodriff's second journey to Australia, the first in 1782 on the *Kitty*. He joined the Navy at the age of six as a servant to his uncle, a master gunner on the HMS *Ludlow Castle*. Australian Dictionary of Biography.

57. **'When any of our comrades died . . .'** Hughes.

58. **'The misery I saw amongst them is indescribable . . .'** This report was provided by the Reverend Johnson. *Historical Records of NSW 1*, Part 2, pp.387–8.

59.   'I find that I am spending the prime of my life ...' Collins letter. 17 October 1791.

60.   'On a cold autumn morning at Sydney Cove...' Currey.

61.   'The treatment I received on the passage...' Morgan.

62.   There will be some who will become suspicious about Bromley ... Tuckey, J. H. *An Account of a Voyage to Establish a Colony* ...

63.   William Appleton is barely four feet tall ... Tipping.

64.   Steel was sent down the same day ... ibid.

CHAPTER 8

65.   Another one dead ... Knopwood, Robert. *Diary of the Reverend Robert Knopwood, 1803–1838.*

66.   'Unto Almighty God ...' From the *Anglican Book of Modern Prayer*, instructions for burial at sea.

67.   '... mere disability brought on by seasickness.' Pateshall, Nicholas. Journal.

68.   ... will regard Knopwood as a fraud ... Fawkner, John Pascoe. *Melbourne's Missing Chronicle.*

69.   Nelson was immediately hit by a musket ball ... Hibbert, Christopher. *Nelson, a Personal History.* 1994.

70.   He's a tall 27-year-old Irishman clinging to handsomeness. Hingston, Richard. *Captain Tuckey of the Congo*; Dictionary of Irish Biography.

71.   'Among the convicts on board ...' Tuckey.

72.   One estimate puts the numbers of death at sea ... Drymon, M. M. *Disguised as the Devil: How Lyme Disease Created Witches and Changed History.* Whythe Avenue Press. 2008.

73.   A 16-year-old forger from London ... Tipping.

CHAPTER 9

74.   'This bay and the harbour in general ...' *Historical Records of Port Phillip.* General orders of David Collins. 20 October 1803.

75.   After entering the Bay the *Calcutta* had turned right ... Descriptions of the Sullivan Bay settlement taken from Tipping, Currey, Hughes and the journals of Tuckey, Pateshall and Knopwood.

76.   'They appeared to have a perfect knowledge of the use of firearms ...' Tuckey.

77.   The feeling appears to be mutual ... Ibid.

78.   Within moments ... Ibid.

79.   'I am sorry to observe that in general ...' quote from Labilliere, Francis Peter. *Early History of the Colony of Victoria.* 1878.

80. **'When I viewed so many of my fellow men . . .'** Tuckey.

81. **'Tis Liberty alone . . .'** From *The Task, Book V. The Winter Morning Walk.*

CHAPTER 10

82. **'The attempt was little short of madness . . .'** Morgan.

83. **'On Christmas Eve when revelries were in full swing . . .'** The exact number of convicts who escaped along with Buckley remains unclear. Only the diary of the Reverend Knopwood includes the names, but his accuracy has always been questionable, along with his spelling and capacity for correctly identifying people. In his journal entry for Sunday 25 December, Knopwood writes: 'Last night a most daring robbery was committed by some person or persons, in the Commissary's marque. While he was in bed they stole a gun which was hung up near the side of the bed, and took a pair of boots which were at the bed side. The sentry saw a man come from it, but thought he was his servant. The hospital tent was likewise robbd.' The following day he notes that at 11 pm, 'the drum beat to arms by reason of some of the convicts had made their escape.' His entry for Tuesday 27 December, says that at 9 pm '6 convicts endeavourd to make their escape; they were beset by a look-out party and one man shot, very much wounded.' It seems the most likely date of the escape was the evening of 26 December, not Christmas Day which has been previously widely mentioned. On Saturday 31 December, Knopwood names missing convicts as 'Mac Allennan, George Pye, Pritchard, M. Warner, Wm. Buckley; Charles Shaw, wounded and brought to the camp; Page, taken same time when Shaw *was shot*, G. Lee, and Wm. Gibson.' There was no convict listed on the *Calcutta* as 'M Warner' and it is more than likely Knopwood has confused the name 'Marmon'. Of the others, Lee and Gibson had escaped on 12 December. Gibson eventually returned to camp and informed Collins of a large river to the north (the Yarra). Buckley himself in *Life and Adventures* says there were 'four of us' who escaped. But in 1837 he told the Reverend George Langhorne that he had made known his plan to escape to 'two other prisoners.' He also mentions using a boat during the escape but there is no record of this taking place. With McAllennan and Marmon eventually returning to camp, it would seem that George Pye and James Taylor were the most likely prisoners to have remained with Buckley until they, too, left him and were never seen again.

84. **'Pity the delusion which some of the prisoners . . .'** General Orders, David Collins, Sullivan Bay. 31 December 1803.

85. **'It is by far the most brutal punishment handed out . . .'** Currey. The two Marines flogged were James Reay and Robert Andrews.

86. **'How is it possible that strong hardy men . . .'** General orders. David Collins, Sullivan Bay. 20 January 1804.

87. **'Some of the most wounding will come from the acid pen . . .'** William Bligh sailed with Captain James Cook on the *Resolution*. In 1789 he was captain of the *Bounty* when crew members mutinied; Bligh and 18 loyalists were placed in a 23-foot boat and spent 47 days sailing to Timor, 6700 kilometres away. Bligh arrived in New South Wales as its fourth governor and left in 1809 following the Rum Rebellion – the only armed takeover of an Australian government. He arrived in Hobart seeking support from Collins. But the pair did not get along and Bligh wrote damaging letters to England about Collins and his conduct. Another high-profile critic of Collins was Joseph Foveaux, who told authorities in London that in Hobart 'a system of the most unexampled profusion, waste and fraud, with respect to money, and stores, had been carried on, almost without the affectation of concealment and sense of shame'.

88. **Two years later, recovering from a cold . . .** Death of Collins, his burial and disinterment from Currey, John. *David Collins: A Colonial Life*.

PART II
CHAPTER 11

89. **'The whole affair was, in fact, a species . . .'** *Life and Adventures*.

90. **Your companions, starving and bitter . . .** Both were never heard from again, although Buckley said he learned years later that one of them had been murdered by an Aboriginal tribe after mistreating one of their women. According to *Life and Adventures*, his two companions left him after watching the *Ocean* preparing to leave for Van Diemen's Land. But Buckley told the Reverend Langhorne that one of his fellow escapers parted from him when they reached the Yarra River, while another came to live with him about six months after he began living with the Wadawurrung. But the man's 'faithless conduct to the Blacks and dissolute behaviour towards their women' forced him to part ways once more with his fellow convict. 'He left and I never heard of him more except by a vague report that he had been killed by the Blacks.'

91. **'I turned a deaf ear . . .'** Narrative of events following Buckley's escape drawn from *Life and Adventures* and *Reminiscenses of James Buckley* with the Reverend George Langhorne.

CHAPTER 12

92. **The voices belong to three aboriginal men . . .** *Life and Adventures.*

93. **There was a stubborn bastard on the Calcutta with you . . .** An excellent description of the biology of the shipworm *Teredo navalis* and the havoc it wreaked on ocean vessels can be found in an article by Sarah Gillman of *Hakai magazine*. 'How a ship-sinking clam conquered the ocean' has been reproduced online in www.smithsonianmag.com, 5 December 2016. Wikipedia also contains a concise description of its abilities.

94. **The master of the *Cinque Ports* is Alexander Selkirk . . .** The *Cinque Ports* was an English galley. It sank a month after Selkirk warned Stradling that it was infested with worms. It had been used by Sir William Dampier as part of an expedition in 1701.

95. **. . . Stradling has had enough of Selkirk's complaints . . .** In one version of events Selkirk told Stradling he would rather be on that island than on a leaking boat, a wish Stradling immediately granted. In 2005 an archaeological expedition to the Juan Fernandez Islands discovered a fragment of a nautical instrument researchers believe belonged to Selkirk. Their findings were published as 'Excavation at Aguas Buenas, Robinson Crusoe Island, Chile, of a gunpowder magazine and the supposed campsite of Alexander Selkirk, together with an account of early navigational dividers.' Takahasi, D. and others, Post Medieval Archeology Journal. Vol. 41. 2007.

96. **When Selkirk is rescued almost four and a half years . . .** Selcraig, Bruce. *Smithsonian Magazine*, July 2005.

97. **The skipper of the *Duke*, Woodes Rogers . . .** Rogers, Woodes. *A Cruising Voyage round the World* (1712). Reprinted in the *The Seafarer's Library*, 1928.

CHAPTER 13

98. **Time you learned something about these people . . .** Descriptions of the origins of Aboriginal Australians drawn from a variety of sources, including Broome, Richard; Frankel, David; Gammage, Bill.

99. **They have hunted diprotodons . . .** Diprotodons were enormous marsupials related to wombats and koalas, believed to have fallen extinct 46,000 years ago. Aboriginal art rock in Queensland is said to depict the creatures and some researchers have suggested the animal may have inspired legends about the mythical Bunyip.

100. **Let's call them the Very First Fleet . . .** One of the latest studies into the arrival of Aborigines in Australia appeared in the *Proceedings of the National Academy of Sciences of the United States of America*, 21 August 2018, by a team of Australian researchers. Another, which studied mitochondrial genomes from historical Aboriginal hair samples, appeared in *Nature*, March 2017.

A summary of some of the work appeared in *The Conversation*, 7 August 2018.

101.   '... explorers will leave behind a scattering of African coins ...' Donnelly, Paul, Silkatcheva, Ana. *The Marchinbar Find – Medieval Travels to Australia from Africa?* Museum of Applied Arts and Sciences, 9 July 2014.

102.   '... miserablist people in the world ...' Dampier, William. *A New Voyage round the World* (1697).

103.   For many there is Bunjil ... Broome, Richard. *Aboriginal Victorians*.

104.   'I was soon afterwards transferred ...' Morgan.

105.   In Central Victoria the Morpor people ... Dawson, James. *The Languages and Customs of Several Tribes of Aborigines in the Western District of Victoria.* Read Books. 2010.

CHAPTER 14

106.   It's one of the reasons you will turn to John Morgan ... Descriptions of Morgan from Bolger, Peter; *Australian Dictionary of Biography*.

107.   '... slowly pacing along the middle of the road with his eyes vacantly fixed ...' Bonwick, James. *The Wild White Man*.

108.   Born in Surrey ... Featherstone, Guy. James Bonwick entry in *Australian Dictionary of Biography*.

109.   'We saw a party of natives plied with drink ...' Bonwick. *The Wild White Man*.

110.   'In order to exist at all he must have had qualities of shrewdness ...' Tudehope, C.M.

111.   Take the surviving crew members of the *Essex* ... Melville published *Moby-Dick* in 1851 and based his character Captain Ahab on one of the survivors of the *Essex*, Owen Chase. In 2000, another retelling of the story, Nathaniel Philbrick's *In the Heart of the Sea: the Tragedy of the Whaleship Essex* won the National Book Award and was turned into an acclaimed movie.

112.   They had originally planned to make their way to the Derwent ... One of the best accounts of the escape from Macquarie Harbour and subsequent cannibalism can be found in Hughes, Robert. *The Fatal Shore*. Pearce's adventures were fictionalised in Marcus Clarke's *For the Term of His Natural Life* and featured in the 2009 movie, *Van Diemen's Land*.

113.   ... his skull being sent to the prolific American author and scientist ... Samuel Morton was a supporter of polygenism, which claimed the Bible proved that each human race had been created separately. He amassed a collection of thousands of human craniums and published claims that the cranial capacity of Caucasians was larger than that of other races. Wade,

Nicholas. *Scientists Measure the Accuracy of a Racism Claim. The New York Times.* 13 June 2011.

114. **'... an unending supply of eels *(buniya)* ...'** Wadawurrung words and definitions from the Wadawurrung language app, produced in partnership with the Wathaurung Aboriginal Corporation and the Victorian Aboriginal Corporation for Languages.

CHAPTER 15

115. **The *Lady Nelson* is an 80-ton brig ...** from Ida, Lee. *The Logbooks of the 'Lady Nelson' with the Journal of Her First Commander Lieutenant James Grant.* Grafton and Co. 1915; Shaffer, Irene. *A Short History of the Lady Nelson.* www.ladynelson.org.au/history/short-history.

116. **Cook is sailing with a set of 'hints' ...** Moore, Peter. *Endeavour: the Ship and the Attitude That Changed the World.* Vintage. 2018.

117. **This is a time when Europeans ...** The phrase 'noble savage' first appeared in English in *The Conquest of Granada*, a play in 1672 by the poet John Dryden. It became a regular literary trope throughout Europe in the 18th and 19th centuries.

118. **'He was a shrewd, sensible, ingenious man ...'** Beaglehole, J. C. *The Life of Captain James Cook.* Stanford University Press. 1974.

119. **From the deck of the *Endeavour* ...** Banks, Sir Joseph. *The Endeavour Journal of Sir Joseph Banks/April 1770.*

120. **Stories are already being passed from clan to clan ...** Moore.

121. **The Prince of Wales is one of the first to employ it ...** The phrase 'mutton dressed as lamb' was first used in print in 1811. www.phrases.org.uk/meanings/mutton-dressed-as-lamb.html.

122. **'The woods are free from underwood ...'** Wharton, William James Lloyd. Captain Cook's journal during his first voyage round the world. Cambridge University Press. 2014.

123. **Water becomes such a lottery that a man ...** Gammage, Bill.

CHAPTER 16

124. **'One of the possible reasons for his survival ...'** Tudehope.

125. **It will come to us courtesy of a Scotsman ...** Corris, Peter. *Australian Dictionary of Biography.*

126. **'They may appear to be some of the most wretched ...'** O'Sullivan, Daniel. *In Search of Captain Cook: Exploring the Man through His Own Words.* I. B. Tauris. 2008.

CHAPTER 17

127. **'Snake . . . *Kadak?* . . .'** Wadawurrung translations from Blake, Barry J. and Wadawurrung language app.

128. **These black heads of the Kallallingurk come from a special quarry . . .** The site of *Wil-im-ee Moor-ring* is now on the Australian National Heritage List.

129. **'Bestowed no labour on the land . . .'** *The Sydney Morning Herald*. 7 November 1838.

130. **One of his guides, Bungin, tells him . . .** Flannery, Tim (ed.). *The Explorers*. Text Publishing. 1998.

131. **These fires he sees are controlled burns.** Descriptions of Aboriginal use of fire from sources including Gammage, Broome.

132. **The introduction of the mustang by Spanish conquistadors . . .** Gwynne, S. C.

133. **It is the same with agriculture.** There is widespread evidence of pre-colonial Aboriginal agriculture. Some of the best summaries are by Gerritsen, Rupert, *Evidence for Indigenous Australian Agriculture. Australasian Science*. July/August 2010; Pascoe, Bruce, *Dark Emu*, and Broome.

134. **If Canopus, the second brightest star in the sky . . .** Bell, Diane. Ngarrindjeri Wurruwarrin: *A World That Is, Was, and Will Be*. Spinifex. 1998.

135. **. . . even the mythical Bunyip.** There are almost a dozen variations of the Bunyip – a rough translation of 'evil spirit' – in Aboriginal mythology. Several scientists have attributed its status to cultural memory and lore going back tens of thousands of years, when early Aboriginal Australians first encountered Australia's megafauna during the Pleistocene epoch. Professor Tim Flannery has explained Buckley's comments about the Bunyip in this way: '. . . we need to remember that Buckley was a rural Cheshireman who doubtless believed implicitly in the faeries and hobgoblins of his homeland. Likewise, the Aboriginal people who were educating Buckley about their environment made no clear division between myth and material reality; instead both were interwoven in a seamless view of the world.' (From: Introduction to *The Life and Adventures of William Buckley*. Text Classics. 2002.)

CHAPTER 18

136. **Take James Murrells . . .** James Murrells (aka Morrills, Jemmy Morril). *ADB*. Gregory, Edmund. Maynard, John.

137. **John Wilson . . .** Chisholm, J. H. *John Wilson*. ADB. Collins letter, 11 June 1795, cited in Currey, J.

138. **But it is Narcisse Pelletier . . .** Anderson, Stephanie and Maynard, John.

CHAPTER 19

139. **'Seldom seen a more fearful section of coastline ...'** The remains of Matthew Flinders, who circumnavigated Australia in 1802–3, were found beneath a London railway station in January 2019, more than 200 years after his death at the age of 40.

140. **'I shall only observe ...'** Lee, Ida. *Logbooks of the Lady Nelson*, 27 January 1802.

141. **'... driven by the world's largest current carrying 130 million cubic metres ...'** Marine Science of Australia. *Oceanography of Australia*. www.ausmarinescience.com/marine-science-basics/oceanography-of-australia.

142. **'They are complete savages ...'** Cited by Boyce, James. *Van Diemen's Land*.

143. **'You can sense the coming cultural collision ...'** Narrative drawn from *Life and Adventures*.

CHAPTER 20

144. **William Todd has been growing frustrated ...** Drawn from Brown, Philip (ed.). *The Todd Journal – Andrew alias William Todd. John Batman's Recorder and his Indented Head Journal, 1835*.

145. **But if men like Joe the Marine ...** Among the Sydney Aboriginals John Batman originally hired to assist him in Van Diemen's Land were Jonninbia ('John Crook'), Warroba ('Pigeon'), Macher ('Mackey'), Numbunghundy ('Sawyer'), Garrammilly ('Jack Radley'), Nillang ('Steward'), Onnorerong ('Waterman'), Quanmurrer ('Joe the Marine'), Bulberlang ('John Peter') and Budgergorry (William). Taylor, Rebe. 'The Wedge Collection and the Conundrum of Human Colonisation'. *Meanjin*. Summer 2017.

146. **Each night he takes out his brown calf leather journal ...** Todd's original journal remains the only continual account of the first five months of European settlement in Port Phillip in 1835. It was rediscovered among the papers of a Mr Evans in Hobart in 1885.

147. **'... the most beautiful sheep pasturage ...'** John Batman journal, 30 May 1835. State Library of Victoria.

148. **... including the towering Billibellary ...** Billibellary (also known as Jika Jika, Jaga Jaga and Billi-billeri) was a joint custodian of the *Wil-im-ee Moor-ring* quarry and its greenstone heads for tomahawks. As a Wurundjeri elder he joined the Native Police Corps, but resigned when he discovered it was being used to hunt down and even kill Aboriginal suspects. He died in 1846 of inflammation of the lungs.

149. **No-one will even be sure of the exact location ...** Most historians now suspect the signing took place on the side of the Merri Creek, which joins the Yarra at Dights Falls.

150. **You open your mouth to say something and . . .** Morgan. Todd journal.

151. **'. . . and a native of Macclesfield . . .'** Macclesfield is about 10 kilometres north-east of Marton. It was a major centre for English silk production in the 18th and 19th centuries.

PART III
CHAPTER 21

152. **William Lushington Goodwin has been waiting . . .** Craig, C. J. *ADB*.

153. **'We are fast becoming priest-ridden and effeminate.'** *The Cornwall Chronicle*. 1 December 1838. Column 4, page 2.

154. **'. . . some of them by nature and habit were cleanly . . .'** Clarke, Thrasycles. *Medical and Surgical Journal of the Female Convict Ship Kains from 11 June 1830 to 25 March 1831*. The National Archives, Kew.

155. **. . . Captain Goodwin 'began to ill use us . . .'** Diary of Charles Picknell, *The Sydney Morning Herald*, 10, 17 and 24 May 1930. Willets, J. 'Free Settler or Felon?' www.jenwillets.com. Parkinson, Northcote C. (ed.). *The Trade Winds: a Study of British Overseas Trade during the French Wars*. Routledge. 1948.

156. **In the middle of 1831 . . .** Sargent, Marion. *The Launceston Examiner*. 15 April 2018.

CHAPTER 22

157. **Early evening at the Cornwall Hotel . . .** The hotel was built by John Pascoe Fawkner in 1824. When it opened it was Launceston's leading hotel, boasting 13 rooms and two storeys. Alexander, Alison. Centre for Tasmanian Historical Studies, University of Tasmania. 2006.

158. **'I'm the greatest landowner in the world . . .'** Bonwick, James. *John Batman: the Founder of Victoria*. Samuel Mullen. 1867.

159. **'A rogue, thief, cheat and liar . . .'** Campbell, Alastair H. *John Batman and the Aborigines*. Kibble Books. 1987.

160. **He might be well known back in London . . .** By the early 1820s Glover was well known as a landscape painter throughout Europe. He moved to Van Diemen's Land in 1831 at the age of 64. The origin of his animosity toward Batman is unclear.

161. **'. . . a horse might run away with a gig for twenty miles . . .'** Batman journal, Bonwick.

162. **Fawkner should already be in Port Phillip . . .** Anderson, H. *Out of the Shadow: The Career of John Pascoe Fawkner*. Cheshire. 1962.

163. **The *Enterprize*, without Fawkner . . .** The crew and passengers of the *Enterprize* arrived on the north bank of the Yarra River on 30 August 1835. Fawkner finally arrived in early October.

164. **James Bonwick has the 19th century version of a man-crush** ... For anyone in any doubt about the veracity of this sentence, read the opening chapter in Bonwick's book about Batman.

165. **The judge was in no mood for leniency** ... *The Sydney Gazette and NSW Advertiser*, 26 October 1816.

166. **Flavell and Tripp were hanged on** ... Ibid. 16 November 1816.

167. **A resident of the local orphan's home** ... Campbell, Alastair.

168. **Events late as the 1970s** ... Billot, C. P. *John Batman: the Story of John Batman and the Founding of Melbourne*. Hyland House. 1979.

169. **... the 'gentleman' bushranger Matthew Brady.** Robson, L. L. *Matthew Brady. ADB.*

170. **... Arthur is a zealous reformer** ... Arthur had taken office in VDL in 1824 after an eight-year stint as superintendent of British Honduras. His despatches from there about the conditions of slaves and the suppression of a revolt have been credited with contributing to the eventual abolition of slavery throughout the Empire in 1834.

171. **Who – except the humourless Arthur – could not appreciate** ... White, Charles. *History of Australian Bushranging, Volume I. The Early Days.*

172. **... a former member of Brady's gang, Thomas Jeffries** ... Jeffries, also known as Mark Jeffries, had a long and violent history. Transported to Australia in 1823, he had been sentenced to 12 months at the Macquarie Harbour Penal settlement after threatening to stab a constable.

173. **In early May Brady and Jeffries are hanged in Hobart** ... *Hobart Town Gazette.* 6 May 1826.

174. **Batman is soon roaming the country** ... Campbell.

175. **'I immediately ordered the men to lay down . . .'** Ibid.

CHAPTER 23

176. **The man with the flattering tongue** ... Batman was originally diagnosed with syphilis in 1833 and was treated during the early settlement of Port Phillip by Dr Barry Cotter, a doctor appointed by Joseph Gellibrand of the Port Phillip Association to act as his agent. McAlister, Moria. 'Dr Barry Cotter – the First Doctor in Melbourne'. www.drbarrycotter.com.

177. **They are little more than trespassers on Crown land** ... The Batman treaty was declared null by the New South Wales government on 26 August 1835 and that finding was officially confirmed by the Colonial Office in London in October.

178. **Todd will be one of many whose lives** ... Brown, P. (ed.). *The Todd Journal.*

179. **Wedge is one of the very few characters** ... Stancombe, G. H., *ADB.*

180. **The following year the Royal Geographic Society . . .** Wedge's report was published in 1836 in the *Journal of the Royal Geographical Society of London*, Vol. 6.

181. **A free man, after all these years . . .** Morgan.

182. **'Nothing,' writes Wedges, 'could exceed the joy . . .'** Wedge letter to Batman, 14 October 1835. Bonwick, J. *Settlement of Port Phillip*.

183. **The man is a collector and very soon . . .** drawn from Taylor, Rebe. 'The Wedge Collection and the Conundrum of Humane Colonisation'. *Meanjin*. Summer, 2017.

184. **'. . . four of Buckley's clubs of various shapes rudely ornamented . . .'** Ibid. There is no telling exactly which of the clubs may have belonged to Buckley. Several items, including clubs and shields, were loaned to the National Museum in Canberra and displayed in 2011.

185. **In early 1836 Charles Darwin . . .** Nichols, Peter. *Evolution's Captain: The Tragic Fate of Robert FitzRoy*. Profile. 2004.

186. **In Van Diemen's Land Darwin climbs Mt Wellington . . .** Darwin, Charles. *The Voyage of the Beagle*. Penguin Classics.

187. **But the man whose theory of natural selection . . .** Ibid; Nicholas, J. M. & F. W. *Charles Darwin in Australia*. Cambridge University Press. 2002.

188. **This can only be a reference to the man . . .** Parry, Naomi. *'Musquito'*. *ADB*.

189. **The most famous had been Pemulwuy . . .** Kohen, J. L. *'Pemulwuy'*. *ADB*.

190. **Swanston is a hardened Scot . . .** Drawn from Hudspeth, W. H., *The Rise and Fall of Charles Swanston*, in 'Papers and Proceedings of the Royal Society of Tasmania for the Year 1948'; and ADB entry 'Charles Swanston'.

CHAPTER 24

191. **The infant colony of what will become Melbourne . . .** The first death in the settlement was that of William Goodwin, child of James Goodwin.

192. **Fawkner will take to his diary later this wintery day . . .** Fawkner journal, 1 July 1836. From Billot, C. P. *Melbourne's Missing Chronicle*.

193. **'. . . the country is somewhat indebted to me . . .'** Bonwick.

194. **Take Christmas Day, 1806 . . .** Billot, C. P.

195. **When Fawkner returns . . .** Ibid.

196. **'Fawkner must be a vindictive, vain-glorious . . .'** Letter from Hamilton Hume to William Westgarth, 12 June 1867. Mitchell Library, NSW. In the same letter Hume mentions that during his expedition from Sydney to Port Phillip in 1824, 'I know for a fact that Buckley followed our tracks from Station Peak to the Meariby Rivulet but did not overtake us – I was by that time as far as "Big Hill", or rather the Dividing Range on my return

to New South Wales.' Station Peak was at that time the name of the highest peak of what is now the You Yangs to the north of Geelong. 'Meariby Rivulet' is possibly a reference to the Werribee River.

CHAPTER 25

197. **... one of the 'fastest land occupations in the history of empires.'** Broome.
198. **'I cannot account for the manner ...'** Billot.
199. **It will be three decades before ...** Ibid.
200. **'Derramuck came this day ...'** Fawkner journal, 3 December 1835.
201. **'Watkins could not make out the words used by Derrimart ...'** Fawkner. *Reminiscences ...*
202. **'Refrain from expressing my thankfulness ...'** Batman to Montague, 30 November 1835.
203. **Decades later Barack will recall how ...** *The Argus*, 12 December 1931.
204. **'Of the two native chiefs, a singular instance of the effects ...'** Bunce, Daniel. *Australasiatic Reminiscences of Twenty Three Years Wanderings in Tasmania and the Australias*, Hendy, J. T. 1857.
205. **Hull relates a recent encounter with ...** Testimony of William Hull from *Report of the Select Committee on the Aborigines*. Victoria Legislative Council Votes and Proceedings, 9 November 1858.

CHAPTER 26

206. **He is a controversial figure in Van Diemen's Land ...** Fox, J.; James, P. C. 'Joseph Tice Gellibrand'. *ADB*.
207. **He is forced to lie under a tree to recover ...** Drawn from 'Gellibrand Memorandum re Port Phillip Expedition Jan–Feb 1836', to Governor Charles La Trobe. Reproduced in 'Letters from Victorian Pioneers'.
208. **'I am quite satisfied that he can only be ...'** Ibid.
209. **But other men see you so differently ...** Brown, P. L. *The Narrative of George Russell ...*

CHAPTER 27

210. **Reed is on board the *Bombay* ...** Renshaw, Will; Fysh, Hudson. 'Henry Reed'. ADB; Welch, Ian. *Henry Reed, Australian Pan-Protestant Evangelical and Businessman. (Working paper)*. Australian National University. 2014.
211. **'The congregation had in it William Buckley ...'** Ibid.
212. **'Bodies almost eaten up by disease ...'** Dray, Stephen. *A Right Old Confloption down Penzance*. Carn Brea Media. 2013.

213. **'He is a man of thought and shrewdness . . .'** Orton report to Wesleyan Missionary Society, August 1836. *Historical Records of Victoria, Vol. 2A: The Aborigines of Port Phillip 1835–1839.*

214. **Langhorne finds a man who . . .** Langhorne, George.

215. **Hepburn is typical of those white men . . .** Drawn from letters by Hepburn in 1853. Bride, Thomas Francis. *Letters from Victorian Pioneers.*

CHAPTER 28

216. **'It appears the natives were fired upon . . .'** Wedge letter to Montagu, 15 March 1836. *Historical Records of Victoria 1.*

217. **It will take years before the details emerge . . .** Drawn from various accounts of the Convincing Ground massacre, including Clark, Ian D., *Scars on the Landscape*, and Pascoe, Bruce, *Convincing Ground: Learning to Fall in Love with Your Country.*

218. **. . . Richard Bourke issues a proclamation warning . . .** Bourke's proclamation that the Aborigines of Port Phillip now came under the protection of the Governor of NSW was issued in the *New South Wales Government Gazette*, 18 May 1836.

219. **He reports back to Sydney . . .** Letter from George Stewart to Colonial Secretary, *HRV Vol. 1.*

220. **Charles Franks is a man of 'strict integrity' . . .** Drawn from reports in *The Cornwall Chronicle*; Rogers, Thomas James. *The Civilization of Port Phillip . . .*; Boyce, James. 1835.

221. **The letter coincides, not surprisingly . . .** *The Cornwall Chronicle*, 30 July 1836.

222. **Henry Hawson must have stepped . . .** Based on a lengthy letter by Hawson in Sydney's *The Colonist*, 22 September 1836.

CHAPTER 29

223. **'It will be one of your most important duties . . .'** Letter, Colonial Secretary to William Lonsdale, 14 September 1836. *HRV Vol. 1.*

224. **Turns out you and Lonsdale have much in common . . .** Penny, B. R. 'Lonsdale, William (1799–1864)'. *ADB.*

225. **A 20 per cent pay rise?** Morgan.

226. **'With boiled meat a biscuit . . .'** Ibid.

227. **Among those surveyed is . . .** 'Return of dwellings, stock and cultivation at Port Phillip, 9 November 1836'. *HRV Vol. 3.*

228. **Barely a week after your meeting with Lonsdale . . .** The murder of Woolmudgin based on various accounts, including sworn deposition of Frederick Taylor at the Melbourne Court Register, 25 October 1836,

Clark, Ian, *Scars in the Landscape; HRV. Vol 2A*; Charles, Florance. *In Pursuit of Frederick Taylor. The Black Sheep* (Journal of the East Gippsland Family History Group).

229. **It will become known as the Murdering Creek massacre . . .** Clark, Ian D.

230. **Frederick Taylor will reach a respectable . . .** From obituary in *The Sydney Morning Herald*, 2 February 1872.

231. **When the charge is heard in court . . .** Melbourne Court register, 3 January 1837. 'J. P. Fawkner assaults private James Duckworth: fined four pounds.' *HRV Vol. 1*.

232. **Later in the year a charge . . .** Ibid.

233. **And, in 1845, Batman's only son . . .** Letter from Eliza Willoughby to her daughter, 30 January 1845. Reproduced in *The Argus*, 12 September 1952.

CHAPTER 30

234. **A Sunday morning in early March, 1837 . . .** The account of the church service and the conversation between the Reverend Langhorne and Buckley comes from George Langhorne's *Reminiscenses of James Buckley. HRV Vol. 2A*.

235. **Bourke's face has a large and vicious scar . . .** King, Hazel. 'Richard Bourke, 1777–1855'. *ADB*.

236. **The Governor has a favourite theory . . .** Statement of Mr George Langhorne in reference to the establishment of the Aboriginal Mission at Port Phillip . . . *HRV, Vol. 2A*, p.187.

237. **'Such nonsense, young man . . .'** Ibid.

238. **Joseph Gellibrand had landed in Geelong in late February . . .** The disappearance of Gellibrand and Hesse was one of the most significant events in the early history of Port Phillip. Despite several searches and many more theories, their bodies were never found. A comprehensive account of the searches – and the impact on the colonial frontier – can be found in Rogers, Thomas James. *The Civilization of Port Phillip . . .*; and *HRV Vol. 1–3*.

239. **Phillip Parker King, travelling with the Governor . . .** from the diary of Phillip Parker King, 3 March 1837. *HRV Vol. 1*.

240. **But you return a week later, seething with anger . . .** Morgan; letter from Lonsdale to Bourke. *HRV Vol. 1*.

241. **But your horse needs to rest . . .** The attack on Buckley's horse has never been fully explained. This description is drawn from *Life and Adventures* and 'William Buckley's horse injured, apparently maliciously' in *HRV Vol. 2A*, p.279.

CHAPTER 31

242. **Fifty lashes? A man was only warming up . . .** Conversation between Fyans and the two Quaker missionaries – George Walker and James Backhouse – from Hughes, Robert. *The Fatal Shore.* Hughes also has a detailed account of the Norfolk Island convict uprising and the central role played by Fyans.

243. **Fyans is an Irishman who survived . . .** Brown, P. L. 'Foster Fyans 1790–1870'. *ADB.*

244. **'The men were very keen after these ruffians . . .'** Hughes.

245. **The recriminations went on for months . . .** Ibid.

246. **Fyans will forge a decent reputation for himself . . .** Official appointment of Fyans contained in a letter from Sir Richard Bourke to Lord Glenelg, 11 September 1837. *HRV Vol. 1.*

247. **'I stared when I saw the monster of a man . . .'** 'Fyans leaves Melbourne for Geelong'. *HRV Vol. 1; 'Reminiscences of Foster Fyans'.* Manuscript, State Library of Victoria.

248. **'I could not calculate on one hour's personal safety . . .'** Morgan.

249. **'Someone – probably Batman or Wedge . . .'** Buckley resignation letter to William Lonsdale, *HRV Vol. 1.*

250. **A petition is sent to Governor Bourke . . .** Ibid.

251. **After months of inquiries and testimony . . .** *Select Committee on Aborigines (British Settlements);* House of Commons, 26 June 1837. *HRV Vol. 2A.*

252. **'It's a difficult thing to apprehend natives . . .'** Fyans' letter to Charles La Trobe, 20 September 1840; *Papers Relative to the Massacre of Australian Aborigines,* House of Commons, London, 1839, pp.88–9. www.archive.org/details/MassacreOfAustralianAborigines.

PART IV
CHAPTER 32

253. **The Theatre Royal is a majestic building . . .** Drawn from various sources including www.theatreroyal.com.au/history-of-the-theatre-royal.

254. **Mean streets, these . . .** Sharman, R. C. 'Solomon, Isaac (Ikey) (1787–1850)'. *ADB.*

255. **Charles Dickens' latest novel, *Oliver Twist* . . .** The novel was first published as a serial with the pseudonym 'Boz' in *Bentley's Miscellany* in 1837–9. A three-volume work appeared in 1838. www.britannica.com/topic/Oliver-Twist-novel-by-Dickens.

256. **There you were, loping down the street . . .** Morgan.

257. **You can't blame John Moses for trying . . .** Descriptions of the play *Wood Demon* drawn from *The Austral-Asiatic Review, Tasmanian and Australian*

Advertiser, 16 January 1838, p.3 and p.7; 'Domestic Intelligence', *Colonial Times*, 16 January 1838, p.7.

258. **Staging the play in Hobart is a coup . . .** Levis, John.

259. **You have woken this morning at . . .** Morgan.

260. **'. . . exhibited as the huge Anglo-Australian giant . . .'** Ibid.

261. **The *Colonial Times* no longer has any sympathy for . . .** 'Hobart Town Police Report', *Colonial Times*, 6 March 1838.

CHAPTER 33

262. **The *Bussorah Merchant*, a 530-ton teak vessel . . .** Government notice, No.2, Colonial Secretary John Montague, *Hobart Town Courier*, 5 January 1838.

263. **So Price was taking no chances . . .** *General regulations*, Price, Morgan. The *Bussorah Merchant*. Tasmanian Archive and Heritage Office.

264. **'. . . an example of ignorance of hygiene . . .'** *The Journey – by Sailing Ship*. Maritime Museum of Tasmania. www.maritimetas.org.

265. **The passenger list, a grim register . . .** Government notice, No.2, Colonial secretary John Montague, *Hobart Town Courier*, 5 January 1838.

266. **This little island they have come to . . .** Drawn from Schultz, Robert J. *The Assisted Immigrants: a Study of Some Aspects of the Characteristics and Origins of the Immigrants Assisted to New South Wales and the Port Phillip District, 1837–1850*. Thesis. Australian National University. December 1971; Pearce, Ian. *Immigration to Tasmania 1803–1946*, Guide to the public records of Tasmania.

267. **But it is the old ones you enjoy meeting most . . .** Morgan; Tipping.

268. **The lieutenant governor is another of those men . . .** Fitzpatrick, Kathleen. 'Franklin, Sir John (1786–1847)'. ADB. Beattie, Owen and Geiger, John. *Frozen in Time: the Fate of the Franklin Expedition*. 2004. Potter, Russell, A. *Finding Franklin: the Untold Story of a 165-Year Search*. 2016.

CHAPTER 34

269. **'He is placed as it were in the very gorge of sin . . .'** Goodridge, Charles. *Statistical View of Van Diemen's Land . . .* Hamilton and Adams. 1832.

270. **Charles Goodridge is another Robinson Crusoe . . .** Goodridge, Charles. *Narrative of a Voyage to the South Seas . . .* 1841.

271. **'The great work of reformation . . .'** Goodridge. *Statistical View of Van Diemen's Land . . .*

272. **Waterfield is a devout and private man . . .** Hanslow, Jan. *Report on Ada Ackerly's Address at the General Meeting*. Port Phillip Pioneers Group. www.portphillippioneersgroup.org.au/pppg5ad.htm.

273. **On 28 April the Reverend . . .** extract from *Diary of the Reverend William Waterfield, Victorian Historical Magazine,* 1914. Issue 11. Vol. 3.

274. **An eccentric Polish explorer . . .** Whitley, G. P. 'Lhotsky, John (1796–1866)'. *ADB.*

275. **'Here he assumed the rank of Gentleman . . .'** *The Tasmanian,* 3 May 1839.

276. **'Buckley must have been a splendid young man . . .'** Lhotsky, John. 'My Conference with Buckley'. *The Tasmanian,* Hobart Town. 26 January 1838, p.5.

CHAPTER 35

277. **The Immigrants' Home is being closed . . .** Morgan.

278. **It is late May 1838, and the government is under pressure . . .** Descriptions of the Cascades Female Factory drawn from *Convict Lives: Women at Cascades Female Factory . . .*; Kippen, Rebecca. *The Convict Nursery at the Cascades Female Factory, Hobart.* Chainletter, No.3, December 2009.

279. **'Miserable place . . . the most unfitting place in the whole colony . . .'** *True Colonist,* 9 March 1838.

280. **But as the Reverend Thomas Ewing . . .** 'Marriages in the District of Hobart', 27 January 1840. Tasmanian Archives.

281. **The Reverend Ewing . . .** Hagger, A. J. 'Ewing, Thomas James (1813–1882)'. *ADB.*

282. **Within a year Ewing's name will be associated . . .** From a presentation by Purtscher, Joyce, 'Suffer Little Children', about the lives of children at the Orphan Schools in the 19th century. www.orphanschool.org.au/suffer.php.

283. **Good thing you married Julia . . .** Morgan.

284. **Your absence from work because of illness . . .** From correspondence in the Archives Office of Tasmania, 4 August–3 September 1841.

285. **By the end of 1842 . . .** *Colonial Times,* 6 December 1842.

286. **In 1848 the papers will carry . . .** *The Britannia and Trades' Advocate,* 15 June 1848.

287. **It will not be until late 1851 . . .** *The Courier,* Hobart Town, 26 July 1851.

288. **By all accounts it is a success . . .** In 1855 Morgan claimed that more than 1000 copies of the first edition had been sold in Van Diemen's Land and began looking for investors to fund the printing of a second edition. *The Tasmanian Daily News,* 27 October 1855, p.7.

289. **Accompanying the book is a sketch of you . . .** Ludwig Becker spent two years in Van Diemen's Land and was a regular attendee at Government House with Sir John Franklin. The historian Marjorie Tipping has said the life-sized portrait of Buckley, which is now on display at the State Library of

Victoria, served as the original likeness for the lithograph that was used as a frontispiece to *Life and Adventures*. It was also used as the basis for a wood engraving by Nicholas Chevalier that appeared in *The Australian Newsletter* in 1857. According to Tipping, '. . . known historical facts, the age of the painting, the technical structure, the materials used and the style, confirm that Ludwig Becker was the artist.' Tipping, Marjorie. 'Portrait of William Buckley, Attributed to Ludwig Becker'. *The La Trobe Journal*. No.1. April 1968.

CHAPTER 36

290. **Perhaps you are hesitant. Nervous . . .** 'Marriages in the District of Hobart, 1853', Tasmanian Archives; *Launceston Examiner*, 15 September 1853.

291. **It's the sort of slur you have let stand in the past . . .** *The Argus*, 28 June 1853, p.5.

292. **In 1855 the Council . . .** *Colonial Times*, 10 April 1855; *The Argus*, 4 May 1855.

293. **According to press reports . . .** Ibid.

294. **Acclaimed as the great old man . . .** According to a report in the *Illustrated Australian News for Home Readers* on 11 October 1869, the funeral procession for Fawkner 'was fully two miles long. At the cemetery the living torrent of persons desirous of playing a last tribute of respect to the memory of the deceased set in shortly after three o'clock and continued pouring in in an unbroken stream until long after the funeral ceremony had concluded.'

295. **Four days before Christmas in 1855 . . .** *The People's Advocate or True Friend of Tasmania* (Launceston), 31 December 1855.

296. **The daily fee at St Mary's is six shillings . . .** *Admissions and Discharges book for St Mary's Hospital*. Library of the University of Tasmania, Special and Rare Collections.

297. **They bury you the following Saturday . . .** *The Tasmanian Daily News*, 4 February 1856.

298. **Just a couple of months after the funeral . . .** *The Argus*, 14 March 1856.

299. **It is a move that incenses John Morgan . . .** *The Tasmanian Daily News*, 19 April 1856.

300. **Six months after the funeral . . .** *The Courier* (Hobart), 25 July 1856.

BIBLIOGRAPHY

Selected books, articles, online resources and source documents

Note: Many 19th and early 20th century titles listed are now fully digitised and available at various websites, including the HathiTrust Digital Library.

Albery, W. *The Sussex Assizes and Quarter Sessions, Crime and Punishments, 1307–1830*, in 'A Millennium of Facts in the History of Horsham and Sussex 947–1947', Horsham, 1947.

Anderson, Hugh. *Out of the Shadow: the Career of John Pascoe Fawkner*. Cheshire, 1962.

Anderson, Stephanie. *Pelletier: the Forgotten Castaway of Cape York*. Melbourne Books, 2009.

Angell, Barbara. *Voyage to Port Phillip, 1803*. Nepean Historical Society, 1984.

Astley, Terry (subaltern). *The Campaign in Holland, 1799*. W. Mitchell, 1861.

Atkinson, Alan. *The Europeans in Australia (Vols. 1–111)*, Oxford University Press, 1998.

Attwood, Bain. *Treating the Past: Narratives of Possession and Dispossession in a Settler Community.* Paper for 'Storied Communities: Narratives of Contact and Arrival in Constituting Political Community', 2006.

Barrett, Charles. *White Blackfellows: the Strange Adventures of Europeans Who Lived among Savages*. Hallcraft, 1948.

Barwick, Diane, E. *Mapping the Past: an Atlas of Victorian Clans 1835–1904*. 'Aboriginal History', Volume 8, 1984.

Batman, John. *The Settlement of John Batman in Port Phillip: from His Own Journal.* George Slater, 1856.

Bell, Jane. *An Extremely Scurrilous Paper: The Cornwall Chronicle 1835–37.* Thesis. University of Tasmania, 1993.

Bernier, Olivier. *The World in 1800.* New World City, 2018.

Billot, C. P. *John Batman: the Story of John Batman and the Founding of Melbourne.* Hyland House, 1979.

Billot, C. P. *The Life and Times of John Pascoe Fawkner.* Hyland House, 1985.

Blainey, Geoffrey. *A History of Victoria.* Cambridge University Press, 2013.

Blainey, Geoffrey. *The Story of Australia's People – the Rise and Fall of Ancient Australia.* Viking, 2015.

Blake, Barry J. *Dialects of Western Kulin, Western Victoria.* La Trobe University, 2011.

Blake, Barry J. (ed.). *Wathawurrung and the Colac Language of Southern Victoria.* Pacific Linguistics, Australian National University, 1998.

Bolger, Peter. *Hobart Town.* Australian National University Press, 1973.

Bolger, Peter. *John Morgan: a Strange Radical.* 'Australian Society for the Study of Labour History', No.18, May 1970.

Bolger, Peter. *John Morgan: Colonial Middle Class Recruit.* Thesis, University of Tasmania, 1965.

Bonwick, James. *Discovery and Settlement of Port Phillip: Being a History of the Country Now Called Victoria, up to the Arrival of Mr Superintendent La Trobe, in October 1839.* George Robertson, 1856.

Bonwick, James. *Early Days of Melbourne.* Jas J. Blundell and Co., 1857.

Bonwick, James. *John Batman, the Founder of Victoria.* Samuel Mullen, 1867.

Bonwick, James. *The Last of the Tasmanians, or, the Black War of Van Diemen's Land.* Sampson, Low, Son and Marston, 1870.

Bonwick, James. *William Buckley: the Wild White Man and his Port Phillip Black Friends.* Geo. Nichols, 1856.

Boyce, James. *1835: the Founding of Melbourne and the Conquest of Australia.* Black Inc., 2013.

Boyce, James. *Van Diemen's Land.* Black Inc., 2009.

Boys, Robert Douglass. *First Years at Port Phillip: Preceded by a Summary of Historical Events from 1768.* Robertson and Mullens, 1935.

Braybrook, Joy. *John Batman: an Inside Story of the Birth of Melbourne.* Xlibris Corporation, 2012.

Bride, Thomas Francis. *Letters from Victorian Pioneers . . .* O'Neil, 1983.

Broome, Richard. *Aboriginal Australians: A History since 1788 (revised edition).* Allen & Unwin, 2010.

Broome, Richard. *Aboriginal Victorians: A History since 1800.* Allen & Unwin, 2005.

Broome, Richard. *Arriving (the Victorians)*. Fairfax, Syme and Weldon Associates, 1984.

Brown, P. L. (ed.). *The Narrative of George Russell of Golf Hill with Russellania and Selected Papers*. Oxford University Press, 1935.

Brown, Richard. *Revolution, Radicalism and Reform: England 1780–1846*. Cambridge University Press, 2000.

Bunbury, Henry. *A Narrative of the Campaign in North Holland, 1799*. T. and W. Boone, 1849.

Campbell, Alastair. *John Batman and the Aborigines*. Kibble Books, 1987.

Campbell, Charles F. *The Intolerable Hulks: British Shipboard Confinement, 1776–1857*. Heritage Books, 1994.

Cannon, Michael (ed.). *Historical Records of Victoria: The Early Development of Melbourne*. Victorian Government Printing Office, 1984.

Cannon, Michael (ed.). *Historical Records of Victoria: Volume 2A, The Aborigines of Port Phillip, 1835–1839*. Victorian Government Printing Office, 1982.

Cannon, Michael (ed.). *Historical Records of Victoria: Volume 2B, Aborigines and Protectors, 1838–1839*. Victorian Government Printing Office, 1983.

Cannon, Michael (ed.). *Historical Records of Victoria: Volume 3, The Early Development of Melbourne 1836–1839*, Victorian Government Printing Office, 1984.

Cannon, Michael. *Old Melbourne Town before the Gold Rush*. Loch Haven Books, 1991.

Carey, J. and McLisky, C. *Creating White Australia*. Sydney University Press, 2009.

Carter, Paul. *The Road to Botany Bay*. University of Minnesota Press, 2013.

Clark, Ian. *Aboriginal Languages and Clans: Historical Atlas of Western and Central Victoria, 1800–1900*. Monash University, 1990.

Clark, Ian. *Scars in the Landscape: a Register of Massacre Sites in Western Victoria, 1802–1859*. Aboriginal Studies Press, 1995.

Clark. Ian D. (ed.). *The Journals of George Augustus Robinson, Chief Protector, Port Phillip Aboriginal Protectorate*. Heritage Matters, 1998.

Clark, Ian D. and Cahir, Fred (eds.). *The Children of the Port Phillip Aboriginal Protectorate: an Anthology of their Reminiscences*. Australian Scholarly Publishing, 2016.

Clark, Ian D. *'You have all this place, no good have children . . .' Derrimut: traitor, savior or a man of his people?* Journal of the Royal Australian Historical Society, December 2005.

Clarke, Keith M. *Convicts of the Port Phillip District*. K. M. and G. Clarke, 1999.

Clements, Nicholas. *The truth about John Batman: Melbourne's founder and 'murderer of the blacks'*. The Conversation, May 2011.

Clendinnen, Inga. *Dancing with Strangers: Europeans and Australians at First Contact*. Text Publishing, 2005.

Collins, David. Edited and with an introduction by John Currey. *Letters to Sir Joseph Banks: London and the Derwent 1798–1808*. Banks Society, 2004.

Connor, John. *The Australian Frontier Wars, 1788–1838*. UNSW Press, 2005.

Cotter, Richard. *No Place for a Colony: Sullivan Bay, Sorrento and the Collins Settlement*. Lacrimae Rerum, 2003.

Crawford, Mr Justice, Ellis W. F. and Stancombe, G. H. (eds). *The Diaries of John Helder Wedge 1824–1835*. Royal Society of Tasmania, 1962.

Crook, William Pascoe. *An Account of the Settlement at Sullivan Bay, Port Phillip, 1803*. Colony Press, 1983.

Curr, E. M. *The Australian Race: Its Origins, Languages, Customs, Place of Landing in Australia and the Routes by Which It Spread Itself over That Continent*. John Ferres Government Printer, 1886.

Currey, John (ed.). *Account of a Voyage to Establish a Settlement in Bass's Straits, to Which Is Added a Description of Port Phillip and an Account of the Landing at the Derwent in 1804 / Edited from the Despatches of David Collins*. Colony Press, 1986.

Currey, John. *David Collins: A Colonial Life*. Melbourne University Press, 2000.

Currey, John. *Records of the Port Phillip Expedition (Vols. 1–3)*. Colony Press, 1993.

Currey, John. *Sullivan Bay: How Convicts Came to Port Phillip and Van Diemen's Land*. Colony Press, 2016.

Dixon, R. M. W. *The Languages of Australia*. Cambridge University Press, 2011.

Donovan, Paul Michael. *Annotated Bibliography of the History of William Buckley and Colonial Indigenous Relations Pertaining to Wathaurong Mythology*. Ballarat and District Industrial Heritage Project, 2013.

Drury, Bob and Clavin, Tom. *The Heart of Everything That Is*. Simon & Schuster, 2013.

Fawkner, John Pascoe. *Melbourne's Missing Chronicle: Being the Journal of Preparation for Departure to and Proceeding to Port Phillip* (edited by C. P. Billot). Quartet Books, 1982.

Fawkner, John Pascoe. *John Pascoe Fawkner's Sullivan Bay Reminiscences*. Lavender Hill Multimedia, 2002.

Feltham, John. *The Picture of London for 1803*. Lewis and Company, 1802.

Female Convicts Research Centre (contributors). *Convict Lives: Women at Cascades Female Factory*. Convict Women's Press, 2012.

Flannery, Tim (ed.). *The Birth of Melbourne*. Text Publishing, 2002.

Flannery, Tim (edited and introduced by). *The Life and Adventures of William Buckley*. Text Publishing, 2002.

Fox, Jacqueline. *Bound by Every Duty: John Lewes Pedder, Chief Justice of Van Diemen's Land*. Australian Scholarly, 2018.

Frankel, David and Major, Janine (eds.). *Victorian Aboriginal Life and Customs: Through Early European Eyes*. Bundoora La Trobe University. Ebureau, 2017.

Futility Closet. The Wild White Man. Podcast 189. www.futilitycloset.com/2018/02/19/podcast-episode-189-wild-white-man/.

Gammage, Bill. *The Biggest Estate on Earth: How Aborigines Made Australia*. Allen & Unwin, 2012.

Garner, Alan, *Strandloper*. Harvill Press, 1996.

Garner, Alan. *The Voice That Thunders: Essays and Lectures*. Harvill Press, 1997.

Goodridge, Charles Medyett. *Narrative of a Voyage to the South Seas, and the Shipwreck of the Princess of Wales Cutter, with an Account of Two Years Residence on an Uninhabited Island*. W. C. Featherstone, 1841.

Goodridge, Charles Medyett. *Statistical View of Van Diemen's Land . . . Forming a Complete Emigrant's Guide*. Hamilton and Adams, 1832.

Gregory, Edmund. *Narrative of James Murrells*. Self-published, 1896.

Gwynne, S. C. *Empire of the Summer Moon*. Scribner, 2010.

Harcourt, Rex. *Southern Invasion, Northern Conquest*. Golden Point Press, 2001.

Hayden, Kevin. *Wild White Man: a Condensed Account of the Adventures of William Buckley Who Lived in Exile for 32 Years (1803–35) amongst the Black People of the Unexplored Regions of Port Phillip*. Marine History Publications, 1976.

Haythornthwaite, Phillip J. *Redcoats: the British Soldiers of the Napoleonic Wars*. Pen and Sword Books Ltd, 2012.

Hill, Barry. *Buckley, Our Imagination, Hope*. In 'William Buckley: rediscovered', Geelong Art Gallery, 2001.

Hitchcock, Tim. *The Streets of London: from the Great Fire to the Great Stink*. Rivers Oram Press, 2003.

Howitt, Alfred William. *Native Tribes of Southeast Australia*. Creative Media Partners, 2015.

Hudspeth, W. H. *Rise and Fall of Charles Swanston*. 'Papers and proceedings of the Royal Society of Tasmania', 1948.

Hughes, Robert. *The Fatal Shore*. Vintage, 2003.

Jackson, Lee. *Dirty Old London: the Victorian Fight against Filth*. Yale University Press, 2014.

Jay, Mike. *The Unfortunate Colonel Despard*. Bantam, 2005.

Jones, Pauline (ed.). *Historical Records of Victoria*. Volume 1: beginnings of permanent government. Victorian Government Printing Office, 1981.

Karskens, Grace. *The Colony: a History of Early Sydney*. Allen & Unwin, 2010.

Kruta, Vladislav. *Dr John Lhotsky: the Turbulent Australian Writer, Naturalist and Explorer*. Australia Felix literary club, 1977.

Labilliere, Francis Peter. *Early History of the Colony of Victoria, from Its Discovery to Its Establishment as a Self-Governing Province of the British Empire*. Sampson Low, Marston, Searle and Rivington, 1878.

Langhorne, George. *Reminiscenses of James Buckley Who Lived for Thirty Years among the Wallawarro or Watourong Tribes at Geelong Port Phillip, Communicated by Him to George Langhorne*. Manuscript. First published in *The Age*, 29 July 1911.

Levis, John. *These Are the Names: Jewish Lives in Australia 1788–1850*. Melbourne University Publishing, 2013.

Lewis, Milton J. *Medicine in Colonial Australia, 1788–1900*. Medical Journal of Australia, 201(1), July 2014.

Maynard, John and Haskins, Victoria. *Living with the Locals: Early Europeans' Experience of Indigenous Life*. National Library of Australia, 2016.

McConvell, Patrick, Kelly, Piers, Lacrampe, Sebastien. *Skin, Kin and Clan: the Dynamics of Social Categories in Indigenous Australia*. ANU Press, 2018.

McPhee, Alex. *The First Chapter in the History of Victoria*. E. W. Cole, 1911.

Memmott, Paul. *Gunya, Goondie and Wurley: the Aboriginal Architecture of Australia*. University of Queensland Press, 2007.

Morton, Joseph C. *The American Revolution*. Greenwood, 2003.

Morgan, John. 'Memorial: to the right honorable the Lords Commissioners of the Admiralty, the right honorable the Lords Commissioners of the Treasury, and to Her Majesty's Secretary of State for the colonies, the right honorable Earl Grey, the humble memorial of John Morgan, now resident in Hobart Town, Van Diemen's Land, and one of the coroners of the territory.' Private circulation, 1852.

Morgan, John. *The Life and Adventures of William Buckley, Thirty-Two Years a Wanderer amongst the Aborigines of the Then Unexplored Country round Port Phillip, Now the Province of Victoria*. Archibald MacDougall, 1852.

Mullaly, Paul R. *Crime in the Port Phillip District, 1835–51*. Hybrid Publishers, 2008.

Munster, Peter M. *Putting Batman and Buckley on the Map of St Leonards: the Story of Early Contact and Settlement at St Leonards, Victoria*. 2004.

Nichols, Mary (ed.). *The Diary of the Reverend Robert Knopwood, 1803–1838: First Chaplain of Van Diemen's Land*. Tasmanian Historical Research Association, 1977.

Pascoe, Bruce. *Convincing Ground: Learning to Fall in Love with Your Country*. Aboriginal Studies Press, 2007.

Pascoe, Bruce. *Dark Emu*. Magabala Books, 2014.

Pascoe, Bruce. *Wathaurong – the People Who Said No*. Wathaurong Aboriginal Co-operative, 2003.

Pateshall, Nicholas. *A Short Account of a Voyage around the Globe in HMS Calcutta 1803–1804.* Edited with an introduction by Marjorie Tipping. Queensberry Hill Press, 1980.

Preston, Diane. *Paradise in Chains: The Bounty Mutiny and the Founding of Australia.* Bloomsbury, 2017.

Pyke, W. T. (ed.). *Savage Life in Australia: The Story of William Buckley the Runaway Convict Who Lived Thirty-Two Years among the Black of Australia.* E. W. Cole, 1889.

Renshaw, Will. *Marvellous Melbourne and Spiritual Power.* Acorn Press, 2014.

Reynolds, Henry. *The Other Side of the Frontier: Aboriginal Resistance to the European Invasion of Australia.* University of New South Wales Press Ltd, 2006.

Robertson, Craig. *Buckley's Hope.* Scribe, 1980.

Rogers, Thomas. '*Friendly' and 'hostile' Aboriginal Clans: the Search for Gellibrand and Hesse.* History of Australia, Volume 13, 2016.

Rogers, Thomas James. *The Civilization of Port Phillip: Settler Ideology, Violence and Rhetorical Possession.* Melbourne University Publishing, 2018.

Rogers, Woodes. *A Cruising Voyage around the World, First to the South Seas . . .* British Library Collections, 1712.

Ryan, Lyndall. *Tasmanian Aborigines: a History Since 1803.* Allen & Unwin, 2012.

Seal, Graham. *The Savage Shore: Extraordinary Stories of Survival and Tragedy from the Early Voyages of Discovery.* Yale University Press, 2016.

Selcraig, Bruce. *The Real Robinson Crusoe.* Smithsonian magazine, 2005.

Schneid, Frederick C. *Napoleon's Conquest of Europe: the War of the Third Coalition.* Praeger Publishers, 2005.

Seal, Graham. *Great Convict Stories: Dramatic and Moving Tales from Australia's Brutal Early Years.* Allen & Unwin, 2017.

Shaw, A. G. L. *A History of the Port Phillip district: Victoria before Separation.* Melbourne University Publishing, 2003.

Shillinglaw, John J. (ed.). *Historical Records of Port Phillip: the First Annals of the Colony of Victoria.* Government Printer, Melbourne, 1870.

Source documents for William Buckley. www.williambuckleyconvict.wordpress.com.

Staniforth, Mark. *Diet, Disease and Death at Sea on the Voyage to Australia, 1837–1839.* International Journal of Maritime History, 1996.

Stephens, Geoffrey. *Knopwood: a Biography.* Moonah, 1990.

Sullivan, Martin. *Men and Women of Port Phillip.* Hale and Ironmonger, 1985.

Taylor, Rebe. *The Wedge Collection and the Conundrum of Humane Colonization.* Meanjin. Summer, 2017.

Tipping, Marjorie. *Convicts Unbound: The Story of the Calcutta Convicts and Their Settlement in Australia.* Viking O'Neil, 1988.

Todd, Andrew alias William. *The Todd Journal*. Geelong Historical Society, 1989.

Tuckfield, Francis. *The Journal of Francis Tuckfield, Missionary to Port Phillip, Southern Australia, 1937*. Unpublished (microform). National Library of Australia.

Tudenhope, Cecily, M. *William Buckley*. Hall's Book Store, 1962.

Tuckey, J. H. *An Account of a Voyage to Establish a Colony at Port Phillip, in Bass's Strait, on the South Coast of New South Wales, in His Majesty's Ship Calcutta, in the Years 1802–3–4*. Longman and co, 1805.

Vaux, James Hardy. *A New and Comprehensive Vocabulary of the Flash Language*. Online edition at Project Gutenberg. www.gutenberg.net.au/ebooks06/0600111.txt.

Vaux, James Hardy. *Memoirs of James Hardy Vaux – Volume 1*. CreateSpace Independent Publishing Platform, 2016.

Walsh, Edward. *A Narrative of the Expedition to New Holland in the Autumn of the Year 1799*. Robinson, 1800.

Waterfield, William. *Extracts from the Diary of the Reverend William Waterfield, First Congregational Minister at Port Phillip, 1838–1843*. Victorian Historical Magazine. Vol. 3 No. 3, March 1914.

Wedge, John Helder. *The Visit to Port Phillip in 1835 of John Helder Wedge*. Margaret Carnegie collection reprint; No.4. Centre for Library Studies, Riverina-Murray Institute of Higher Education, 1986.

Welsh, Frank. *Australia: A New History of the Great Southern Land*. Overlook Press, 2006.

Westgarth, William. *Personal Recollections of Early Melbourne and Victoria*. CreateSpace Independent Publishing, 2015.

Westgarth, William. *The Colony of Victoria: Its History, Commerce and Gold Mining; Its Social and Political Institutions down to the End of 1963; with Remarks, Incidental and Comparative, upon the Other Australian Colonies*. Sampson Low, Son and Marston, 1864.

Wilkins, J. M. *The Life and Times of Captain William Lonsdale 1799–1864*. Self-published, 1991.

Wilton, Elizabeth. *On the Banks of the Yarra: a Story of William Buckley and John Batman*. Rigby, 1969.

Winfield, Rif. *British Warships in the Age of Sail 1793–1817: Design, Construction, Careers and Fates*. Chatham Publishing, 2014.

Woodriff, Daniel. *Captain of HMS Calcutta and the Sullivan Bay Settlement of 1803–4 (edited and with notations by Richard Cotter)*. Lavender Hill Multimedia, 2002.

INDEX

Discover a
new favourite